Entrepreneurship

Entrepreneurship: A Contemporary Perspective emphasizes theories and practices related to entrepreneurship as it is found in the real world. The book provides in-depth insights into entrepreneurship concepts and offers practical learning solutions through its many and varied case studies. The book explores the attributes of successful entrepreneurial ventures in a changing business environment and explains how key concepts, approaches and practices have evolved over time. The unique focus of this textbook is that it steps away from the traditional views of entrepreneurship and instead looks at entrepreneurship through a number of distinct lenses, including gender, geopolitical trends, and the social environment. The book also examines the optimal conditions and strategies for the survival and sustenance of entrepreneurial ventures in an ever-changing business world. With a future-facing focus, *Entrepreneurship: A Contemporary Perspective* shines a light on what entrepreneurship will be like in the next few – likely transformative – decades. Suitable for students at advanced undergraduate and postgraduate levels, this textbook will find a home wherever modern entrepreneurship is taught and studied.

Adnan ul Haque, Doctor of Business Administration (DBA), PMI-PMP, PMI-ACP, MBA, MPA, is a fulltime faculty and course developer at Yorkville University, Canada.

Entrepreneurship

A Contemporary Perspective

Edited by Adnan ul Haque

Routledge
Taylor & Francis Group
LONDON AND NEW YORK

Designed cover image: Getty Images

First published 2026
by Routledge
4 Park Square, Milton Park, Abingdon, Oxon OX14 4RN

and by Routledge
605 Third Avenue, New York, NY 10158

Routledge is an imprint of the Taylor & Francis Group, an informa business

British Library Cataloguing-in-Publication Data
A catalog record for this book is available from the British Library.

Library of Congress Cataloging-in-Publication Data
Names: Haque, Adnan Ul, 1983– editor.
Title: Entrepreneurship : a contemporary perspective / edited by Adnan Ul Haque.
Description: Abingdon, Oxon ; New York, NY : Routledge, 2026. |
Includes bibliographical references and index.
Identifiers: LCCN 2024061133 (print) | LCCN 2024061134 (ebook) |
ISBN 9781032824024 (pbk) | ISBN 9781032824031 (hbk) |
ISBN 9781003504351 (ebk)
Subjects: LCSH: Entrepreneurship.
Classification: LCC HB615 .E577869755 2026 (print) | LCC HB615 (ebook) |
DDC 338/.04–dc23/eng/20250530
LC record available at https://lccn.loc.gov/2024061133
LC ebook record available at https://lccn.loc.gov/2024061134

ISBN: 978-1-032-82403-1 (hbk)
ISBN: 978-1-032-82402-4 (pbk)
ISBN: 978-1-003-50435-1 (ebk)

DOI: 10.4324/9781003504351

Typeset in Galliard
by Newgen Publishing UK

Access the Support Material: www.routledge.com/9781032824024

Contents

Disclaimer:

All names and businesses referenced in the case studies are fictional and created specifically for the purpose of this publication. These characters and scenarios are designed to support the learning objectives of this chapter and do not depict real individuals or enterprises.

Tables

Contributors

Tahmina Akhter, PhD, is a distinguished professor at Yorkville University's Bachelor of Business Administration program. She is known for her strong academic background and dedication to impactful research. She holds a PhD from the University of Waterloo and a second M.Sc. from Toronto Metropolitan University, both in Applied Mathematics. Prior to relocating to Canada, Dr. Akhter served as an Assistant Professor of Mathematics at the University of Asia Pacific in Dhaka, Bangladesh. In Canada, she has held roles as a sessional instructor and a postdoctoral fellow in the Applied Mathematics Department at the University of Waterloo. Dr. Akhter's research spans a range of fields, including statistical analysis and modeling, pharmacokinetics, mathematical medicine, and fluid dynamics, reflecting her passion for the interdisciplinary applications of mathematics. She is also widely recognized for her ability to inspire and motivate others, a commitment that is evident in both her teaching and her research. Dr. Akhter's enthusiasm and dedication have made her a respected and influential figure in her field, fostering academic and personal growth in her students and colleagues alike.

Manjot Kaur Brar holds a Bachelor of Business Administration (BBA) in Project Management from Yorkville University. She has extensive experience in the hospitality industry. Her area of interest includes project management, entrepreneurship, and business ethics.

Riffat Faizan, DBA, is an adjunct professor at Yorkville University and research scientist at the Scientific Societal and Behavioral Research Center (SSBRC), Canada. She has over a decade of academic teaching experience, both nationally and internationally. She holds a Doctor of Business Administration from the Royal Academy of Economics and Technology in Switzerland. As a professional researcher, Dr. Faizan has authored numerous papers published in Scopus, ABS, and impact factor journals. She has had the privilege of chairing sessions and delivering keynote addresses at international conferences. With two decades of experience in networking, logistics operations, and managing corporate clients across Canada and globally, she also has expertise in building international teams, working with a core focus on reliability and integrity across diverse cultures and regions.

Rokhsareh Farsad, ME, is a dedicated faculty member and researcher at Yorkville University in Ontario, Canada, with a strong commitment to advancing the Sustainable Development Goals (SDGs). Her work encompasses developing sustainability curricula and conducting impactful research on environmental issues and sustainable practices.

Rokhsareh emphasized the importance of engaging students emotionally to foster a deeper understanding of and commitment to sustainability. She believes that by stimulating emotional connections, students can become environmentally conscious and proactive individuals. Rokhsareh holds a master's degree in English literature and has collaborated with various educational institutions, underscoring the significance of communication skills in shaping students' academic and personal growth.

Siyath Thamuditha Gallage is a research scholar with a Bachelor of Business Administration in Project Management from Yorkville University, Toronto, Ontario, Canada. He has been actively involved in various projects affiliated with Yorkville University, including participating in project management seminars, contributing to research papers, and organizing a Career Expo event. His areas of interest include agile project management methodologies such as Scrum and Kanban, finance, smart city solutions, and environmentally sustainable practices.

Pavlos Gkasis, PhD, is the Associate Dean of the Bachelor of Business Administration in the Project Management Program at Yorkville University, Toronto, Ontario, Canada. Dr. Pavlos Gkasis has worked as a professor and economist with 19 years of combined academic and professional experience. As an academic leader and professor, he has achieved excellence in administration, research, scholarly activity, and research-led teaching. He has authored, coauthored, and led multiple funded research projects. His research interests include International Business, Technological Diffusion, Knowledge Spillovers, Multinational Enterprises, Foreign Direct Investment, Macroeconomic Analysis, Financial Economics, International Economics and Trade, Political Economy, and Migration.

Irfan ul Haq, MBA, PMP, is an adjunct professor at Yorkville University and a dedicated researcher at the Scientific Societal and Behavioral Research Center (SSBRC), Canada. As an active blogger, he explores societal and behavioral issues, bringing fresh perspectives to contemporary challenges. He has contributed to national and international projects, collaborating with diverse teams across the globe. Irfan holds an MBA from Anglia Ruskin University, UK, and is a certified Project Management Professional (PMP). Currently pursuing a PhD, his research interests include entrepreneurship, project management, stress management, and sustainable practices.

Harmandeep Kaur is a research scholar with a Bachelor of Business Administration (BBA) specializing in Project Management from Yorkville University. She volunteers as a researcher at the Scientific Societal and Behavioral Research Center (SSBRC) and actively participates in diverse research initiatives within the field of business management. She has extensive experience in customer care, hospitality, and tourism management. Her work has been published in Scopus and other reputable indexed journals. Her academic and professional pursuits center around project management, gender studies, organizational behavior, entrepreneurship, sustainable business practices, and leadership.

Pardeep Singh Malhi holds a Bachelor of Business Administration (BBA) in Project Management from Yorkville University. His area of research includes project management, entrepreneurship, and business ethics.

Oluchi E. Oti, DBA, is a dynamic business and academic strategist known for her visionary approach and transformative impact on the corporate and educational landscape. With a career span of over two decades, Oluchi has earned a reputation for her keen foresight, innovative problem-solving skills, and a relentless drive for excellence. Beyond her consultancy roles, she champions a holistic approach to business strategy, emphasizing innovation, sustainability, and organizational resilience in a rapidly evolving global economy. Her commitment to driving strategic initiatives that foster long-term success and stakeholder value continues to set benchmarks in the business and education community.

Diya Nitinbhai Patel holds a Bachelor of Business Administration (BBA) in Project Management from Yorkville University. She is an independent researcher with a focus on entrepreneurship, project management, and business ethics. In addition to her research, Diya volunteers at the Scientific Societal and Behavioural Research Center (SSBRC) contributed to studies in these fields. Her work aims to explore the intersection of business practices, management strategies, and ethical frameworks in entrepreneurial settings. As a researcher, Diya is committed to advancing knowledge in these domains and supporting the development of ethical and sustainable business practices.

Anuraj Sangha is an independent researcher and blogger with a Bachelor of Business Administration (BBA) in Project Management from Yorkville University. Her research interests focus on entrepreneurship, project management, and business ethics. Anuraj currently volunteers as a researcher at the Scientific Societal and Behavioral Research Center (SSBRC), where she contributes to ongoing research initiatives.

Ali Sher, PhD, is a professor of business at Yorkville University. He received his PhD in Engineering Management with a concentration in Information & Process Engineering and MS in Computer Science from George Washington University. He has published in prominent peer-reviewed journals, including International Technology Management Review, Journal of Interactive Learning, and Journal of Online Learning and Teaching. Prior to joining Yorkville University, Dr. Sher taught at the business schools of the University of New Brunswick, George Mason University, Rochester Institute of Technology, and DeVry University. Earlier in his career, he worked for the World Bank and International Finance Corporation, Washington DC, where he was responsible for developing and managing financial information systems for worldwide emerging market stock database clients.

Negar Sohaee, DBA, MBA, is a professor of the business administration at Yorkville University, with over six years of teaching experience in both in-person and online formats. She serves on the Ontario Campus Curriculum Committee and has contributed to research on sustainability education, AI's impact on HR, and autonomous vehicles in logistics. Dr. Sohaee's recent publications include chapters on entrepreneurship and employability competencies, showcasing her commitment to bridging practical business insights with academic excellence in her teaching.

Abdul Naveed Tariq, PhD, is a professor and program coordinator of the Honors Bachelor of Commerce – Business Management (BBM) program at the School of Management and Entrepreneurship (SME), Seneca Polytechnic, Toronto, Canada.

He holds a PhD in Management from the University of Putra Malaysia and has over 25 years of international experience in higher education. Dr. Naveed has held academic positions at various institutions across North America, the Far East, South Asia, the Middle East, and North Africa. In addition to his teaching responsibilities, he has been actively involved in university administration, research, quality accreditation processes, and curriculum design and development on a global scale.

Arif Toor, PhD, has extensive teaching experience in the field of management and business studies. He has taught business and accounting courses universities in Canada, the UK, and the Middle East. He has a PhD from the University of Toronto and manages his training consultancy business in Downtown Toronto. He is a firm believer in participatory learning that is student-centered.

About the Editor

Adnan ul Haque
DBA, Faculty of Business, Yorkville University, Canada
Director of Research, Scientific Societal and Behavioral Research Center (SSBRC)

Adnan is a Business Faculty member and Research Scientist at Yorkville University. He also serves as the Director of Research at the Scientific Societal and Behavioral Research Center (SSBRC) and as the Editor-in-Chief of the *Scientific Societal & Behavioral Research Journal* (*SSBRJ*). He holds a Doctor of Business Administration (DBA) in Organizational Behavior from the University of Wales Trinity Saint David, United Kingdom. His research specializes in gender-related occupational stress through a cultural lens.

Dr. Haque has received the Best PG Research Student Award from the University of Sunderland, London, and earned distinctions in PGD in business and management from ATHE, London, as well as a diploma in research and leadership from the University of

Copenhagen, Denmark. He also completed his MPA in HRM and BPA (Hons) from the University of Karachi with management and sciences distinctions. He is a certified Project Management Professional (PMP) and Agile Certified Practitioner (PMI-ACP).

As a seasoned business and management lecturer, Senior Researcher, and Session Chair and Keynote Presenter at international conferences, Dr. Haque is an expert in his field. He also serves as an external PhD examiner for universities worldwide. His consultancy experience spans roles as a Corporate Trainer in Stress Management and Professional Development for multinational corporations and an HR consultant for IT and logistics firms in the UK, Canada, and Pakistan.

Dr. Haque's research interests include organizational behavior, entrepreneurship, project management, human resources management, sustainability, Industry 4.0, knowledge hiding, occupational stress, supply chain management, innovative work behavior, and leadership styles. Specializing in occupational stress, he has published numerous research articles and presented keynotes at international conferences. He also contributes as an editor for books and special issues with renowned publishers such as Taylor & Francis, IGI, and Springer.

Preface

Entrepreneurship has been an instrumental driver of global economic growth and development, innovative disruptions, and social change. This book is designed to provide readers with a comprehensive understanding of the entrepreneurial landscape by blending conceptual frameworks, key theories, practical applications and real-world insight. Academics, professionals, scholars, readers, and aspiring entrepreneurs benefit from this textbook to understand and explore the contemporary issues of entrepreneurship in the modern era. It provides insight into critical issues, opportunities, and challenges faced by entrepreneurs.

This book offers a holistic view to readers by presenting topics that individuals experience in their entrepreneurial journey, ranging from fundamental principles to distinct challenges and emerging trends. It enhances the body of knowledge by enabling readers to address challenges; develop the required knowledge, skills, and abilities (KSAs) to operate in dynamic economies; and ensure successful operations.

Chapter 1 provides a general overview and explores the nature of entrepreneurship. It identifies the conventional types of entrepreneurs, followed by the entrepreneurial process. It also highlights opportunity recognition, feasibility planning, and essential traits associated with successful entrepreneurs.

Chapter 2 clarifies the concept by distinguishing types and types of entrepreneurship. It highlights the emerging forms of entrepreneurship in the modern era, supported by real-world examples to explain the role of societal and economic factors in shaping these distinct entrepreneurial ventures.

Chapter 3 introduces readers to concepts of design thinking and managing resources in entrepreneurship. It explores a human-centered approach enabling entrepreneurs to navigate complex challenges in dynamic environments. This chapter also highlights the role of design thinking in advancing critical thinking, enhancing innovation, improving customer engagement, and effective and efficient resource management to survive and thrive in a competitive landscape.

Chapter 4 critically examines gender and entrepreneurship by comparing male and female entrepreneurs. It attempts to identify the challenges and barriers women face in terms of resource accessibility and opportunity recognition. The chapter highlights the role of risk aversion in leading investor preferences and biases toward women's participation in specific industries. It also explores societal constraints and the need for innovative inclusivity and calls for policymakers to develop level playing fields for both male and female entrepreneurs.

Chapter 5 draws a comparison between volatile and stable economies to understand financial constraints and support systems in entrepreneurial ecosystems. For broader generalizability, four emerging economies, namely, Brazil, Nigeria, Pakistan, and Vietnam, are compared with advanced economies, namely, Canada, Germany, Japan, and the UK. It offers recommendations to support entrepreneurial ventures in diverse economic environments.

Chapter 6 provides details about the ingredients of successful business plans and market segmentation. It also highlights the importance of environmental scanning tools, including PEST, SWOT, ETOP, and QUEST analysis, that help entrepreneurs assess opportunities, trends, and challenges in environments and develop strategies for survival and growth.

Chapter 7 discusses essential financial considerations for entrepreneurs. It distinguishes between controllable and uncontrollable factors affecting entrepreneurial success. Furthermore, it highlights the importance of strategic planning, adaptability, and leadership.

Chapter 8 provides details about the role of operations management in entrepreneurial success. It compares the manufacturing and service industries to gain insight into the optimal utilization of resources, reducing costs, and enhancing customer satisfaction. It also provides details about the role of strategic management in operational efficiency along with the significance of effective stakeholder management in a competitive environment.

Chapter 9 focuses on essential marketing strategies and their effective usage by entrepreneurs in the modern era. Key business areas, including sustainable growth, brand awareness, and building customer loyalty, are explored through modern-day marketing tools and techniques, including digital marketing, content marketing, experiential marketing, influencer marketing, and the Search engine optimization (SEO).

Chapter 10 helps readers understand the evolving future of entrepreneurship while managing different types of risk interlinked with entrepreneurship. It also evaluates the significance of data-driven decision-making and emerging technologies, including blockchain and artificial intelligence (AI), in helping entrepreneurs mitigate various types of risk and achieve long-term sustainable growth.

Chapter 11 provides insight into transgender entrepreneurship. Lack of funding, systematic discrimination, and social stigma are barriers affecting transgender entrepreneurs. It also discusses the emerging opportunities in the market, the rise of the digital economy and gradually growing awareness, leading to the development of inclusivity in the corporate world that helps these individuals in successful operations.

Chapter 12 focuses on entrepreneurial stress, which is part of an entrepreneurial journey. It explores the causes and consequences of stressors affecting the physical and mental well-being of entrepreneurs. It also highlights the importance of resilience and structural support in addressing those stressors. The chapter provides recommendations related to the ability of entrepreneurial stressors to thrive in competitive environments.

Chapter 13 evaluates the transformative role of AI in the entrepreneurial ecosystem. It reflects the opportunities and challenges interlinked with the adoption of AI, especially the unpreparedness of existing businesses, the skills gap, and regulatory concerns.

Chapter 14 examines entrepreneurial leadership and decision-making. It highlights the strategic decision-making process, intuition and logic, pragmatism, ethics, and vision to succeed in a competitive landscape. The chapter also explores the leadership role in resource management, team formation, and crisis management.

Chapter 15 discusses factors for failure in intrapreneurship by providing details about their unique challenges. It offers real-world examples of companies that have faded due to their rigid stance. The chapter offers invaluable lessons that can help companies willing to embrace innovative ideas from the workforce.

The last chapter focuses on challenges emerging in the modern era and types of business models. It provides details about the adaptation of business models to operate effectively in the evolving entrepreneurial landscape. It also explores the role of customer development, flexible strategies, and risk mitigation in sustaining entrepreneurial growth and success.

This book compels readers to critically evaluate the factors and trends emerging in the entrepreneurial landscape; addresses constraints and opportunities in constantly evolving environments; enables them to approach situations through lessons learned from real-world examples; and encourages them to embrace entrepreneurship for innovation, social impact, and personal growth and development. In academics, it will guide students in developing knowledge and skills to transform concepts and theories into practical applications. In a professional setting, it will enable entrepreneurs to learn about the best practices to operate in a volatile, uncertain, complex, and ambiguous environment.

I hope that this book inspires readers to transform their ideas into impactful realities that create lasting value.

Adnan ul Haque
Author, Entrepreneurship: A Contemporary Approach

Chapter 1

Brief Overview and Nature of Entrepreneurship

Adnan ul Haque and Harmandeep Kaur

1.0 Introduction

An entrepreneur is an individual motivated to earn profit by running their own venture while accepting risk and bringing their own innovations (Haque, 2024). Veena (2024) states that a person or small group of partners who embark on an innovative journey to establish a new firm are referred to as 'entrepreneurs.' An aspirant entrepreneur actively searches for a certain business activity and is willing to take distinct yet calculated types of risk. As a result, should the idea succeed, this individual will also stand to gain the most. The process of carrying out business activity is regarded as entrepreneurship (Haque, 2024). Hence, innovativeness, risk, and business activities are arguably the remaining features of entrepreneurship. Nonetheless, the work of Zahra (2021) argues that entrepreneurship is often viewed through the lens of commercial activities, but it goes beyond commercial activities because the idea behind entrepreneurship is to create value.

This unique value can be created in diverse domains, such as social, environmental, and cultural domains. Nonetheless, with the passage of time, entrepreneurship has emerged as a dynamic field of study because of its innovation and key role in economic development. Entrepreneurial efforts sometimes include innovation. Large corporations may attempt to mimic this element by encouraging "intrapreneurship" (Veena, 2024). Employees are encouraged to address issues from an entrepreneurial perspective, which might result in a novel idea for the company. Even if the corporation gives these workers more autonomy, it still controls the project and bears all the risk. Entrepreneurs are beneficial to all businesses, both large and small.

However, according to Shane and Venkatraman (2000), entrepreneurship is the process of creating a novel company, adding value through innovation, and improving the market as it already exists. Therefore, it is reasonable to argue that those who are able to see potential opportunities and transform them into a workable plan are referred to as entrepreneurs. This chapter discusses the value of learning about entrepreneurship, its traits, different kinds of entrepreneurship, benefits and drawbacks, and the essential features associated with it.

1.1 The Importance of Studying Entrepreneurship

According to Hisrich and Peters (2017), innovations and global prosperity depend on entrepreneurship. This explanation suggests that entrepreneurship is crucial for fostering innovation, creating jobs, and igniting the economic growth engine. Thus, developing a

DOI: 10.4324/9781003504351-1

comprehensive understanding of entrepreneurship enables individuals to grasp adequate knowledge regarding the creation of new ventures and develop a foundation to compete and sustain in cutthroat competition as well as a constantly changing environment. The following are some of the reasons for studying entrepreneurship discussed in this chapter.

1.1.1 Developing Core Entrepreneurial Skills

Entrepreneurship equips individuals with essential skills for starting and growing successful businesses. It fosters creative thinking and opportunity identification through idea generation and problem-solving techniques. The curriculum includes crafting business plans, which help set goals and anticipate challenges (Wasim et al., 2024). Additionally, it teaches risk assessment and management, covering the financial aspects necessary for informed decision-making. Students learn marketing principles and networking, which are crucial for attracting and keeping customers. The curriculum also emphasized resilience and adaptability by navigating uncertainties and overcoming setbacks. It develops leadership and interpersonal skills, preparing individuals to lead confidently in their ventures.

1.1.2 Developing Knowledge Related to Business

Studying entrepreneurship is crucial for existing and emerging entrepreneurs to increase their business knowledge because it covers several important business functions, namely, marketing, management, operations, and finance. Students learn theories and apply them to real-world situations through experiential learning. The development of business plans helps deepen understanding through market analysis and financial projections. Education also sharpens critical thinking and problem-solving skills. Additionally, it teaches market dynamics and economic management, which are crucial for making informed decisions. Lastly, networking opportunities with industry experts enrich the learning experience by providing real-world insights.

1.1.3 Promoting Innovation and Creativity

Learning about entrepreneurship significantly boosts innovation and creative thinking by fostering a mindset that embraces uncertainty and values modern concepts (McGoldrick, 2024; Wasim et al., 2024). It helps people increase their ability to take calculated risks and hone their problem-solving skills so that they can take on difficult assignments via case studies and real-world projects. Programs often include brainstorming sessions and design thinking exercises, which promote creative thinking and group idea generation. People are encouraged by this education to see challenges as opportunities for personal growth and cultivate a resilient and adaptable entrepreneurial mindset (Haque, 2024). The development of relationships with mentors and seasoned professionals/business owners promotes innovation and offers useful knowledge (Haque, 2024).

1.1.4 Providing Opportunities for Personal Development

Studying entrepreneurship offers significant personal development opportunities beyond just business skills. It encourages self-reflection and helps individuals recognize their strengths and motivations, which is vital for career decisions. The proactive mindset cultivated through entrepreneurship promotes risk-taking and initiative (Haq et al. 2024). Additionally, hands-on projects and case studies foster resilience and adaptability, whereas decision-making skills are enhanced through analyzing risks and making informed choices. Team-based projects develop collaboration and leadership abilities, and activities such as pitching ideas improve communication skills (Kaur et al., 2024). Finally, entrepreneurship education highlights the importance of effective time management while enabling individuals to prioritize tasks and set goals efficiently. Nonetheless, many studies have confirmed that entrepreneurs experience a greater level of stress due to inadequate time management (Haq et al., 2024; Haq et al., 2024; Haque, 2024).

1.1.5 Increasing the Likelihood of Success

Learning about entrepreneurship increases the likelihood of success by providing essential knowledge in areas such as marketing and finance, risk management, and, most importantly, offering comprehensive knowledge about the creation of structured business plans. It facilitates networking with seasoned professionals and provides access to resources such as incubators. Additionally, hands-on experiences prepare students for challenges they can encounter in the real world. All in all, it fosters the tenacity, adaptability, and inventiveness necessary to thrive in the competitive business environment.

1.1.6 Providing Opportunities for Business Networking

Studying entrepreneurship gives aspiring business owners important networking opportunities. Through the many guest speakers and corporate executives that universities invite, students gain access to influential individuals. Students may receive guidance from seasoned mentors via mentorship programs. Programs could work with startup incubators to help people network with other entrepreneurs and investors. Strong alumni networks may provide opportunities for collaboration and mentorship. Additionally, students can expand their professional networks and obtain real-world experience via internships and industry placements.

1.1.7 Filling the Skills Gap by Offering a Well-Rounded Education

An education in entrepreneurship establishes a strong foundation for the establishment and operation of a business because of the extensive range of subjects that are addressed. You will acquire a comprehensive understanding of the essentials of business, such as finance, strategy, operations, and marketing. Coursework places strong emphasis on analytical and problem-solving skills via the use of real-world examples and projects. Students may hone their public speaking and presentation skills via activities such as presenting business concepts. They can also learn to manage their money wisely and become effective leaders by focusing on financial literacy and leadership principles.

1.1.8 Creating Local Job Opportunities Through Entrepreneurship

Encouraging people to establish their own enterprises and pursue studies in entrepreneurship substantially contributes to the local job generation. Entrepreneurs with the requisite skills and experience propel local economies via small and medium-sized enterprises

(SMEs). These firms bolster the supply chain and associated enterprises by generating jobs and stimulating demand for local products and services as they expand. Furthermore, entrepreneurial education helps individuals create local opportunities, thereby minimizing brain drain and maintaining employment (McGoldrick, 2024; Wasim et al., 2024).

1.1.9 Contributing to Economic Growth

Entrepreneurship increases employability, which increases economic competitiveness and results in better products and services as well as happier consumers (Kritikos, 2014; McGoldrick, 2024; Nexford University, 2024). With respect to business analytics research, retail techniques may be significantly impacted by an understanding of customer buying trends. Furthermore, every corporation must comprehend the importance of key elements of a business plan, such as the executive summary and market research. A company's sustainability is ensured by making precise financial projections and providing sufficient resources. Understanding the target market, the competitive landscape, and the need for a detailed breakdown of revenue and expenses are all necessary for creating a successful business plan (Kritikos, 2014). Understanding financial performance and projections is essential for navigating the difficulties of launching and growing a business, and this knowledge may be enhanced with the use of resources such as the SCORE website (McClure, 2022). Two ways in which entrepreneurship fosters economic progress are through innovation and employment creation. SMEs, often started by entrepreneurs, contribute significantly to GDP in most countries (World Bank Group, 2019).

1.1.10 Advancing in Innovation and Technology

Technology entrepreneurship is an investment in a project that brings together and employs skilled people and diverse assets to generate and capture value for the company. Technology entrepreneurship differs from other types of entrepreneurial activity (e.g., social entrepreneurship, small business management, and self-employment) in that it involves collaborative experimentation and the production of new products, assets, and their attributes, which are inextricably linked to advancements in scientific and technological knowledge as well as the firm's asset ownership rights (Bailetti, 2012). Many modern innovations originate from entrepreneurial ventures, which foster technological growth (Schumpeter, 1934). This makes entrepreneurship essential for staying competitive in today's digital economy.

1.2 Characteristics of Entrepreneurship

Creativity, resource management, opportunity recognition, and risk-taking are just a few of the most common characteristics of entrepreneurship (Drucker, 1985). Although entrepreneurs generate revenue, they do take calculated risks; however, most importantly, entrepreneurs must address complexities, connectedness and context (Haque et al., 2017). Entrepreneurship involves not only identifying and exploring opportunities in the environment but also ensuring that those opportunities are effectively organized and used to maximize the entrepreneur's advantage (Drucker, 1985).

1.2.1 Innovation

The first characteristic that comes to mind is "innovation" when any individual thinks about entrepreneurship (Haq et al., 2024). The emergence of entrepreneurship is based on the fundamentals of innovation. In other words, innovation is the heart of entrepreneurship. It is also argued that entrepreneurs disrupt established models by introducing new goods, services, or procedures (Schumpeter, 1934). They are visionary and creative problem solvers who are always looking for ways to improve and adjust accordingly to the demands of the market (Hisrich et al., 2017). In other words, they are innovative solution finders rather than wasting time and resources on worrying about problems.

1.2.2 Risk-Taking

Although they frequently take calculated risks, by nature, entrepreneurs are risk-takers (Kuratko, 2016). In other words, they are not risk averse; they might be calculative, but they would certainly take the risk of making things work out. In contrast to those who gamble carelessly, entrepreneurs make sound judgments resulting from intuition and in-depth research, weighing and assessing potential rewards against possible losses in a careful manner. Undoubtedly, entrepreneurs remain resilient in the face of challenges; they are keen to learn and grow from their failures and overcome obstacles by developing distinct strategies (Hisrich et al., 2017).

1.2.3 Vision and Opportunity Recognition

Another key characteristic frequently associated with entrepreneurs is vision and opportunity recognition. They recognize possibilities where many ordinary individuals remain unsure because they have a clear map (vision for the future). They have the unique ability to identify and make the most from the existing gaps in the market (Shane and Venkataraman, 2000). It would not be incorrect to state that they are farsighted rather than hindsight oriented. They do create innovative and unique solutions to cater to unfulfilled needs because of their farsightedness (vision).

1.2.4 Proactiveness

The preparedness for the situation and taking all probable scenarios before proceeding is regarded as proactiveness (Kaur and Haque, 2024). Entrepreneurs are aggressive in developing and pursuing business prospects through proactive approaches (Lumpkin and Dess, 1996). They frequently outperform their competitors by making necessary adjustments in their plans and operations through prompt decisions, particularly in a fast-paced environment, due to their proactive approach (Kuratko, 2016).

1.2.5 Resourcefulness

Entrepreneurs are credited for making the most of scarce resources. As resources are limited, entrepreneurs can use and improvise with resources through their innovative entrepreneurial capabilities (Haq et al. 2024; Haque, 2024). They can use their personal and professional relationships, connections, and available capital to not only drive but also maximize the growth of their business (Stevenson and Jarillo, 1990). Professional networking is a vital trait for entrepreneurs, as it allows them to delimit access restrictions to resources and attain them in a quicker manner than the common masses do.

1.2.6 Leadership and Team Building

Entrepreneurs require strong leadership not only to motivate their team but also to guide them in times of crisis (Hisrich et al., 2017). To scale or expand the business, both leading and developing teams are essential because they help meet long-term strategic goals (Kuratko, 2016).

1.2.7 Flexibility and Adaptability

In constantly changing markets, entrepreneurs need to be adaptive and agile (flexible). One essential component behind success is the ability to ensure that it remains effective in prompt response to changes (Morris et al., 2011). Successful entrepreneurs frequently adapt quickly to emerging facts and problems, allowing them to modify their plans as needed.

1.2.8 Customer-Focused

Being an entrepreneur requires having a thorough awareness of the demands and preferences of customers. Entrepreneurs who are strong concentrate on providing value to clients and addressing certain issues (Kuratko, 2016). Technological development and imaginative thinking are frequently driven by consumer desires.

1.2.9 Commitment and Passion

The intense enthusiasm that entrepreneurs have for their businesses helps them overcome challenging times. Since entrepreneurs typically labor for years to achieve meaningful benefits, this passion frequently translates into long-term commitment (Hisrich et al., 2017).

1.2.10 Financial Acumen

Effective money management is essential for any entrepreneur. This entails obtaining finance as well as being aware of profit margins and cash flow (Kuratko, 2016). Maintaining profitability is essential to keeping the organization afloat, even if monetary gains can occasionally be not the major driver.

1.2.11 Social Responsibility

Nowadays, most entrepreneurs rank social responsibility as their highest priority and thus include sustainability and moral behavior in their business plans (Porter and Kramer, 2011). This can generate additional value and positively contribute to society in the shape of positive societal change.

1.3 Types of Entrepreneurships

However, there is a separate chapter in the book discussing the types of entrepreneurs. This section provides an overview of most types of entrepreneurship. Entrepreneurship can be divided into various categories:

1.3.1 Small Business Entrepreneurship

Small business entrepreneurship involves providing services on a small level or ventures that typically serve local markets (Belyh, 2022). These business owners offer solutions for issues that arise within their local communities. The goal of small business entrepreneurship is to turn a sufficient profit to support themselves.

1.3.2 Large-scale Entrepreneurship

Large-scale entrepreneurship, typically associated with large companies, extends beyond offering goods and services for the local community (Belyh, 2022). The aim is to reach as many people as possible with their exciting idea, business, or service. The ability of large companies to generate financing independently does not determine their level of entrepreneurship. They receive investment through crowdsourcing platforms, venture capital firms, and angel investors. These business owners are inventors as well as service providers. They search for funding to support their creativity and introduce novel concepts in their sectors.

1.3.3 Scalable Startups

Businesses aim for large-scale growth, often relying on venture capital (Blank, 2013). According to Belyh (2022), entrepreneurs successfully scale their startups, identify gaps in the market and create a unique idea to address those identified gaps. These business owners epitomize innovation, developing a concept that changes the world in a drastic manner. They come up with concepts that drastically alter the world. Scalable startups are particularly common in the IT industry.

1.3.4 Social Entrepreneurship

This type of entrepreneurship focuses on solving social problems through innovative solutions (Dees, 2001). A social entrepreneur is a businessperson whose mission is to improve society (Belyh, 2022). This group of individuals wants to benefit the public while still turning a profit from their businesses. Social entrepreneurs provide invaluable solutions at little or no cost; they are not motivated primarily by profit but rather focus their efforts on social goods.

1.4 The Entrepreneurial Process

There are five stages in the entrepreneurial process (Fayolle, 2007). These include idea development, opportunity assessment, planning, firm formation/launch, and growth. The details will be discussed in a later chapter, but for starters, it helps the entrepreneur grow as well as distinguish themselves from competitors.

1.4.1 Opportunity Identification

According to Smith and Hendricks (2023), opportunity identification is the realization of an undiscovered business idea with high potential profits. It requires the ability to use knowledge efficiently, be aware of how data evolve, and scan the corporate environment with keenness. Entrepreneurs often identify gaps in the market that others overlook. Opportunity identification involves assessing demand and recognizing unmet needs (Kirzner, 2015). For example, opportunity identification, considered the first stage of the entrepreneurial process, is a critical skill for entrepreneurs (Kirzner, 2015).

1.4.2 Feasibility and Planning

According to Laverty and Littel (2020), a feasibility study enables a company to consider where and how it works, its competitors, any roadblocks, and the capital needed to start. The business plan then provides a framework for executing entrepreneurial ambition. Entrepreneurs conduct market research, assess their business model's feasibility, and develop a business plan that outlines how the venture will operate.

1.4.3 Resource Mobilization

Resource mobilization is the process by which a corporation decides which assets it has and plans to acquire more assets if necessary. Learning about corporate resources and mobilization will help you prepare for a meaningful career in which this may help a company achieve its goals. Securing the right resources—capital, talent, and networks—is essential. Entrepreneurs often start with limited resources and must acquire them efficiently (Bhide, 2000).

1.4.4 Launch and Growth

Effective plans must be put in place from the beginning to launch and expand an entrepreneurial endeavor. Setting attainable goals, carrying out in-depth market research, and having a sharp vision are essential. Once resources are secured, the venture is launched. Entrepreneurs must regularly monitor performance, adapt to market changes, and scale operations for growth (Stevenson and Jarillo, 1990).

1.5 Advantages and Disadvantages of Entrepreneurship

While entrepreneurship offers many rewards, it also comes with significant challenges. Understanding both sides helps individuals make informed decisions about pursuing entrepreneurial ventures. Entrepreneurs have the potential to generate wealth through business success, thus reflecting complete independence (Carland et al., 1984). In addition, it gives them the satisfaction of personal fulfillment. Many entrepreneurs find fulfillment in being their own boss and pursuing their passion (Gartner, 1988). Entrepreneurship provides individuals with a path to financial independence and personal fulfillment (Carland et al., 1984).

Nonetheless, there are also disadvantages of entrepreneurship. Risk and uncertainty are two of the greatest drawbacks largely associated with entrepreneurship. Entrepreneurs face significant risks, including market volatility, financial losses, and business failure (Knight, 1921). Moreover, many entrepreneurs struggle to balance the demands of their businesses with their personal lives (Boyd and Gumpert, 1983). There are many benefits of being a business owner, such as increased freedom and self-reliance, and potential for increased income (Maciá and Maciá, 2022), whereas there are some drawbacks of becoming an entrepreneur, such as being able to handle newly gained independence and inevitable economic risks.

1.6 Entrepreneurial Uniqueness and Key Personality Traits

According to Rana (2023), outstanding businesspeople have a certain set of abilities and traits that allow them to recognize opportunities when others do not. They can produce creatively, take measured chances, form enduring bonds with others, and endure hardships. Personality traits and cognitions are integral parts of entrepreneurship. The shortcomings of the trait method for entrepreneurship are addressed by the cognitive approach. Its goal is to use cognitions to understand how entrepreneurs act. Cognitive components such as scripts, self-efficacy, cognitive styles, and heuristics have been the focus of most of the related research. Successful entrepreneurs often share certain personality traits and cognitive skills that help them navigate the challenges of building a business.

Research has shown that entrepreneurs often exhibit traits such as risk tolerance, resilience, and creativity (McClelland, 1961). These traits help them persist through challenges and innovate solutions. Entrepreneurs tend to possess unique personality traits, such as high-risk tolerance and persistence, which contribute to their success (McClelland, 1961).

Alves and Wenjing (2022) reveal that entrepreneurs possessing extraordinary entrepreneurial skills have certain common traits: they have strong cognitive flexibility, they recognize a broad range of options and possibilities, and they are not bound by inherent concepts. Entrepreneurs also think differently, exhibiting higher levels of optimism, creativity, and problem-solving abilities (Baron, 2004). This helps them see opportunities where others see obstacles. Passion is a driving force behind many entrepreneurial ventures. Entrepreneurs who are deeply passionate about their ideas tend to be more resilient in the face of failure (Cardon et al., 2009).

Bibliography

Alves, J., and W. Yang. "Cognitive Mechanisms in Entrepreneurship Competence: Its Implication for Open Innovation." *Journal of Open Innovation: Technology, Market, and Complexity* 8, no. 2 (2022): 65. https://doi.org/10.3390/joitmc8020065.

Bailetti, T. "Technology Entrepreneurship: Overview, Definition, and Distinctive Aspects." *Technology Innovation Management Review* 2 (2012): 5–12.

Baron, R. A. "The Cognitive Perspective: A Valuable Tool for Answering Entrepreneurship's Basic 'Why' Questions." *Journal of Business Venturing* 19, no. 2 (2004): 221–239.

Belyh, A. "The 13 Different Types of Entrepreneurs (With Examples)." *FounderJar*, 2022. www.founderjar.com/types-of-entrepreneurs/.

Bhide, A. *The Origin and Evolution of New Businesses.* Oxford: Oxford University Press, 2000.

Blank, S. *The Startup Owner's Manual: The Step-by-Step Guide for Building a Great Company.* K&S Ranch, 2013.

Boyd, D. P., and D. E. Gumpert. "Coping with Entrepreneurial Stress." *Harvard Business Review* 61, no. 2 (1983): 44–64.

Carland, J. W., F. Hoy, and J. A. Carland. "Differentiating Entrepreneurs from Small Business Owners: A Conceptualization." *Academy of Management Review* 9, no. 2 (1984): 354–359.

Cardon, M. S., J. Wincent, J. Singh, and M. Drnovsek. "The Nature and Experience of Entrepreneurial Passion." *Academy of Management Review* 34, no. 3 (2009): 511–532.

Dees, J. G. "The Meaning of 'Social Entrepreneurship'." Stanford University, 2001.

Drucker, P. F. *Innovation and Entrepreneurship: Practice and Principles.* New York: Harper & Row, 1985.

Fayolle, A. *Entrepreneurship and New Value Creation: The Dynamic of the Entrepreneurial Process.* Cambridge: Cambridge University Press, 2007.

Gartner, W. B. "Who is an Entrepreneur? Is the Wrong Question." *American Journal of Small Business* 12, no. 4 (1988): 11–32.

Haq, I., A. U. Haque, and N. A. A. Rahim. "Entrepreneurial Stress and Mental Well-Being: Pre- and Post-COVID-19 Comparative Analysis of SMEs in Canada." *Forum Scientiae Oeconomia* 12, no. 1 (2024): 53–71.

Haq, I. U., A. U. Haque, H. Kaur, and N. A. A. A. Rahim. "Occupational Stress Affecting Innovative Capabilities and Innovative Work Behavior of Migrant Entrepreneurs." *Polish Journal of Management Studies* 9, no. 2 (2024): 238–253. https://doi.org/10.17512/pjms.2024.29.2.12.

Haque, A. U. "How Occupational Stress Impacts the Innovative Work Behavior and Innovative Entrepreneurial Capabilities of Migrant Entrepreneurs in Contrasting Economies?" In *Migration and Entrepreneurship in the Global Context*, edited by D. Hyams-Ssekasi and E. Daskalaki, 15–30. Cham: Palgrave Macmillan, 2024. https://doi.org/10.1007/978-3-031-34067-3_2.

Haque, A. U., E. Aydin, and E. Uysal. "A Comparison of Effectiveness of Global Leaders and Domestic Leaders in Electronic Retail Industry." *Global Journal of Management and Business Research (G)* 17, no. 3 (2017): 11–20.

Hisrich, R. D., M. P. Peters, and D. A. Shepherd. *Entrepreneurship.* New York: McGraw-Hill Education, 2017.

Kaur, H., and A. U. Haque. "The Impact of Occupational Stress on the Performance of Employees in Competitive Sectors: Systematic Review." *International Journal of Applied Business and Management Studies* 9, no. 1 (2024): 1–7.

Kaur, H., A. U. Haque, and P. Gkasis. "The Impact of Varying Styles of Leadership on Team Dynamics and Project Success." *Forum Scientiae Oeconomia* 12, no. 3 (2024): 51–69. https://doi.org/10.23762/FSO_VOL12_NO3_3.

Knight, F. "Risk, Uncertainty and Profit." Boston: Houghton Mifflin Company, 1921.

Kritikos, A. S. "Entrepreneurs and their Impact on Jobs and Economic Growth." *IZA World of Labor*, 2014. Accessed November 1, 2024. https://wol.iza.org/articles/entrepreneurs-and-their-impact-on-jobs-and-economic-growth/long.

Kirzner, I. M. *Competition and Entrepreneurship.* Chicago: University of Chicago Press, 2015.

Kuratko, D. F. *Entrepreneurship: Theory, Process, Practice.* 10th ed. Boston: Cengage Learning, 2016.

Laverty, M., and C. Littel. "11.3 Conducting a Feasibility Analysis." *Entrepreneurship | OpenStax*, January 16, 2020. Accessed November 1, 2024. https://openstax.org/books/entrepreneurship/pages/11-3-conducting-a-feasibility-analysis.

Lumpkin, G. T., and G. G. Dess. "Clarifying the Entrepreneurial Orientation Construct and Linking it to Performance." *Academy of Management Review* 21, no. 1 (1996): 135–172.

Maciá, F., and F. Maciá. "The Advantages and Disadvantages of Being an Entrepreneur." *Human Level*, 2022. Accessed November 1, 2024. www.humanlevel.com/en/blog/digital-marketing/advantages-disadvantages-entrepreneur.html.

McClelland, D. C. *The Achieving Society.* Princeton, NJ: Van Nostrand, 1961.

McClure, B. "How to Analyze a Company's Financial Position." *Investopedia*, 2022. Accessed November 1, 2024. www.investopedia.com/articles/fundamental/04/063004.asp.

McGoldrick, J. "Why is it Important to Study Entrepreneurship?" *Nexford University*, 2024. Accessed November 1, 2024. www.nexford.edu/insights/why-is-it-important-to-study-entrepreneurship.

Morris, M. H., D. F. Kuratko, and J. G. Covin. *Corporate Entrepreneurship & Innovation*. Boston: Cengage Learning, 2011.

Nexford University. "What is Entrepreneurship: How to Become an Entrepreneur." *Nexford University*, 2024. Accessed November 1, 2024. www.nexford.edu/insights/what-is-entrepreneurship.

Porter, M. E., and M. R. Kramer. "Creating Shared Value." *Harvard Business Review* 89, no. 1/2 (2011): 62–77.

Rana, A. "The Unique Skills and Characteristics of Successful Entrepreneurs." *LinkedIn*, 2023. Accessed November 1, 2024. www.linkedin.com/pulse/unique-skills-characteristics-successful-amit-rana?utm_source=share&utm_medium=member_ios&utm_campaign=share_via.

Schumpeter, J. A. *The Theory of Economic Development: An Inquiry into Profits, Capital, Credit, Interest, and the Business Cycle*. Cambridge, MA: Harvard University Press, 1934.

Shane, S., and S. Venkataraman. "The Promise of Entrepreneurship as a Field of Research." *Academy of Management Review* 25, no. 1 (2000): 217–226.

Smith, E., and B. Hendricks. "Opportunity Recognition: Definition, Importance & Examples." *Study.com*, 2023. Accessed November 1, 2024. https://study.com/academy/lesson/opportunity-recognition-or-definition-examples.html.

Stevenson, H. H., and J. C. Jarillo. "A Paradigm of Entrepreneurship: Entrepreneurial Management." *Strategic Management Journal* 11, no. 5 (1990): 17–27.

Veena. "What is Entrepreneurship?" *Stanford Online*, 2024. Accessed November 1, 2024. https://online.stanford.edu/what-is-entrepreneurship.

Wasim, J., M. H. Youssef, I. Christodoulou, and R. Reinhardt. "The Path to Entrepreneurship: The Role of Social Networks in Driving Entrepreneurial Learning and Education." *Journal of Management Education* 48, no. 3 (2024): 459–493. https://doi.org/10.1177/10525629231219235.

World Bank Group. "Small and Medium Enterprises (SMEs) Finance." 2019. Accessed November 1, 2024. www.worldbank.org/en/topic/smefinance#:~:text=SMEs%20account%20for%20the%20majority,(GDP)%20in%20emerging%20economies.

Zahra S. A. (2021). International entrepreneurship in the post Covid world. *Journal of World Business, 56*, no. 1, 101143. https://doi.org/10.1016/j.jwb.2020.101143

Case Study: A Fresh Graduate's Entrepreneurial Journey

Harmandeep Kaur and Adnan ul Haque

Background

Jessica, a recent graduate, found herself struggling to secure a job in her field. Frustrated by the lack of opportunities, she decided to take a different route and start her own venture. Having pursued her Bachelor of Business Administration (BBA) during the COVID-19 pandemic, where most of her courses were online, she was deeply inspired by the potential of online education. Her entrepreneurial ambitions were driven by her goals to provide creative and innovative tech solutions. This led her to focus on establishing herself in the e-learning market. This creative approach was in response to the growing e-learning market. However, her entrepreneurial journey was far from easy.

Jessica faced several key challenges, including a lack of entrepreneurial experience, limited financial resources, and constant pressure to survive in a highly competitive and dynamic market. Despite these hurdles, she remained determined to turn her vision into reality.

The Entrepreneurial Process

Jessica starts out by pointing out a need in the market for online education—specifically, customized learning resources for students with varying learning preferences. While creating a minimum viable product, she asks for input from potential customers. Jessica ensured that she used professional networking sites and reliable sources to investigate funding methods; she explored how to pitch her idea and what could be interrelated pitch challenges. She explored various methods to fund her business, especially bootstrapping and angel investors, to start her venture. She connected with different professionals, mentors, gurus, and other tech industry executives to seek guidance and invaluable insights. She was successful in connecting with those experts through a pitch competition. Nonetheless, Jessica must manage the stress of uncertainty, contend with market competition, and strike a balance between opportunity and risk. She is inspired and encouraged by her determination and is excited to take on the challenges ahead.

Conclusion

Modern-day entrepreneurship is illustrated through the example of Jessica's experience. Resilience, creativity, and resourcefulness are the three main characteristics of an entrepreneur that are shown by Jessica. Despite the challenges of uncertainties and several types of risks she was facing, she did not give up. Instead, she saw them as stepping stones to learn and accomplish her goals and dreams.

Reflection Questions

- As an entrepreneur, what are the key traits shown by Jessica?
- Highlight the challenges faced by Jessica in the entrepreneurial process, and how does she tackle them?
- Explain how Jessica balanced the risks and benefits of entrepreneurship.
- After reviewing the case, what strategies would you recommend to Jessica that could strengthen her position in her entrepreneurial journey?
- Explain the core principles reflected in chapter one through Jessica's journey.

Chapter 2

Types and Kinds of Entrepreneurship

Adnan ul Haque and Irfan ul Haq

2.0 Introduction

This chapter offers an extensive overview of the key distinct types and kinds of entrepreneurship. The development of a comprehensive understanding of the distinction between these concepts is crucial because individuals frequently confuse them. The characteristics, along with motivation, are largely associated with the kinds of entrepreneurship, whereas types of entrepreneurship explore the concepts related to the nature of entrepreneurial ventures. In other words, the essence of endeavors (nature and scope) is linked with types, whereas motivation and fundamental characteristics are associated with kinds of entrepreneurship. The broadly categorized major types and several kinds of entrepreneurship developed over time are discussed in this chapter.

2.1 Types of Entrepreneurs

The company's size and structure, along with the business scope, define the types of entrepreneurs. Numerous different types have emerged recently, indicating the manifesto of entrepreneurs, as the context plays a vital role in their emergence (Morris et al., 2011). Although a wide range of types are operating, some of the key types that are commonly found across the globe are discussed below:

2.1.1 Small-Scale Business Entrepreneurs

Regardless of the type of economy, whether it is advanced or emerging, small businesses play a significantly important role in the economic growth and development of a country (Storey, 1994; Faizan and Haque, 2016; Haq et al., 2024; Haque, 2024). Small businesses, such as internet cable operators, retail businesses, grocery shops, and restaurants, usually operate locally (Storey, 1994). According to a survey carried out by the U.S. Small Business Administration (2019), these small-scale businesses often employ fewer than 500 people, and interestingly, most are family-owned businesses. For example, the cofounder of Paul Mitchell hair products, John Paul DeJoria, began his entrepreneurial venture with a relatively small budget and steadily expanded it by concentrating on local sales and services. His business started from scratch with limited resources, and gradually, what started as a small personal business eventually evolved into a global brand with the passage of time (DeJoria, 2017).

DOI: 10.4324/9781003504351-2

2.1.2 *Innovators (Pioneers/Trend Setters)*

Although innovators would be discussed later under the types of entrepreneurs, this would also apply to kinds too. Schumpeter (1934) explained that innovator entrepreneurs are those who innovate products and/or services that serve as a breakthrough in the market. These are products and services that change the dynamics of the market. Interestingly, many are categorized as small enterprises; certain innovators—such as biotech companies or tech startups—expanding their companies to become major industry players (Hisrich et al., 2017). Facebook's creator, Mark Zuckerberg, is one of the innovators that drastically changed worldwide communication and advertising; therefore, it would be regarded as an innovator because his business today has transformed social relationships and commerce to a greater extent (Kirkpatrick, 2011).

2.1.3 *Silver (Seniors/Second Run) Entrepreneurs*

Those individuals who decide to take a late career or second run in life are regarded as silver entrepreneurs. They are often referred to as senior entrepreneurs because, usually post-retirement, they decide to start their own entrepreneurial venture (Kautonen et al., 2017). In pursuit of fulfilling their lifelong goals and ambitions or just remaining active, these silver entrepreneurs start their businesses using their financial resources, networks and connections, and rich experience. For example, Mc-Donald's Ray Kroc, in the later stage of his life, bought McDonald's and continued expanding the business during his entrepreneurial career. At the age of 52, he started the franchise business of McDonald's, which later emerged as a franchise empire, eventually leading to the transformation of the fast-food industry while creating chains (franchises) (Love, 1995).

2.1.4 *Social Entrepreneurs*

According to Yunus (2010), the focus of social entrepreneurs is on starting businesses that address social or environmental issues while providing some sort of solution to those problems. The creation of social value remains their main goal, which means that social service is first, whereas the second objective is to earn profit (Mair and Marti, 2006). Providing education, clean water, and access to healthcare facilities in underprivileged areas are types of such businesses. Hence, the business operates with the intention of improving the social conditions of others. For example, the founder of TOMS Shoes, Blake Mycoskie, is a prime example of a social entrepreneur. He created a unique social business model—the "one-for-one" model. Under this concept, one pair of shoes sold means that one needy and deserving person is awarded a pair of shoes. In other words, with each sale, there is a donation of one pair of shoes to a needy person. His company has been successful not only by making profits but also by addressing societal issues (Mycoskie, 2011).

2.1.5 *Migrant Entrepreneurs*

Migrant entrepreneurs are those who move from one place to another within the country in pursuit of better business opportunities (Gogol, 2024; Haq et al., 2024; Haque, 2024). Usually, driven by the need to provide economic stability, especially in unknown surroundings, migrant entrepreneurs are people who start firms in one region or location and later move to another region or location (Kloosterman and Rath, 2001). Frequent interaction with migrant groups or communities from which these entrepreneurs are themselves helps them because they target these groups. They have cultural awareness and knowledge about the customs and preferences of those migrant communities. For example, a Scottish entrepreneur runs a small eatery business in London and sells traditional Scottish dishes such as Neeps, Haggis, and Tatties. Since they specialize in it, the Scottish community in London will be their target audience.

2.1.6 Immigrant Entrepreneurs

Haque (2024) argued that immigrant entrepreneurs are those individuals who start their own entrepreneurial venture in a different country. Thus, it is more about crossing international boundaries, whereas migrants are crossing only regional boundaries (Haq et al., 2024). In other words, immigrant entrepreneurs travel to a different country with the intent of starting their own venture there (Portes and Rumbaut, 2014). Aliaga-Isla and Rialp (2013) argued that by generating employment opportunities and constantly developing creative ideas in their host nations, they reflect the key role of immigrant entrepreneurs in economic growth at the international stage. For example, the cofounder of Google, Sergey Brin, is an immigrant entrepreneur, as noted that he moved from the Soviet Union to the United States of America. Importantly, online advertising and internet search engines have advanced significantly because of Brin's efforts (Vise, 2005).

2.1.7 Minority Entrepreneurs

Women and ethnic minorities are among the underrepresented or underprivileged groups that are regarded as minority entrepreneurs (Fairlie and Robb, 2008). In addition, Faizan and Haque (2016) argued that minority entrepreneurs are marginalized groups that, although they face several distinct challenges—including financial constraints, limited access to bank loans, or market opportunities—have a high rate of success because they focus on niche markets. For example, the owner of FUBU, Daymond John, is a successful minority entrepreneur. He specifically focused on the African American community to address their needs and respond to their demands. Urban streetwear was the underserved market that he targeted to establish himself (John, 2016), and later, his brand created appeal among a global audience.

2.1.8 Digital or Online Entrepreneurs

With the emergence of the internet, the growth of digital marketing has created e-commerce platforms, and online entrepreneurs capitalized on opportunities by selling their products, services, or ideas online (Chaffey, 2019). It is also important to note that the internet economy has facilitated this type of entrepreneurship because it is one of the easiest platforms to set up a business and even operates in the international market by creating an appeal for the global audience. For instance, Amazon's founder, Jeff Bezos, is a classic example of an online entrepreneur who started his operations with an online bookshop, which later transformed into one of the largest e-commerce platforms in the world. In other words, it started being small but subsequently expanded to become one of the largest e-commerce systems worldwide. By using a digital platform, Bezos illustrated how a digital entrepreneur could transform the entire retail sector (Stone, 2013).

2.2 Kinds of Entrepreneurs

In comparison to types, the kinds of entrepreneurs are driven by motivation. In other words, mindset and motivation play a vital role in the approaches carried out by entrepreneurs. Hence, it could be stated that different kinds of entrepreneurs have a distinct business approach due to varying motivations and sets of beliefs that shape their sense of the world around them (Cherry, 2024). Interestingly, the early work of Drucker (1985) noted that the actions of entrepreneurs are driven by motivation and fundamental characteristics. The wide range of the continuum has revolutionized innovation-driven models to merely sustain the survival model based on meeting the needs of consumers, which are presented by these major kinds of entrepreneurs.

2.2.1 Managers

Operational responsibilities and administrative roles are taken by entrepreneurial managers, who are focused primarily on the effective and efficient management of business activities. Most commonly, they prioritize the sustenance and expansion of existing systems while exhibiting very limited interest in innovation (Mintzberg, 1973). Furthermore, the work of Kuratko (2016) explained that instead of demonstrating creativity or taking risks with experimentation, these entrepreneurs quite often emphasize long-term strategic planning and stability. One practical example would be Starbucks' Howard Schultz, who at times has been viewed from the entrepreneurial lens as the managerial entrepreneur. He ensured that Starbucks' expansion was through a greater emphasis on consistent quality, enriching the experiences of the customers, and maintaining operational excellence so that it was more of a managed brand rather than experimenting with the brand by introducing unique and innovative features (Schultz, 2011).

2.2.2 The Wannabes

The wannabes were defined for the first time by Filion (1991) by stating that these types of individuals aspire to be entrepreneurs; however, they usually do not have the required set of skills, undivided commitment, and sufficient risk tolerance that restrict them from achieving their ambition. Owing to inadequate planning and reluctance to take decisive action, their business ventures never materialized. In other words, the plan to start an entrepreneurial venture might not take flight because they are unsure about their actions and often lack sufficient concrete planning. Morris et al. (2011) argued that such individuals lack a proper strategy or genuine vision, while glamour interlinked with entrepreneurship is the reason behind their motivation to start an entrepreneurial venture. For example, some early entrepreneurs labeled "wannabes" were involved in the dot-com bubble, such as Webvan, owing to their innovative concepts that promised enormous potential, yet the idea lacked long-term strategies or business models. These enterprises often fail due to owners' inadequate execution of their strategies or a lack of understanding of the industry's realities (Cassidy, 2002).

2.2.3 Survivalists

According to Welter et al. (2017), instead of grasping the opportunity, survivalist entrepreneurs become involved in business because it is necessary for them to survive. In other words, unlike other entrepreneurs who are commencing business to innovate and have the desire to establish their own venture, these entrepreneurs are driven by the need to generate income from their ventures so that they can make both ends meet. Perhaps these entrepreneurs are often the type of people who have many financial commitments and have lost their job for some reason, and as a result, they start their own venture to pay their bills and other expenses. Interestingly, the work of Banerjee and Duflo (2011) revealed that these types of entrepreneurs are mostly found in environments where employment opportunities are, and therefore, they start to operate their own small venture to generate relatively modest revenue. For example, we can see that in several emerging economies, there are roadside kiosks or food stalls and taxi and/or rickshaw drivers operating their own businesses. These are all small vendors and business owners engaged in products and services, following a survivalist business model. The passion or motivation to engage in entrepreneurship is not based on the ambition to have their own successful venture but is compelled to fulfill their daily living needs (Banerjee and Duflo, 2011).

2.2.4 Pushers

According to Shane and Venkataraman (2000), external pressures such as economic hardship and constraints, the desire to escape from an unsatisfactory job, and societal pressures are motivations behind pushing entrepreneurs. In other words, pushers are pushed by external motivators rather than having any clear vision about operating a business. For instance, the founder of Under Armour, Kevin Plank, realized that there was no efficient football apparel, which served as the key factor behind the commencement of business operations. Frustration (an external factor) plays a vital role and therefore creates a product to overcome this problem (Cunningham et al., 2020).

2.2.5 Pullers

In contrast to pushers, pullers are propelled into commencing business by their enthusiasm and/or clear vision to make the most opportunities (Gartner, 1985). Individuals with a keen desire for innovation and experimentation (internal motivators) are pullers, which drive them to pursue their passion (Kuratko, 2016). In other words, they are innovators following their instinctive desires to follow their passion and make the majority of the available opportunities (Kuratko, 2016). For instance, one may define SpaceX and Tesla's founder, Elon Musk, as puller entrepreneurs. Vance (2017) explained that he is driven to pursue a career in business by realizing the opportunity, as he followed his passion (intrinsic factor) because he wanted to address global problems such as energy crises and pollution. Thus, he recognized the opportunity and developed sustainable solutions by exploring space and energy conservation.

2.2.6 Calculators

Extensive analytical skills are the key characteristic of calculator entrepreneurs. They make decisions based on thorough research and in-depth data-driven analysis (Hisrich et al., 2017). Interestingly, such individuals take many perspectives into consideration and focus on different angles before proceeding with decisions. In other words, they are more calculative in their approach and avoid unnecessary risks before proceeding with their plans (Hisrich et al., 2017). They are also referred to as investment averse by nature unless they view such investments as likely to reap rewards. According to Stevenson and Jarillo (1990), calculator entrepreneurs are focused mainly on the maximization of returns and the reduction of risk, whereas they are less motivated to follow their desire. The Chief Executive Officer of Berkshire Hathaway, Warren Buffet, is an example of a calculator entrepreneur. He is renowned for making calculated decisions about investments, and his financial decisions are based on data-driven analysis (Lowenstein, 2008). Moreover, detailed and careful risk assessment and extensive research play pivotal roles in making informed decisions about investments (Lowenstein, 2008).

2.2.7 Innovators

According to Schumpeter (1934), entrepreneurs who are developing new goods, services, processes, or ideas that could drastically change current sectors or even lead to the development of a whole new market are regarded as innovator entrepreneurs. According to Kuratko (2016), risk-taking skills are a key feature of innovators, as they disrupt the traditional mode of operations in sectors and industries. They often challenge the status quo and traditional norms in sectors and industries (Kuratko, 2016). Again, as used earlier, the example of Elon Musk, SpaceX and Tesla's founder would also fit as a classic innovator entrepreneur because he not only challenged the existing status quo but also disrupted operations in the energy sector. His ambition and vision to provide sustainable energy and space exploration drove him to become an entrepreneur (Vance, 2017).

2.2.8 Revolutionary Visionaries

Beyond simple inventions, entrepreneurs who are better known for their revolutions based on their farsightedness (vision) are regarded as revolutionary visionaries (Drucker, 1985). Hence, the main objective of these revolutionaries is to ensure that there is significant positive change in industries as well as in society. In other words, these are entrepreneurs with a bold approach who bring innovative ideas or business models that challenge conventional methods in particular fields. According to Shane and Venkataraman (2000), their vision to revolutionize sectors or change society usually makes them pioneers in the development of business strategies and launching disruptive technologies, products, services, or processes. For example, Grameen Bank's founder, Muhammad Yunus, is an example of a visionary/revolutionary entrepreneur. Microcredits and microfinance are the concepts he developed; thus, he is the pioneer of these concepts, which not only offered poor and underprivileged people financial services but also played a vital role in reducing poverty on a global scale (Yunus, 2010). The traditional banking business model was challenged by offering a sustainable alternative that revolutionized the banking system and global poverty reduction.

2.2.9 *Futurepreneurs*

Young entrepreneurs aged between 18–29 who are willing to start their own business are regarded as futurepreneurs. These types of entrepreneurs are in the process of starting their venture by seeking funds, mentorship, and support from a network to pursue their dream of having their own business. This group is still in its embryonic stages because there are limited data. However, it is about aspiring individuals looking for guidance to start their own businesses.

2.3 Conclusion

From the above discussions, it is concluded that the economic environment, social circumstances, and personal motivations play crucial roles in the formation of the types and kinds of entrepreneurs. The kinds and types of entrepreneurs are explored in this chapter to explain that although the prime objective of entrepreneurship is usually value creation, the ways and techniques utilized to accomplish this objective are relatively distinct.

The types of entrepreneurs are many, but keeping the scope of this book, only notable ones are discussed, such as small-scale businesses, innovators, social entrepreneurship, silver entrepreneurship, migrant entrepreneurship, immigrant entrepreneurship, minority entrepreneurship, and online entrepreneurship. Nonetheless, the nature and scope of entrepreneurial ventures are key factors in shaping these types. Characteristics and motivation are significant attributes that determine the type of entrepreneurship. Some notable kinds include managers, survivalists, innovators, wannabes, pushers, pullers, revolutionary visionaries, and futurepreneurs.

Nonetheless, the above in-depth analysis reveals that different entrepreneurial ventures are the result of different entrepreneurial approaches. The context is very important to consider while pursuing a business. It is concluded that the process of entrepreneurship is dynamic in nature; thus, individuals must consider all environmental factors, along with the societal needs and changing preferences of the audience, before the commencement of their entrepreneurial journey. As entrepreneurship progresses, novel forms and varieties are expected to emerge in the future, thereby further enhancing the dynamics of the entrepreneurship field.

Bibliography

Aliaga-Isla, R., and A. Rialp. "Systematic Review of Immigrant Entrepreneurship Literature: Previous Findings and Ways Forward." *Entrepreneurship & Regional Development* 25, no. 9–10 (2013): 819–844.

Banerjee, A. V., and E. Duflo. *Poor Economics: A Radical Rethinking of the Way to Fight Global Poverty*. New York: PublicAffairs, 2011.

Cassidy, J. *Dot.con: The Greatest Story Ever Sold*. New York: Harper Perennial, 2002.

Chaffey, D. *Digital Marketing: Strategy, Implementation, and Practice*. New York: Pearson Education, 2019.

Cherry, K. "What is a Mindset and Why it Matters." *Verywell Mind*, 2024. Accessed November 1, 2024. www.verywellmind.com/what-is-a-mindset-2795025#:~:text=Your%20mindset%20is%20a%20set, range%20of%20situations%20in%20life.

Cunningham, J. A., B. Harney, and C. Fitzgerald. *Effective Technology Transfer Offices: A Business Model Framework*. Berlin: Springer, 2020.

DeJoria, J. P. *Good Fortune: How I Made My Fortune by Making a Difference.* New York: Random House, 2017.

Drucker, P. F. *Innovation and Entrepreneurship.* New York: Harper & Row, 1985.

Fairlie, R. W., and A. M. Robb. *Race and Entrepreneurial Success: Black-, Asian-, and White-Owned Businesses in the United States.* Cambridge, MA: MIT Press, 2008.

Faizan, R., and A. U. Haque. "The Relationship between Societal Attributes, Feminine Leadership & Management Style: Responses from Pakistan's Urban Region Female-Owned Businesses." *European Journal of Business and Management* 8, no. 23 (2016): 171–191.

Filion, L. J. "Vision and Relations: Elements for an Entrepreneurial Metamodel." *International Small Business Journal* 9, no. 2 (1991): 26–40.

Gogol, F. "Migrants vs. Immigrants: What's the Difference?" *Stilt.* 2024. Accessed November 1, 2024. www.stilt.com/blog/2020/08/migrants-vs-immigrants-whats-the-difference/.

Gartner, W. B. "A Conceptual Framework for Describing the Phenomenon of New Venture Creation." *Academy of Management Review* 10, no. 4 (1985): 696–706.

Haq, I., A. U. Haque, and N. A. A. Rahim. "Entrepreneurial Stress and Mental Well-Being: Pre- and Post-COVID-19 Comparative Analysis of SMEs in Canada." *Forum Scientiae Oeconomia* 12, no. 1 (2024): 53–71.

Haq, I. U., A. U. Haque, H. Kaur, and N. A. A. A. Rahim. "Occupational Stress Affecting Innovative Capabilities and Innovative Work Behavior of Migrant Entrepreneurs." *Polish Journal of Management Studies* 9, no. 2 (2024): 238–253. https://doi.org/10.17512/pjms.2024.29.2.12.

Haque, A. U. "How Occupational Stress Impacts the Innovative Work Behavior and Innovative Entrepreneurial Capabilities of Migrant Entrepreneurs in Contrasting Economies?" In *Migration and Entrepreneurship in the Global Context*, edited by D. Hyams-Ssekasi and E. Daskalaki, 15–30. Cham: Palgrave Macmillan, 2024. https://doi.org/10.1007/978-3-031-34067-3_2.

Hisrich, R. D., M. P. Peters, and D. A. Shepherd. *Entrepreneurship.* New York: McGraw-Hill Education, 2017.

John, D. *The Power of Broke: How Empty Pockets, a Tight Budget, and a Hunger for Success Can Become Your Greatest Competitive Advantage.* New York: Crown Business, 2016.

Kautonen, T., S. Down, and M. Minniti. "Ageing and Entrepreneurial Preferences." *Journal of Business Venturing* 29, no. 6 (2017): 952–970.

Kirkpatrick, D. *The Facebook Effect: The Inside Story of the Company That Is Connecting the World.* New York: Simon & Schuster, 2011.

Kloosterman, R., and J. Rath. "Immigrant Entrepreneurs in Advanced Economies: Mixed Embeddedness Further Explored." *Journal of Ethnic and Migration Studies* 27, no. 2 (2001): 189–201.

Kuratko, D. F. *Entrepreneurship: Theory, Process, Practice.* 10th ed. Boston: Cengage Learning, 2016.

Love, J. F. *McDonald's: Behind the Arches.* New York: Bantam Books, 1995.

Lowenstein, R. *Buffett: The Making of an American Capitalist.* New York: Random House, 2008.

Mair, J., and I. Marti. "Social Entrepreneurship Research: A Source of Explanation, Prediction, and Delight." *Journal of World Business* 41, no. 1 (2006): 36–44.

Mintzberg, H. *The Nature of Managerial Work.* New York: Harper & Row, 1973.

Morris, M. H., D. F. Kuratko, and J. G. Covin. *Corporate Entrepreneurship & Innovation.* Boston: Cengage Learning, 2011.

Mycoskie, B. *Start Something That Matters.* New York: Spiegel & Grau, 2011.

Portes, A., and R. G. Rumbaut. *Immigrant America: A Portrait.* 4th ed. Berkeley: University of California Press, 2014.

Schultz, H. *Onward: How Starbucks Fought for Its Life Without Losing Its Soul.* Emmaus, PA: Rodale Books, 2011.

Schumpeter, J. A. *The Theory of Economic Development: An Inquiry into Profits, Capital, Credit, Interest, and the Business Cycle.* Cambridge, MA: Harvard University Press, 1934.

Shane, S., and S. Venkataraman. "The Promise of Entrepreneurship as a Field of Research." *Academy of Management Review* 25, no. 1 (2000): 217–226.

Stevenson, H. H., and J. C. Jarillo. "A Paradigm of Entrepreneurship: Entrepreneurial Management." In *Entrepreneurship*, edited by Á. Cuervo, D. Ribeiro, and S. Roig, 7–18. Berlin: Springer, 2007.

Stone, B. *The Everything Store: Jeff Bezos and the Age of Amazon*. New York: Little, Brown, 2013.

Storey, D. J. *Understanding the Small Business Sector*. New York: Routledge, 1994.

U.S. Small Business Administration. "Small Disadvantaged Business." *U.S. Small Business Administration*, 2019. Accessed November 1, 2024. www.sba.gov/federal-contracting/contracting-assistance-programs/small-disadvantaged-business.

Vance, A. *Elon Musk: Tesla, SpaceX, and the Quest for a Fantastic Future*. New York: HarperCollins, 2017.

Vise, D. A. *The Google Story: Inside the Hottest Business, Media, and Technology Success of Our Time*. New York: Delta, 2005.

Welter, F., D. Audretsch, T. Baker, and W. B. Gartner. "Everyday Entrepreneurship – A Call for Entrepreneurship Research to Embrace Entrepreneurial Diversity." *Entrepreneurship Theory and Practice* 43, no. 3 (2019): 311–321.

Yunus, M. *Building Social Business: The New Kind of Capitalism That Serves Humanity's Most Pressing Needs*. New York: PublicAffairs, 2010.

Case Study: The Evolution of an Entrepreneur

Adnan ul Haque, Harmandeep Kaur and Irfan ul Haq

Background

In his late 30s, after losing his job during an economic downturn, Noah began this journey as a "survivalist entrepreneur." Initially, he wanted only to make sufficient money to provide food and shelter for his family. For this purpose, he decided to start a small business selling homemade crafts online.

The Shift

Noah changed his mindset when he observed that his business was gradually gaining increasing progress in the market. Upon realizing that the business could be scaled by the introduction of a line of eco-friendly products, he transitioned from being a "Survivalist" to an "Innovator." Previously, he was a push-entrepreneur, but now he was more of a Pull entrepreneur. Innovative packaging was designed to attract environmentally conscious consumers, and funds were aggressively allotted to research and development (R&D). A lasting impact on the environment and society was also sought by Noah, as noted earlier, who also transitioned into a puller rather than a pusher. Rapid growth was experienced by his business, and the characteristics of a managerial entrepreneur began to be adopted with a focus on scaling operations and improving efficiency through continuous improvement and research.

Conclusion

The fluid nature of entrepreneurship is highlighted by Noah's journey. Entrepreneurs often start in one category but gradually evolve into another category, based on experiences and the growth of their business operations.

Reflection Questions

Initially, what type of entrepreneur was Noah, and what served as the motivation for the transition in his entrepreneurial approach?

- How did the survivalist mindset of Noah shift to an innovation-oriented approach?
- With business expansion, what traits of managerial entrepreneurship did Noah embrace?
- How did external market factors influence Noah's transition from one type of entrepreneur to another?
- To ensure that there is sustainable continuous growth, what implementation strategies would you recommend to Noah?

Chapter 3

Categories, Design Thinking, and Managing Resources

Adnan ul Haque

3.0 Introduction

In the modern era, the role of entrepreneurship in economic growth and development is undeniable (Faizan and Haque, 2016; Haq et al., 2024; Haq et al., 2024; Haque, 2024). Nonetheless, the challenges and opportunities faced by entrepreneurs are unique. To survive and thrive, distinct strategies are adopted so that businesses can survive in complex business environments (Haque et al., 2017). Similarly, to effectively meet the demands of the market, adaptability and innovation help entrepreneurs adopt strategies effectively. Design thinking—a human-centered iterative methodology—is one such approach that helps entrepreneurs prioritize empathy, innovation, and creativity and find impactful practical solutions. This chapter explores the linkages between design thinking and various categories of entrepreneurship, that is, small-scale business, social entrepreneurship, scalable startups, intrapreneurship, and large-scale enterprises. The chapter reflects on how the association between design thinking and the identified categories enables entrepreneurship to mitigate risk, promote steady growth, and enhance innovation and creativity. Additionally, the chapter explores the design thinking steps used by entrepreneurs in a rapidly changing and uncertain environment. Lastly, the chapter delves into certain ways in which design thinking impacts each category through practical (real-world) examples.

3.1 Categories of Entrepreneurship

All four major kinds of entrepreneurship operating in the modern era are (a) small-scale ownership, (b) scalable startups, (c) social entrepreneurship and (d) intrapreneurship. Knowing these categories enables individuals to analyze many strategies for starting new businesses, including both opportunities and limitations (McCormick, 2022). Han (2022) defined design thinking as an approach as well as a mindset to bring innovation and solve problems through human-centered design. However, it is important to understand that it is distinct from other ideation processes and innovations because it has more to explore from a user-centric perspective and is solution-based rather than problem-based (Han, 2022). The implementation of design thinking significantly helps every kind of business. While operating in dynamic environments, entrepreneurs use design thinking because it stresses human-centered, iterative processes that encourage innovation, creativity, and adaptability (Brown, 2009). These are all vital aspects for the growth and survival of businesses in complex environments (Haque, 2024). The next section of this chapter explores the design thinking linkage with each entrepreneurial category.

DOI: 10.4324/9781003504351-3

3.1.1 Design Thinking and Scalable Startups

Innovative and creative technological solutions play a vital role not only in the quick expansion of scalable startups but also in grasping sizable markets (Brown, 2009; Han, 2022). Design thinking allows startups to concentrate on the needs of the consumer, test ideas rapidly and regularly, and improve continuously as per given feedback, thus fitting very adequately within this strategy (Brown, 2009).

According to Laoyan (2024), there are five stages in design thinking: empathizing (looking into the problem), defining (framing the problem statement), ideating (brainstorming to create a solution), prototype (creating different inexpensive versions), and testing (selecting the best after testing all prototypes). For example, design thinking helped Airbnb transform from a startup to a recognized hospitality platform worldwide (Hockenberry and Epstein, 2014). Accommodation in booking travel was a problem that was addressed through design thinking. Initially, the founders faced difficulty attracting the audience and creating appeals in the market. Guests and hosts were interviewed by applying design thinking's "empathize" stage to assess their needs, which led to further improvements in operations by ensuring that it was a trustworthy and user-friendly platform (Hockenberry and Epstein, 2014). By continuously improving its operations and business model to fit customer demands, this iterative development strategy helped Airbnb expand rapidly. Iterative and swift innovation as part of design thinking is often used in the empathy stage and prototyping state so that scalable startups effectively use it to address their needs. Through the acceleration of innovation cycles, most scalable startups gain competitive advantages that are created through design thinking (Brown, 2009). On the other hand, Ries (2011) found that startups grow by considering feedback from customers and quick prototyping. One of the major benefits of design thinking is that real-time and quick feedback is obtained, which helps startups reduce the likelihood of major operational risks and failures (Blank, 2013). Nonetheless, the drawback of design thinking is that if businesses spend more time in the prototype and testing stages rather than actively working toward growth and expansion, scaling could be delayed (Liedtka, 2011).

3.1.2 Small-Scale Ownership and Design Thinking

Typically, operating in localized markets, these small-scale organizations rely heavily on consumer loyalty and personal relationships to be successful. Through the empathy stage and ideation stage, design thinking enables small-scale owners to customize their products precisely according to consumer needs and demands (Dunne and Martin, 2006). Through routine interactions with consumers, a small, family-owned restaurant can learn about its preferences and thus use design thinking to rethink its decor, cuisine, or service style (Liedtka and Ogilvie, 2011). Hence, regular engagement is important to reimagine the operations as well as designs. By prototyping, such as introducing and experimenting with new dishes on a limited-time basis, they enable themselves to gather vital feedback, which could significantly help them adapt and adjust their business model to stay relevant in a competitive environment (Liedtka and Ogilvie, 2011).

According to Liedtka (2011), design thinking could lead to a customer-centered innovative approach that could help small-scale organizations improve their competitiveness, especially given the scarcity of resources. Furthermore, the work of Beckman and Barry (2007) revealed that small organizations could benefit from design thinking to perform small-scale experimentation without becoming involved in financial risk like larger organizations. Strong loyalty can be developed by matching their offerings to consumer demands, which is one of the greatest advantages of design thinking for small businesses (Brown, 2009; Liedtka and Ogilvie, 2011). However, the drawback for small-scale businesses is that, owing to a lack of implementation expertise and limited resources, they struggle in applying the process of full-scale design thinking (Liedtka and Ogilvie, 2011). Things become further complicated when owners are juggling many roles and when time is limited (Liedtka and Ogilvie, 2011).

3.1.3 Design Thinking and Intrapreneurship

The central concept of design thinking is 'innovation', which drives intrapreneurship (Kelly, 2023). When individuals carry out innovation within an existing organization, it is regarded as intrapreneurship (Kelly, 2023). In other words, it could be argued that the application of entrepreneurial ideas inside current companies reflects a focus on creativity and innovation. Hence, innovation is a common element of design thinking and intrapreneurship. For instance, 3M scientist Spencer Silver was researching in a laboratory to develop tougher adhesives and accidentally discovered a light adhesive that would not bond to surfaces but would stick (Kelly, 2023). Arthur Fry was another scientist (3M) who was frustrated with bookmarks falling out of his choir hymnal (Kelly, 2023). Thus, he came up with the idea of using light adhesives as bookmarks. Eventually, the two scientists developed a revolutionary product—widely regarded as the Post-It Note (Kelly, 2023). Another large corporation, Google, has incorporated design thinking to inspire team innovation and creativity. The policy of "20% time" motivates and encourages staff members to concentrate on initiatives outside of their usual responsibilities, which leads to the creation of products such as Google Maps and Gmail (Schmidt and Rosenberg, 2014).

Following the design thinking process, these advancements came from employing empathy to pinpoint internal requirements and prototype new innovative solutions. Importantly, internal obstacles such as a risk aversion culture and rigid structures destroy intrapreneurship. Design thinking creates environments for experimentation and reframes issues in ways that fit business objectives, thereby enabling intrapreneurs to overcome these obstacles (Zahra, 1991). Large corporations use design thinking frequently to encourage internal creativity and enable intrapreneurs to lead new projects. Martin (2009) stated that usually, change-resistant corporate environments benefit from design thinking, as they offer risk mitigation by developing structured and organized innovation procedures. Dunne and Martin (2006) argued that internal resistance to new ideas decreases as design thinking helps intrapreneurs formulate user-friendly solutions aligned with business plans and corporate strategies. On the other hand, Liedtka (2011) argued that intrapreneurs could find it significantly difficult because of rigid and inflexible corporate structures, which hamper the flexible and iterative nature of design thinking.

3.1.4 Design Thinking and Social Entrepreneurships

The prime focus of social entrepreneurship is on establishing businesses that are not only financially viable but also address social and societal issues (Brown and Wyatt, 2010). In other words, financial stability and addressing societal problems are objectives of social entrepreneurship. Since design thinking stresses empathy, which fits the social entrepreneur's objective to a greater extent (Brown and Wyatt, 2010), empathy allows them to cater to human needs; thus, design thinking specifically is suitable for social entrepreneurs in commencing their business activities (Brown and Wyatt, 2010). For instance, TOMS Shoes employs a one-for-one social business model. According to this business model, with the sale of one pair of shoes, a pair of shoes is donated to a needy child in an emerging economy. TOMS developed a brand that creates social consciousness and appeals to consumers because they empathize with both consumers and beneficiaries.

Social entrepreneurs benefit significantly from design thinking's iterative method because they not only prototype but also test ideas without making enormous upfront expenditures and investments, especially when resource constraints are a significant challenge for them (Brown, 2009). For example, IDEO's not-for-profit wing, IDEO.org, incorporates design thinking to address social challenges through creative solutions, such as providing access to clean water in emerging economies through the development of scalable solutions and affordable prototypes resulting from feedback from consumers (Brown and Wyatt, 2010).

The emphasis of design thinking on empathy and iterative prototyping helps social entrepreneurs stay in line with their social objectives while also enabling innovation with limited resources. Through design thinking, social entrepreneurs handle the complexity of societal issues in a manner that is impactful and financially viable (Bornstein, 2007; Dees, 1998). In underserved markets, social entrepreneurs benefit from the human-centered approach of design thinking because it helps them develop solutions that are not only sustainable but also significantly impactful (Brown and Wyatt, 2010). However, the major drawback is that design thinking might create a situation where social entrepreneurs might find it difficult to strike the right balance between social impact and financial viability (Dees, 1998). At times, it could relatively slow down progress if the focus is not on scaling solutions but rather on placing greater emphasis on iteration (Dees, 1998).

3.1.5 Design Thinking in Large-Scale Businesses

Competitive advantages and a culture of innovation are fostered through the efficient and effective use of design thinking in large-scale businesses. In other words, it serves as an important catalyst for not only providing competitive advantage but also developing a culture of innovation. However, the prominent challenge for these organizations is ensuring flexibility in their operations and design thinking due to structural complexities and processes. According to Kelley and Kelley (2013), the culture of experimentation fosters collaboration among different departments because of the effective adoption of the principles of design thinking. Hence, it could be argued that design thinking plays a vital role in breaking down silos. For instance, Procter & Gamble (P&G) redefined its product development process by embracing design thinking principles. The principles help P&G promote collaboration among diverse teams in the 'empathize' stage and 'define' stage so that customer feedback is constructively used for innovation (Brown, 2009). The swift prototyping and testing of unique concepts results from this human-centered approach (Martin, 2009). Additionally, the time-to-reach market is significantly reduced when a product is closely aligned to meet the needs and preferences of consumers through design thinking (Martin, 2009).

Moreover, large corporations also benefit from design thinking due to its iterative nature, which helps in the effective fulfillment of customer expectations and adaptation to changing market demands (Liedtka, 2011). According to Hansen and Birkinshaw (2007), design thinking not only helps large businesses adapt and innovate but also sustains growth, especially with advancements in technologies and changing consumer behavior and preferences. Hence, competitiveness in the market increases, and product offerings are also enhanced in a constructive manner because of effective design thinking. Nonetheless, it is important for large-scale businesses to keep close watch of the challenges arising from design thinking (Taneja and Toombs, 2014). The norms and practices established in large organizations are often structured and rigid; thus, it is often difficult to develop a flexible culture, leading to failure in the iterative learning and implementation process (Taneja and Toombs, 2014). Hence, it could be argued that design thinking offers a significant platform to gain competitive advantage, but the greatest challenge is the structural process and norms in place. To benefit from design thinking, organizations must embrace openness and innovation.

3.2 Finding Sources of New Venture Ideas

Extensive market research, feedback from customers, and practical (first-hand) experience within the industry are some of the prominent sources that inspire ideas for new businesses (McCormick, 2022). Opportunity recognition is another key component at the core of entrepreneurship that is understood through the creation of proper awareness of these sources (Kirzner, 2015). Considering some of the sources for opportunity recognition in light of real-world examples helps in understanding and clarifying concepts. Commonly, inspiration occurs to entrepreneurs from their own business, sector, or industry fields. For example, Warby Parker's founder was frustrated with expensive eyewear; thus, this first-hand experience drove him to develop a fashionable substitute at an affordable price (Wasserman, 2012). On the other hand, inspiration for new ideas could emerge from the careful observation of underprivileged market segments. For example, Dollar Shave Club carefully observed inefficiencies in the razor business and thus developed subscription services to fill these gaps. Technological advancements, namely, the IoT, blockchain, and artificial intelligence (AI), have also led to the creation of innovative solutions. In other words, opportunities to develop innovative solutions are often driven by technological advancements. For example, Tesla, by using advanced technologies—especially batteries—transformed the automotive industry (Popomaronis, 2020).

3.3 Opportunity Identification and Changing Thought Process

Recognizing opportunities in the market involves exploring unfulfilled needs or detecting inefficiencies, which could serve as a foundation for developing a solution (Kirzner, 2015). Nonetheless, to recognize opportunities and change existing thought processes, entrepreneurs consider "creative destruction" by moving away from traditional methods of operations while embracing change (Schumpeter, 1942; Haque, 2024). Schumpeter (1942) explained creative destruction as the process by which fresh and creative ideas replace outdated technologies or goods. While exploring opportunity recognition, it is important to consider conventional opportunity recognition. McCormick (2022) argued that conventional opportunity recognition is an approach that uses industry analysis, consumer surveys, or observations to focus primarily on exploring gaps in existing markets. It is important to conduct this research before these markets are entered. For instance, Amazon first saw potential growth in the demand for online book sales before it entered the market. On the other hand, creative opportunity recognition occurs when entrepreneurs create opportunities through disruption and innovative and creative thinking. For example, Netflix shifted from a pay-for-use business model (renting DVDs) to a subscription-based streaming business model, which led to the revolutionary transformation of the entertainment industry (Van Alstyne et al., 2016).

3.4 Design Thinking: An Overview

Greater emphasis on human-centered innovation is a key aspect of a problem-solving method—design thinking (Brown, 2009). Iterative prototyping, creativity and innovation, and empathy are encouraged by this approach to address distinct complex issues (Dunne and Martin, 2006).

The five stages of design thinking include empathize, define, ideate, prototype, and test (Kelly, 2023).

- Empathize: Having knowledge and understanding about the target audience's needs for whom businesses are designed.
- Define: Clearly, state and express the issue (problem) businesses want to address.
- Ideate: Generate a spectrum of creative solutions (ideas) through brainstorming.
- Prototype: Formulate clear, simple, and cost-effective designs (samples) of the proposed solution.
- Test: Refine the solution as per the gathered feedback and suggestions.

According to Brown (2009), the chance of failure is greatly reduced, creative experimentation is enhanced, and customer demands are prioritized because of the iterative nature of design thinking. Thus, it helps not only small-scale businesses but also large corporations. However, design thinking could be highly time-consuming, particularly for businesses that are facing the situation of delivering quick results in a short time, reflecting greater pressure (Liedtka, 2011). In addition, a culture shift is required for design thinking, as most organizations are familiar with efficiency-driven and linear procedures (Liedtka, 2011).

3.5 Using Design Thinking to Advance New Venture Development

According to Hockenberry and Epstein (2014), entrepreneurs can apply design thinking in the creation of new ventures by enabling businesses to reach their target audience so that the goods and/or services produced in actuality satisfy their needs and demands. This approach eventually led to the growth and expansion of new businesses (Hockenberry and Epstein, 2014). Airbnb presents the classic case of applying design thinking to improve and further refine its platform based on suggestions and feedback from early customers (Hockenberry and Epstein, 2014). In other words, Airbnb founders ensured that the platform was user-friendly and positively enriching customer experiences (Hockenberry and Epstein, 2014).

3.6 Guidelines for Using Design Thinking in Venture Development

It is important for entrepreneurs to have empathy for their consumers; therefore, they must understand customers' pain points (Tuttle, 2021; Patel et al., 2024). For instance, the creators of Mint.com interviewed many users to learn about their painful experiences (frustration) with tools offering personal financial solutions (Tuttle, 2021; Patel et al., 2024). Only if entrepreneurs understand the pain of their customers can they develop products and/or services that eliminate the identified pain (problem).

Entrepreneurs should develop iterations and prototypes (Kelly, 2023). It is important that entrepreneurs develop prototypes, carry out tests with actual users, and refine (iteration process) the products and/or services according to the suggestions and feedback received rather than delaying and waiting for a perfect solution (Madsen, 2024). For instance, Dropbox is an example reflecting that prior to launching the actual product, a simple explainer video was launched to gauge interest (Madsen, 2024). This approach helped them identify pain points, and consumer feedback was given before developing the actual product.

Entrepreneurs should be ready to change if feedback from the user highlights that there is a fundamental flaw or a large miss in the comprehensive transformation of ideas into opportunities. It is also important that entrepreneurs are open to embracing the change and accept the critique to further refine the product and/or services. For example, Slack was originally used as an internal communication tool for a gaming business; however, after realizing its greater potential, it was transformed into an important workplace collaboration tool (Butterfield, 2019).

3.7 Conclusion

It is concluded that irrespective of their size and type, from small-scale businesses to large-scale enterprises, they face different types of challenges and constraints in the development of products and/or services. Nonetheless, there are opportunities arising from these constraints and challenges. The role of design thinking in converting recognized ideas to viable business opportunities has been established through an extensive review of the literature as well as real-world examples. Moreover, the entrepreneurship field is constantly evolving and currently covers a broad spectrum of fields. Design thinking helps businesses efficiently and effectively identify opportunities, optimize resource allocation and management, and create creative and innovative entrepreneurial ventures that appeal to their target audience. Design thinking's iterative and user-friendly approach corresponds to an uncertain, complex, and constantly evolving environment. It also enables entrepreneurs to address complexities in an effective and efficient manner so that they can create not only innovative and creative solutions but also relevant and practical ones.

Bibliography

Beck, T., A. Demirgüç-Kunt, and V. Maksimovic. "Financial and Legal Constraints to Growth: Does Firm Size Matter?" *The Journal of Finance* 60, no. 1 (2005): 137–177.

Beckman, S. L., and M. Barry. "Innovation as a Learning Process: Embedding Design Thinking." *California Management Review* 50, no. 1 (2007): 25–56.

Blank, S. *The Four Steps to the Epiphany*. K&S Ranch, 2013.

Bornstein, D. *How to Change the World: Social Entrepreneurs and the Power of New Ideas*. Oxford University Press, 2007.

Brown, T. *Change by Design: How Design Thinking Transforms Organizations and Inspires Innovation*. Harper Business, 2009.

Brown, T., and J. Wyatt. "Design Thinking for Social Innovation." *Stanford Social Innovation Review*, 2010. Accessed November 1, 2024. https://ssir.org/articles/entry/design_thinking_for_social_innovation.

Butterfield, S. "The Making of Slack." *Harvard Business Review*, 2019.

Dees, J. G. "The Meaning of Social Entrepreneurship." *Stanford Social Innovation Review*, 1998.

Dunne, D., and R. Martin. "Design Thinking and How it will Change Management Education: An Interview and Discussion." *Academy of Management Learning & Education* 5, no. 4 (2006): 512–523.

Faizan, R., and A. U. Haque. "The Relationship between Societal Attributes, Feminine Leadership & Management Style: Responses from Pakistan's Urban Region Female-Owned Businesses." *European Journal of Business and Management* 8, no. 23 (2016): 171–191.

Han, E. "What is Design Thinking & Why is it Important?" *Harvard Business Review*, 2022. Accessed November 1, 2024. https://online.hbs.edu/blog/post/what-is-design-thinking.

Hansen, M. T., and J. Birkinshaw. "The Innovation Value Chain." *Harvard Business Review* 85, no. 6 (2007): 121–130.

Haq, I., A. U. Haque, and N. A. A. Rahim. "Entrepreneurial Stress and Mental Well-Being: Pre- and Post-COVID-19 Comparative Analysis of SMEs in Canada." *Forum Scientiae Oeconomia* 12, no. 1 (2024): 53–71.

Haq, I. U., A. U. Haque, A. Kaur, and N. A. A. A. Rahim. "Occupational Stress Affecting Innovative Capabilities and Innovative Work Behavior of Migrant Entrepreneurs." *Polish Journal of Management Studies* 9, no. 2 (2024): 238–253. https://doi.org/10.17512/pjms.2024.29.2.12.

Haque, A. U. "How Occupational Stress Impacts the Innovative Work Behavior and Innovative Entrepreneurial Capabilities of Migrant Entrepreneurs in Contrasting Economies?" In *Migration and Entrepreneurship in the Global Context*, edited by D. Hyams-Ssekasi and E. Daskalaki, 15–30. Cham: Palgrave Macmillan, 2024. https://doi.org/10.1007/978-3-031-34067-3_2.

Hockenberry, M., and J. Epstein. "The Airbnb Story." *Fast Company*, 2014.

Liedtka, J., and T. Ogilvie. *Designing for Growth: A Design Thinking Toolkit for Managers*. Columbia University Press, 2011.

Kelly, K. "6 Famous Examples of Intrapreneurship." *Forum*, 2023. https://forummagazine.org/6-famous-examples-of-intrapreneurship.

Kelley, T., and D. Kelley. *Creative Confidence: Unleashing the Creative Potential Within Us All*. Crown Business, 2013.

Kirzner, I. M. *Competition and Entrepreneurship*. University of Chicago Press, 2015.

Laoyan, S. "How to Solve Problems Using the Design Thinking Process." *ASANA*, 2024. Accessed November 1, 2024. https://asana.com/resources/design-thinking-process.

Madsen, C. B. "How Dropbox Validated a Billion-Dollar Idea with One Simple Experiment." *LinkedIn*, 2024. Accessed November 1, 2024. www.linkedin.com/pulse/how-dropbox-validated-billion-dollar-idea-one-simple-berthou-madsen-kvrdf/.

Martin, R. *The Design of Business: Why Design Thinking is the Next Competitive Advantage*. Harvard Business Press, 2009.

McCormick, H. "4 Types of Entrepreneurship: Which One is Right for You." *CFE*, 2022. Accessed November 1, 2024. https://cfe.umich.edu/4-types-of-entrepreneurship-which-one-is-right-for-you/.

Patel, N. S., S. Puah, and Z-F. K. Kok. "Shaping Future-Ready Graduates with Mindset Shifts: Studying the Impact of Integrating Critical and Design Thinking in Design Innovation Education." *Frontiers in Education* 9 (2024). https://doi.org/10.3389/feduc.2024.1358431.

Popomaronis, T. "5 Tips for Recognising a Meaningful Business Opportunity When You See One". (2020, May 11). www.stamfordadvocate.com/business/article/5-Tips-for-Recognizing-a-Meaningful-Business-15261546.php

Ries, E. *The Lean Startup: How Today's Entrepreneurs Use Continuous Innovation to Create Radically Successful Businesses.* Crown Business, 2011.

Schmidt, E., and J. Rosenberg. *How Google Works.* Grand Central Publishing, 2014.

Schumpeter, J. A. *The Theory of Economic Development: An Inquiry into Profits, Capital, Credit, Interest, and the Business Cycle.* Harvard University Press, 1934.

Taneja, S., and D. A. Toombs. "The Role of Design Thinking in the Creation of Innovation in Organizations." *Business Horizons* 57, no. 4 (2014): 493–501.

Tuttle, G. "What is Design Thinking and Why is it Important?" *wework*, 2021. Accessed November 1, 2024. www.wework.com/ideas/professional-development/creativity-culture/what-is-design-thinking.

Van Alstyne, M. W., G. G. Parker, and S. P. Choudary. *Harvard Business Review*, 2016. Accessed November 1, 2024. https://hbr.org/2016/04/pipelines-platforms-and-the-new-rules-of-strategy.

Wasserman, N. *The Founder's Dilemmas: Anticipating and Avoiding the Pitfalls That Can Sink a Startup.* Kauffman Foundation Series on Innovation and Entrepreneurship. Princeton University Press, 2012.

Zahra, S. A. "Predictors and Financial Outcomes of Corporate Entrepreneurship: An Exploratory Study." *Journal of Business Venturing* 6 (1991): 259–285.

Case Study: Design Thinking Incorporated by an Immigrant Entrepreneur

Harmandeep Kaur and Adnan ul Haque

Background

In search of better and unique opportunities, Indian immigrant entrepreneur Tarun moved to Canada. In North America, he observed a growing demand for eco-friendly and sustainable packaging solutions because environmental consciousness and awareness are developing among businesses and consumers. Using his experience in product design and a strong engineering academic background, Tarun started a specialized business in biodegradable packaging materials.

Opportunity Recognition

With careful observation of Canadian businesses' struggle in finding an alternative that is sustainable, affordable, and eco-friendly packaging material, the entrepreneurial journey of Tarun began. An opportunity in the market for an environmentally and cost-effective responsible package solution was seen by him, and the credit went to his prior knowledge of sustainable design and material science.

Applying Design Thinking

Tarun adopted a design-thinking approach to develop his product. Local customers and business owners were engaged so that they had a clear understanding of their packaging needs. Their concerns about durability, environmental impact, and cost were taken into consideration by him. The next stage was the ideation stage, where multiple packaging designs that could meet these requirements were brainstormed, and Tarun also led that session.

Next, Tarun created various kinds of prototypes related to packaging materials, which were tested by a few early adopters in the local market. Feedback from these businesses was constructively used by Tarun to ensure that the design was further refined and improved in terms of durability and quality while ensuring that the designs remained eco-friendly and cost-effective.

Challenges

Tarun faced several challenges as an immigrant entrepreneur. In Canada, a different regulatory environment had to be navigated by ensuring that he learned and developed awareness about the local laws related to environmental standards and sustainable business practices. In the beginning, funding options were limited, and there were immense difficulties in establishing relationships with Canadian investors because he did not have sufficient experience and had a limited network.

Success and Growth

A product that was well received by the market was created by the excellent design thinking of Tarun after facing many challenges. Customer needs were empathized with by him, and his product was iteratively improved, which allowed long-term contracts with local businesses to be secured, eventually leading to expansion into larger markets across Canada. Partnerships with environmental organizations were looked for by Tarun after his business grew, further strengthening his brand's commitment to sustainability. His venture proved to be a leading provider of eco-friendly packaging in the region, proving how a customer-centric approach and design thinking can lead to entrepreneurial success.

Reflection Questions

- How did Tarun find the opportunity to start an eco-friendly packaging business in Canada? What specific market gaps did he see, and how did his background influence his entrepreneurial decision?
- What steps of the design thinking process did Tarun follow in developing his business? How did each stage (empathizing, ideation, or prototyping) contribute to the final product offering?
- How was feedback from customers incorporated by Tarun into the development of his packaging designs? Why is the input from concerned parties about the design thinking process important for new ventures and startups?
- As an immigrant entrepreneur, what were the challenges Tarun faced, and how did he overcome those challenges?
- How did Tarun create environmentally friendly packaging while ensuring that it remained affordable? Why is this balance important for businesses operating in the sustainable products sector?
- Considering Tarun's success in local markets, what strategies should he adopt to scale his business further? How can design thinking continue to play a role in a company's future innovations and growth?
- How did Tarun adapt to the cultural and regulatory differences between India and Canada? What role did understanding the local market environment play in shaping his business strategy?

Chapter 4

Entrepreneurship and Gender

Harmandeep Kaur

4.0 Introduction

Overall success, resource allocation and optimization, and recognition of opportunities are some of the critical aspects that are influenced by gender to a certain extent. In other words, the role of gender is critical in entrepreneurship. Interestingly, the inclusive entrepreneurial ecosystem develops and grows because of the challenges, opportunities, and distinct capabilities demonstrated by male and female entrepreneurs. Perhaps, opportunities as well as challenges faced by contrasting genders shape and develop an all-inclusive entrepreneurial ecosystem. From a gender perspective, this chapter critiques the product development model, evaluates how the entrepreneurial environment influences outcomes, explores how gender shapes and formulates the differentiation between ideas and opportunities. With respect to gender, understanding the complexities of entrepreneurship can be better examined through these elements.

4.1 Distinguishing Between Ideas and Opportunities

In this section, ideas and opportunities are differentiated and explained through the lens of gender. Real-life examples are used to reflect on how each gender recognizes opportunities and the response in terms of praise and recognition from industries and mass consumers.

4.1.1 Defining Ideas and Opportunities

It is essential to differentiate between ideas and opportunities to understand the core of entrepreneurship. According to the work of Shane and Venkataraman (2000), creative concepts are regarded as ideas that have the potential to transform into products or services. Nonetheless, it is not always the case that all types of ideas can be converted into actual and viable business opportunities. In contrast, opportunities are ideas that could result in financial viability and are often aligned with the needs of the market (Shane and Venkataraman, 2000).

4.1.2 Gender Differences in Opportunity Recognition

Opportunity recognition is often approached differently by men and women because of varying socialization processes and environmental factors, as shown by the number of studies. When industries are aligned with societal roles or personal experiences, opportunities

DOI: 10.4324/9781003504351-4

are often recognized by women entrepreneurs, particularly in sectors such as consumer services, education, and healthcare (Brush et al., 2009). These sectors not only correspond with traditional gender roles and responsibilities but also influence the types of entrepreneurial ventures likely to be pursued by female entrepreneurs. In contrast, higher-risk sectors such as finance and technology are frequently dominated by male entrepreneurs because, despite significant uncertainty, there is potential for high returns. This disparity, which is not solely attributable to personal interests, also reflects access to networks and broader societal and social norms that facilitate opportunity recognition (Eddleston and Powell, 2012).

To support this notion, the example of the founder of Samasource, Leila Janah, is presented. She recognized an opportunity to address poverty on a global platform by outsourcing her digital work to emerging economies. She embodies social entrepreneurship, as her business venture showed greater and stronger commitment to social impact. However, in comparison, the founder of Tesla and SpaceX, Elon Musk, commences his operations in high-risk sectors that rely on technical expertise and innovation, commonly indicating greater male dominance in these high-risk sectors. Elon Musk is more famous and praised than Leila Janah is. Hence, female entrepreneurs are more comfortable operating in low-risk sectors, whereas male entrepreneurs prefer high-stake sectors.

Nonetheless, a single case should not be used as a standard to draw generalizations; however, it could be stated that gender's approach to risk may be a deciding factor for industry choice. In other words, this example shows that the pursuit of entrepreneurial opportunity may be affected by gender to a certain extent. Although recent studies reveal that innovative entrepreneurial capabilities are more evident among female entrepreneurs than among male entrepreneurs, this is often due to female resilience in dealing with stressors (Haq et al., 2024). Interestingly, Faizan and Haque (2016) reported that social welfare and community services are typically prioritized by female entrepreneurs, which might lead them to avoid high-risk and aggressive sectors to explore their opportunities. Nonetheless, this distinction indicates that there is a need for educational training and relevant assistance to raise awareness and encourage women to expand their entrepreneurial pursuits.

4.1.3 Critical Analysis of Opportunity Recognition

The distinction between ideas and opportunities is not merely confined to academic concepts because support programs, along with policy-related implications, are crucial for nurturing and developing entrepreneurship. Awareness among female entrepreneurs about certain opportunities may be relatively low (Eddleston and Powell, 2012). Thus, they need further increased educational programs. These programs should aim not only to increase awareness but also to highlight the need for proper recognition and re-evaluation of existing entrepreneurial support systems. The chances of success of female-led entrepreneurial ventures increase to a significant extent, especially outside the conventional sector, due to frameworks and programs designed to assist women in building professional networks and relevant skills (Eddleston and Powell, 2012).

4.2 The Entrepreneurial Environment and Gendered Outcomes

This section explores the existing entrepreneurial environment and its linkage with gender-based performance, opportunities, and challenges.

4.2.1 The Role of the Entrepreneurial Environment

Business success is significantly influenced by various attributes found in the entrepreneurial environment. These attributes include the legal framework, cultural norms, professional and social networks, and access to capital (Haque, 2024). Nonetheless, the impact of these distinct factors can vary significantly between male and female entrepreneurs (Brush et al., 2014).

4.2.2 Access to Capital and Financial Constraints

For female entrepreneurs, one of the significant barriers remains limited access to financial resources (Faizan and Haque, 2016). The Diana Report published in 2014 revealed that there is a significant gap in the gender gap in pay and entrepreneurial activities (Brush et al., 2014). Notably, capital venture funding for women constitutes less than 3% of total capital investments (Brush et al., 2014). In other words, there is a substantial difference between the funding that males and females receive from the government and from institutions (Haq et al., 2024). Moreover, within investment circles and funding institutions, there is unconscious bias, which is the root cause behind this inequality (Baker and Henry, 2013). This unconscious bias often results in favoring male entrepreneurs because there is a perception that they are more capable of handling distinct risks interlinked with ventures operating in sectors expecting greater growth.

In addition, the study of Backer and Henry (2013) revealed that the non-confrontational approach in negotiations among women often leads to the perception that males are effective negotiators, thus increasing the likelihood of receiving higher venture capital funding. This reluctance to fund female-led ventures limits the funding cycle for women, ultimately reducing future funding opportunities. For instance, the founder of The Muse, Kathryn Minshew, faced immense difficulties related to funding in her entrepreneurial journey. Although she successfully ran a popular platform, there was greater skepticism among investors regarding the viability of her business model. This skepticism occurred especially because there was implicit bias among investors that her team was predominantly female. Ironically, instead of focusing on the potential of the business, investors were more focused and interested in the dynamics of teams, reflecting the bias that female entrepreneurs often face while fundraising for their ventures.

4.2.3 Legal and Cultural Barriers

In contrast to males, females face unique legal restrictions that add further complications to their efforts to commence their own ventures (Faizan and Haque, 2016). For example, in some economies, to obtain loans and start their own venture, women often require approval from male guardians (Faizan and Haque, 2016). In emerging economies, these legal barriers significantly discourage women from setting up their own ventures (Pasha et al., 2020).

Similarly, the entrepreneurial participation of women is often restricted by cultural expectations and social norms in societies (Faizan and Haque, 2016). Families are prioritized over careers in many cultures, which hinders their participation in entrepreneurial activities. For instance, previously, women faced legal restrictions in Saudi Arabia that made it difficult for them to own property or start entrepreneurial ventures without male consent. The role of women in emerging economies is associated mostly with domestic affairs and family care, indicating that cultural obstacles hinder their participation in entrepreneurial activities. However, the trends have changed due to recent reforms. In other words, the situation has substantially improved with recent reforms that allow females greater freedom to participate and engage in entrepreneurial activities. Nonetheless, entrepreneurial opportunities and capabilities for women are adversely affected by legal and cultural barriers (Faizan and Haque, 2016).

4.2.4 Critical Analysis of the Entrepreneurial Environment

The need for systemic change highlights the challenges women face in accessing capital and navigating cultural and legal barriers (OECD, 2022; World Bank, 2022). According to a report from the World Bank (2022), the entrepreneurial potential of women remains restricted by discriminatory cultural norms and legal barriers in certain regions across the globe. It is also noted in the report that in some regions, business registration and securing property rights are rigid, discouraging women's engagement and participation in entrepreneurial activities (World Bank, 2022). Interestingly, recent research confirms that female entrepreneurs often face greater obstacles than their counterparts do, especially in securing capital funding and loan attainment (OECD, 2022). In addition, the rate of rejection for loans is higher for female entrepreneurs than for male entrepreneurs; thus, female entrepreneurs can secure only small loan amounts, indicating gender bias (OECD, 2022). Collaboration among support organizations, policymakers, and financial institutions is important to create an environment conducive to women's entrepreneurial success (IFC, 2021).

Recently, efforts have been made to ensure a level playing field for all genders. Increasing the visibility of female entrepreneurs, offering customized training programs for female entrepreneurs, and implementing policies that ensure equal access to funding are important steps (IFC, 2021). In addition, social media awareness and support campaigns and mentoring programs should be developed to increase female entrepreneurs' engagement and equalize access to loan and funding opportunities (IFC, 2021).

4.3 The Product Development Model and Gender Shortcomings

This section examines the product development model and gender shortcomings. It explains the contrasting approaches in the market for male and female entrepreneurs.

4.3.1 Understanding the Product Development Process

Various stages, such as ideation (idea-generating stage), prototyping (making different models as samples), market testing (before launching the product or service, tests are carried out), and launch (making the product available to the consumers), are part of the product development model. A marketable product is the outcome that is created through the transformation of an idea at each essential stage. In other words, each phase (stage) is important for ensuring smooth transformation of an idea into a reliable and marketable product and/or service. On the other hand, the needs of women and other marginalized groups may not be addressed if these processes are led by male perspectives. It can be argued that because the sectors and processes are highly male dominated (Faizan and Haque, 2016), marginalized groups, as well as women, might not benefit from designs that only take a male perspective into consideration, which is a biased approach.

4.3.2 Gender Bias in Product Development

Bose et al. (2011) argued that historically, male users have been kept in mind byproduct designers and companies. In other words, the product was developed while keeping male consumers in mind. Thus, significant gaps in the market have formed due to this bias, as the needs of female consumers are not properly addressed byproduct designers and companies (Bose et al., 2011). The National Highway Traffic Safety Administration conducted a study that revealed that during the safety test, average male body-model dummies were predominantly used in crash tests (Bose et al., 2011; Reuther, 2024). As a result, women's injury rate is higher than that of men in car crashes (Bose et al., 2011). Considering the example of the fitness industry, women's needs are clearly ignored to a greater extent. With male users in mind, most products are designed, ranging from gym equipment to fitness trackers. Nonetheless, this gap is being filled by female entrepreneurs, as they focus on developing fitness products for women (Wang et al., 2022). Women's unique health needs are now being considered in the product designs of companies such as LIVESTRONG and Fitbit.

4.3.3 Women-Led Innovation: FemTech as a Response

In response to gender biases, female entrepreneurs step up by providing solutions that meet women's specific needs (Wang et al., 2022). The development of innovative products has been the focus of interest. In other words, these female entrepreneurs fill these gaps by incorporating innovation in products used by women, especially with the rise of FemTech technology designed to improve women's health (Wang et al., 2022). The example of Ida Tin identified a vital gap in the market for women's health tracking tools and developed an application, the Clue app. She created one of the leading menstrual tracking applications, which helped many women better understand their health patterns (Gellman, 2017). The significance of diversity in entrepreneurship as well as product development is illustrated by this success because the solution caters to the need and demand of a larger audience.

4.3.4 Critical Analysis of the Product Development Process

Within entrepreneurship, the systemic need for diverse teams is highlighted by gender biases, which are especially evident in product development phases (Reuther, 2024). Inclusive products that resonate with a broader consumer base are more likely to be produced by companies that prioritize gender diversity in their development teams (Reuther, 2024). By ensuring that every stage of product development includes diverse perspectives, businesses can cater to the needs of different types of consumers by creating innovative solutions. It is evident that innovative work behavior plays a significant role in product development, which eventually leads to the success of entrepreneurs (Haque, 2024).

4.4 Critical Analysis: Gender and Entrepreneurial Outcomes

This section critically examines the gaps in the approach toward male and female entrepreneurs. This reflects the double standard of success parameters and the scaling of women-led enterprises.

4.4.1 The Double Standard of Success

The lens of gender is usually used to measure entrepreneurial success, demonstrating double standards. Praise is often given to male entrepreneurs for taking risks and exhibiting high ambition, whereas recognition is often reserved for women regarding balancing work and family. Societal perceptions are shaped by this double standard, and emphasizing entrepreneurial success is depicted through a risk approach. Research indicates that fewer risks are taken by female entrepreneurs than by their male counterparts, typically due to a lack of financial safety nets and cultural pressures (Klyver and Grant, 2010; Haq et al., 2024). Nonetheless, it is usually demonstrated over the passage of time by women-led enterprises that greater commitment to sustainability and its attainment is visible among their work, despite slower growth perceptions about their entrepreneurial venture. This highlights the reality that the need for success criteria in entrepreneurship should be modified to include many approaches and techniques. Focusing exclusively on metrics that show male success needs to be changed. This reality underscores the need to redefine success metrics in entrepreneurship to encompass different paths and strategies.

4.4.2 Scaling Women-Led Businesses

While small businesses are often managed excellently by women entrepreneurs, unique challenges are posed by the scaling of these ventures. A significant number of small businesses are owned globally by women; however, greater obstacles are faced by them in accessing the networks and funding that are necessary for expansion. Crucial mentorship and funding are provided by programs such as the African Women Entrepreneurs Program (AWEP), which specifically aims to support women entrepreneurs in scaling their businesses (Elmi et al., 2021).

Women entrepreneurs often excel in managing small businesses, but scaling these ventures poses unique challenges. Women own a significant number of small businesses globally; however, they face greater obstacles in accessing the networks and funding necessary for expansion. Programs such as the African Women Entrepreneurs Program (AWEP) provide crucial mentorship and funding specifically aimed at supporting women entrepreneurs in scaling their businesses (Elmi et al., 2021). The impact of AWEP is an essential aspect to explore. Thousands of women entrepreneurs in Africa have been successfully empowered by the AWEP, with training and resources provided to grow their businesses. Access to networks and financial resources is facilitated by these initiatives, helping women overcome the barriers that are often imposed on their growth potential. AWEP has successfully empowered thousands of women entrepreneurs in Africa, providing them with training and resources to grow their businesses (Elmi et al., 2021). By facilitating access to networks and financial resources, these initiatives help women overcome the barriers that often limit their growth potential.

4.4.3 *Critical Analysis of Gendered Outcomes*

The gendered dynamics of entrepreneurial outcomes are understood as critical for the development of effective support systems. It is recognized that women entrepreneurs often face unique challenges, allowing tailored interventions from policymakers and support organizations. By fostering environments that support women in scaling their businesses, greater gender equity in entrepreneurship can be achieved.

Understanding the gendered dynamics of entrepreneurial outcomes is critical for developing effective support systems. Recognizing that women entrepreneurs often face unique challenges allows policymakers and support organizations in creating tailored interventions. By fostering environments that support women in scaling their businesses, society can work toward achieving greater gender equity in entrepreneurship.

4.5 Conclusion

The entrepreneurial landscape is significantly shaped by gender, with resource access, opportunity recognition, and overall business outcomes being influenced. The systemic barriers faced by female entrepreneurs, including limited access to capital, cultural biases, and product development shortcomings, are highlighted in this chapter. Addressing these issues requires a concerted effort from policymakers, investors, and the entrepreneurial community to create a more inclusive and fairer environment. The distinct challenges and perspectives of female entrepreneurs are recognized, allowing an entrepreneurial ecosystem that enables all individuals, regardless of gender, to thrive and succeed in fostering.

Bibliography

Baker, T., and C. Henry. “Gender and the Financing of New Ventures: A Study of the Impact of Gender on New Venture Financing.” *Journal of Small Business Management* 51, no. 3 (2013): 451–71.

Bose, D., M. Segui-Gomez, and J. R. Crandall. “Vulnerability of Female Drivers Involved in Motor Vehicle Crashes: An Analysis of US Population at Risk.” *American Journal of Public Health* 101, no. 12 (2011): 2368–73.

Brush, C. G., A. de Bruin, and F. Welter. “A Gender-Aware Framework for Women’s Entrepreneurship.” *International Journal of Gender and Entrepreneurship* 1, no. 1 (2009): 8–24.

Brush, C. G., P. G. Greene, L. Balachandra, and A. E. Davis. *Diana Report: Women Entrepreneurs 2014: Bridging the Gender Gap in Venture Capital*. Wellesley, MA: Babson College, 2014.

Eddleston, K. A., and G. N. Powell. “Nurturing Entrepreneurs’ Work–Family Balance: A Gendered Perspective.” *Entrepreneurship Theory and Practice* 36, no. 3 (2012): 513–41.

Elmi, M., N. Spencer, J.-A. Francis, S. Dei, S. Soumare, G. Y. Mo, and H. Parameswaran. “The State of Women’s Entrepreneurship: A Focus on Black Women Entrepreneurs.” Women Entrepreneurship Knowledge Hub, Black Business and Professional Association, 2021. Accessed November 2, 2024. https://wekh.ca/wp-content/uploads/2021/02/The_State_of_Womens_Entrepreneurship_Black_Entrepreneurs.pdf.

Faizan, R., and A. U. Haque. "The Relationship between Societal Attributes, Feminine Leadership & Management Style: Responses from Pakistan's Urban Region Female-Owned Businesses." *European Journal of Business and Management* 8, no. 23 (2016): 171–91.

Gellman, L. "Ida Tin's Battle to Build Clue, a Period-Tracking App." *The New Yorker*, 2017. Accessed November 2, 2024. www.newyorker.com/business/currency/ida-tins-battle-to-build-clue-a-period-tracking-app.

Haq, I., A. U. Haque, and N. A. A. Rahim. "Entrepreneurial Stress and Mental Well-Being: Pre- and Post-COVID-19 Comparative Analysis of SMEs in Canada." *Forum Scientiae Oeconomia* 12, no. 1 (2024): 53–71.

Haq, I. U., A. U. Haque, H. Kaur, and N. A. A. A. Rahim. "Occupational Stress Affecting Innovative Capabilities and Innovative Work Behavior of Migrant Entrepreneurs." *Polish Journal of Management Studies* 9, no. 2 (2024): 238–53. https://doi.org/10.17512/pjms.2024.29.2.12.

Haque, A. U. "How Occupational Stress Impacts the Innovative Work Behavior and Innovative Entrepreneurial Capabilities of Migrant Entrepreneurs in Contrasting Economies?" In *Migration and Entrepreneurship in the Global Context*, edited by D. Hyams-Ssekasi and E. Daskalaki, 15–30. Cham: Palgrave Macmillan, 2024. https://doi.org/10.1007/978-3-031-34067-3_2.

International Finance Corporation (IFC). "Promoting Women Entrepreneurship." World Bank Group, 2021. Accessed November 2, 2024. www.ifc.org/en/what-we-do/sector-expertise/gender/entrepreneurship.

Klyver, K., and S. Grant. "Gender Differences in the Determinants of Entrepreneurial Intentions." *International Journal of Gender and Entrepreneurship* 2, no. 1 (2010): 44–59.

OECD. "How Fragile Contexts Affect the Well-Being and Potential of Women and Girls." OECD Development Co-operation Directorate, OECD Publishing, Paris, 2022. Accessed November 2, 2024. https://one.oecd.org/document/DCD(2022)12/en/pdf.

Pasha, H. A. *Pakistan National Human Development Report 2020.* Islamabad: United Nations Development Programme, Pakistan, 2020.

Reuther, K. K. "Shrink It and Pink It: Gender Bias in Product Design." *Harvard Advanced Leadership Initiative Social Impact Review*, 2024. Accessed November 2, 2024. www.sir.advancedleadership.harvard.edu/articles/shrink-it-and-pink-it-gender-bias-product-design.

Shane, S., and S. Venkataraman. "The Promise of Entrepreneurship as a Field of Research." *Academy of Management Review* 25, no. 1 (2000): 217–26.

Wang, F.-J., C.-H. Hsiao, and T.-T. Hsiung. "Marketing Strategies of the Female-Only Gym Industry: A Case-Based Industry Perspective." *Frontiers in Psychology* 13 (2022): 928882. https://doi.org/10.3389/fpsyg.2022.928882.

World Bank. "Nearly 2.4 Billion Women Globally Don't Have Same Economic Rights as Men." World Bank Group, 2022. Accessed November 2, 2024. www.worldbank.org/en/news/press-release/2022/03/01/nearly 2-4-billion-women-globally don-t-have-same-economic-rights-as-men.

Case Study: A Single Mother's Path to Entrepreneurship

Diya Nitinbhai Patel, Harmandeep Kaur and Adnan ul Haque

After her divorce, a single mother of two kids, named Shanaya, found herself in a challenging financial situation. She turned to entrepreneurship to create financial stability out of a need to provide for her children and with limited formal education. Shanaya decided to start a small business selling custom cakes and pastries after receiving praise for her homemade cakes at family events as she enjoyed baking.

Everything was not smooth during her first days of the venture. Funding was among the first challenges faced by Shanaya. Banks were reluctant to offer her a loan; owing to her limited credit history and being a single mother, she struggled to keep up with the bills. Securing capital to buy baking equipment and renting kitchen space seemed impossible without collateral or assistance from an external source. The process was lengthy and involved additional hurdles that were not often faced by male entrepreneurs. Eventually, Shanaya obtained a small loan from a local microfinance organization that specifically supported women's entrepreneurial ventures.

Being a mother and an entrepreneur, balancing her responsibilities was another significant challenge. Shanaya juggled between managing business-related responsibilities and attending to the needs of her children with limited childcare support. Shanaya was exhausted and sometimes had to turn down business opportunities after her long hours in the kitchen because too many personal and professional responsibilities collided, especially caregiving responsibilities. Poverty added further challenges to women entrepreneurs. In her business dealings, Shanaya also faced gender biases and skepticism. Assuming her domestic responsibilities would hinder her entrepreneurial success because she was a single mother. Thus, potential customers as well as some suppliers questioned her abilities, skills, and ability to effectively run a business. Nonetheless, she still pushed her way through those difficulties by wisely availing local women's business networks and support in the use of mentorship programs.

Shanaya gradually developed her customer base by focusing on customized cakes with no compromise on quality standards and constructively promoted her work through social media. With the passage of time, she stabilized her business, which enabled her to hire a part-time assistant. This allowed her additional time to focus on the expansion of her business and spend more time with her children. Shanaya's story depicts the determination and resilience in the face of difficulties demonstrated by a single mother in search of entrepreneurial success. The case is more intriguing because the caregiving responsibilities and intersection of gender frequently pose unique barriers.

Reflection Questions

- As a single mother in the early stages of her entrepreneurial venture, what were the key challenges faced by Shanaya? How were these challenges different from those faced by male entrepreneurs?
- What role did gender play in creating disparity in access to financing? For female entrepreneurs, what alternative solutions could help mitigate this issue?
- What strategies did Shanaya consider managing both personal responsibilities and business demands? Did her role as a caregiver impact her entrepreneurial efforts, if so, how?
- Did the local female entrepreneurs' network contribute to her success, if so, how? If not, why? Do you think that networking and mentorship are important for entrepreneurial success?
- Upon reflecting on Shanaya's case, what policy or structural changes would help support women or single mothers in their entrepreneurial journey?

Chapter 5

Financial Challenges for Entrepreneurs in Volatile and Stable Economies

Arif Toor, Ali Sher and Adnan ul Haque

5.0 Introduction

Entrepreneurship is a dynamic and critical driver of economic growth, innovation and job creation. Entrepreneurs often face significant financial challenges that can impede the success and sustainability of their businesses. The impact of these challenges is particularly severe in emerging and volatile economies where there is no stable government policy to support entrepreneurship. We use representative emerging economies, such as Pakistan, Brazil, Nigeria, and Vietnam, and compare the literature with advanced economies, such as Canada, Germany, Japan and the UK, which are characterized by stable economic environments. This chapter explores and compares the financial challenges encountered by entrepreneurs in both emerging and advanced economies, drawing on literature to highlight similarities, differences and implications for policy and practice. The chapter highlights key issues such as access to capital, financial management practices, risk management and the role of external stakeholders in mitigating financial constraints. We also consider the implications of this comparison for the role of government policies and institutional support in each of our selected jurisdictions.

It is well established that entrepreneurship plays a pivotal role in promoting economic growth and innovation across advanced and emerging economies (Haq et al., 2024; Haque, 2024). Research has shown that entrepreneurs often confront a range of financial hurdles, including but not limited to access to adequate capital, which can significantly impact the viability of new and aspiring entrepreneurs' ventures (Kerr and Nanda, 2009). Understanding these challenges within diverse national contexts—such as Pakistan, Brazil, Nigeria, and Vietnam—and advanced economies such as Canada, Germany, Japan, and the UK—is essential for devising effective support mechanisms and policies conducive to promoting entrepreneurial success. This chapter aims to synthesize the literature to provide insights into the financial challenges faced by entrepreneurs in both emerging and advanced economies, shedding light on both commonalities and distinct issues. The following are the salient points of our work:

5.1 Access to Capital

In the context of emerging economies, access to capital remains one of the most fundamental challenges faced by entrepreneurs. In countries such as Pakistan, Brazil, Nigeria, and Vietnam, entrepreneurs frequently encounter barriers such as high interest rates, limited financing options, and stringent collateral requirements, which hinder their ventures'

DOI: 10.4324/9781003504351-5

development. For example, in Pakistan, although there has been improvement in the entrepreneurial ecosystem, many startups still rely on informal sources such as funding from family and/or friends and personal savings due to a shortage of capital and higher collateral demand (Zahra et al., 2009). Additionally, despite the increase in local investments, many entrepreneurs face challenges in scaling their businesses and accessing sufficient funding (Cosgrove et al., 2023). In Nigeria, capital generation is a visible challenge (Ajim Capital, 2023). Fundings has increased over time, but many entrepreneurs still face significant barriers in accessing financial resources because of regulatory uncertainties, financing models, and limited financial knowledge (Ajim Capital, 2023b). Similarly, in Brazil, entrepreneurs are constrained by rigid lending requirements and high inflation rates, which frequently lead to informal borrowing and personal savings (ApexBrasil, 2021).

In contrast, while Canada and other advanced economies benefit from government-supported initiatives and strong financial infrastructure, emerging economies have systematic gaps in accessing capital. Access to traditional bank loans is relatively easier because, owing to established financial systems, early-stage ventures face challenges in accessing capital from venture capitalists and angel investors (Carter et al., 2003). However, there are established government initiatives and venture capital networks that play crucial roles in bridging these gaps (Block and Sandner, 2009). Nonetheless, government roles in both types of economies remain crucial for effective access to funding. For example, the Kamyab Jawan Program in Pakistan, which aims to support youth entrepreneurship with financial assistance, is a positive step; however, an inclusive environment for diverse types of entrepreneurship is still not developed (Aazim, 2021; Cosgrove et al., 2023). Thus, informal funding is a frequent practice in emerging economies, and government-backed schemes are focused on advanced economies to assist entrepreneurs in accessing capital. Additionally, alternative financing models can help start and scale business ventures across the globe (Cosgrove et al., 2023).

5.2 Financing Requirements and Collateral Obligations

Formal financial institutions in emerging economies often impose tougher requirements for collateral and guarantees, making it difficult for SMEs to obtain funding for their projects (Faizan and Haque, 2016; Haq et al., 2024). Qualifying for bank loans is most difficult for startups, as they typically lack a proven record of financial performance sufficient access for collateral. This has created a financial environment heavily reliant on collateral-based lending, excluding many entrepreneurs who do not have tangible assets to pledge as security. The resilience of collateral, in return, reduces funding for the entrepreneurial population (Zahra et al., 2009; Akhtar and Liu, 2018; Bokhari and Syed, 2019). This challenge is compounded by high interest rates and transaction costs associated with borrowing, further limiting access for financially constrained entrepreneurs (World Bank, 2022).

Interest is the price paid for using someone else's money, and this cost is especially significant in emerging economies. In Pakistan, the central bank's interest rate has been 22% since June 2023, which is highest among emerging markets and comparatively higher than that of developed economies (IMF, 2023, cited from Mangi, 2023). The high interest rate is one of the barriers to limiting financial access for entrepreneurs in Pakistan. In Brazil, a high interest rate, political instability, and high inflation deter entrepreneurial investments (ApexBrasil, 2021). Similarly, in Nigeria, high risks, rigid government policies, and a lack of alternative financing models limit access to capital (Ajim Capital, 2023). In Vietnam, state-owned banks do not have favorable terms for new entrepreneurs (Vietnam Country Climate and Development Report, 2022), deterring entrepreneurs from starting their ventures.

In contrast, advanced economies such as the UK, Germany and Japan have a well-established financial system, offering a diverse range of financing options. For example, banks in Germany are known for their support to SMEs, with low interest and government-backed schemes, making it simpler and easier to gain access to capital (Germany Trade and Invest, 2023). Similarly, in the UK, the startup loan program helps entrepreneurial activities prosper (British Business Bank, 2020). In Japan, grants for SMEs are a government initiative along with low interest rates (Kushida, 2023). The Canadian banking system's availability and reliability of financial solutions, including venture capital funding and government-supported financing programs, further encourage entrepreneurs (Government of Canada, 2023). Most of these financial institutions offer term loans, lines of credit, and commercial mortgages. A variety of financial products are accessible to businesses with solid credit histories and collaterals, enabling entrepreneurs to fund day-to-day operations, expansion projects, and capital expenditures. The banking sector in advanced economies is relatively stable compared with that in emerging economies. The interest rate is also low, and a variety of financial solutions are available in advanced economies.

5.3 Risk Aversion, Perception, Practices, and Support

Banks and financial institutions in emerging economies tend to exhibit risk-averse behavior, preferring established businesses with proven track records and tangible collateral (Haque, 2024). Startups and innovative ventures, which typically carry greater risks, struggle to attract financing despite their potential for growth and job creation (Zahra et al., 2009; Akhtar and Liu, 2018; Bokhari and Syed, 2019). In emerging economies such as Pakistan, risk aversion is often exacerbated by economic volatility, political instability, fluctuating exchange rates, and overall economic volatility. In Nigeria, infrastructural deficits and political instability contribute to risk aversion among investors to lend money to startup businesses (Ajim Capital, 2023a). Similarly, in Vietnam, financial transparency is low, while the venture capital market is poorly developed, discouraging investors from engaging in innovative projects (Vietnam Country Climate and Development Report, 2022).

In contrast, the Canadian financial system is highly risk tolerant. The financial system is credit-based, where independent organizations are responsible for collecting, managing, and reporting financial data to consumers (Carter et al., 2003; Block and Sandner, 2009). This has enabled Canadian banks and other financial institutions to make informed decisions and reduce barriers to capital for aspiring entrepreneurs with good credit scores. Other advanced economies, such as Germany, Japan, and the UK, benefit from strong risk management practices (British Business Bank, 2020; Germany Trade and Invest, 2023; Kushida, 2023).

5.3.1 Financial Management Practices

Effective financial management practices are critical for the sustainability of entrepreneurial ventures in both emerging and advanced economies. In Pakistan, entrepreneurs often lack formal financial training, leading to challenges in budgeting, cash flow management, and financial reporting (Razzaq et al., 2024). The lack of financial management education among entrepreneurs leads to the perception among investors that there is a limited chance of reaping higher returns in the future (Ahmed, 2007; Aazim, 2021). Similarly, in Vietnam, the perceptions of investors about entrepreneurs are no different, thus making investors risk averse (Nguyen and Research Team, 2016; Tran and Lo, 2024). Nigeria has more corruption, which makes it difficult for small businesses to secure funds. In Brazil, the situation is different, as basic financial management practices are reasonably better than those in other emerging economies are, yet unstable macroeconomic practices deter investors (Godke Veiga and McCahery, 2019). Canadian entrepreneurs may face difficulties in financial planning and forecasting, which are exacerbated during economic downturns (Magerman, 2007). The financial management system of Germany, Japan, and the UK is an integral part of entrepreneurial education (International Monetary Fund – IMF, 2024; OECD, 2024). Education programs and mentorship networks play pivotal roles in enhancing financial literacy and management capabilities in both contexts.

5.3.2 Risk Management

Entrepreneurs in both emerging and advanced economies must navigate diverse risks associated with market volatility, regulatory changes, and competitive pressures. In Pakistan and Nigeria, political instability and security concerns add layers of complexity, impacting investor confidence and access to international markets (Khan, 2007; Ogwu et al., 2022). In Vietnam, entrepreneurs face risk due to unpredictable market conditions and changing government regulations (Nguyen and Research Team, 2016; Tran and Lo, 2024). Brazil faces high inflationary pressures and inconsistent governmental policies that destabilize market conditions (Godke Veiga and McCahery, 2019).

On the other hand, Canadian entrepreneurs grapple with technological disruptions and global economic uncertainties, necessitating robust risk mitigation strategies. There is a stable political system. Effective risk management frameworks and insurance mechanisms are critical for enhancing resilience in both entrepreneurial ecosystems (Petig and Shangjing, 2018). In Japan and Germany, technological disruption poses risk, but economies are relatively strong and thus can absorb shocks better than emerging economies can (IMF, 2024; OECD, 2024). The UK, facing the challenge after Brexit, must further refine its risk mitigation strategies to support small businesses and startups. (McKenzie et al., 2023).

5.3.3 Role of Government Policies and Institutional Support

Government policies and institutional support mechanisms significantly influence entrepreneurial outcomes in both emerging and advanced economies. In Pakistan, regulatory reforms aimed at easing business registration processes and providing tax incentives for startups are pivotal (Li and Rama, 2015). However, bureaucratic inefficiencies and corruption remain challenges (Yousaf, 2021). In Vietnam, there has been substantial improvement in policies to support entrepreneurial ventures, yet high taxes and inefficient public services are hindering entrepreneurial operations (Nguyen and Research Team, 2016; Tran and Lo, 2024). Credit lines and tax incentives for SMEs in Brazil constitute positive steps, but the complex legal environment and constantly changing regulations negatively affect entrepreneurs (Godke Veiga and McCahery, 2019).

In contrast, Canada has a strong network of government-supported programs to improve capital access, such as the Business Development Bank of Canada (BDC) and Export Development Canada (EDC), which provide loans and venture capital to SMEs (Magerman, 2007; Bank of Canada, 2023). Supportive policies such as research and development tax credits and innovation grants bolster entrepreneurial activities, alongside robust incubator and accelerator programs (Raspotnik et al., 2020). Collaboration between the public and private sectors is crucial for creating an enabling environment for entrepreneurial growth and innovation (OECD, 2019). Similarly, Germany, Japan, and the UK offer institutional support to entrepreneurs (McKenzie et al., 2023; IMF, 2024; OECD, 2024).

Overall, the difference in risk perception between advanced and emerging economies plays a significant role in the future of entrepreneurial ventures, as stable and mature financial systems in advanced economies strengthen entrepreneurial activities, while significant hurdles are faced by entrepreneurs in accessing credit and venture capital in emerging economies.

5.4 Availability of Venture Capital and Angel Investors

Unlike more developed economies, emerging economies such as Pakistan, Brazil, Nigeria, and Vietnam lack a robust ecosystem of venture capital and angel investors who are willing to provide risk capital to early-stage ventures. The venture capital industry in Pakistan is nascent and faces challenges such as limited fund sizes, regulatory hurdles, and a conservative investment approach (Zahra et al., 2009; Akhtar and Liu, 2018; Bokhari and Syed, 2019). Additionally, venture capital firms in Pakistan prefer already established businesses, which creates a challenge for startups to secure funding from them (Raza, 2020). Similarly, in Brazil, Vietnam, and Nigeria, angel investors are reluctant to support early-stage startups (ApexBrasil, 2021; Vietnam Country Climate and Development Report, 2022; Ajim Capital, 2023).

In contrast, Canada boasts a vibrant venture capital ecosystem, with numerous venture capital firms and angel investors actively investing in high-potential startups and growth-stage companies. Venture capital funding provides entrepreneurs with equity financing to scale operations, develop new products, and enter new markets (Block and Sandner, 2009; Government of Canada, 2023). Angel investors, who often provide early-stage financing and mentorship, play a crucial role in supporting innovative ventures with high growth potential. Similarly, in advanced economies such as the UK, Germany, and Japan, angel investing networks and well-established venture capital platforms supported by the government encourage innovation and startup growth (British Business Bank, 2020; Germany Trade and Invest, 2023; Kushida, 2023).

5.5 Informality and Access to Informal Financing

Many entrepreneurs in Pakistan rely on informal sources of financing, such as family savings, personal networks, and microfinance institutions. While these sources provide essential funding for small businesses, they often come with higher costs and limited scalability (Akhtar and Liu, 2018; Bokhari and Syed, 2019; Farooq et al., 2022). Informal financing sources tend to lack the institutional support, transparency, and legal protections associated with formal financial channels, which can hamper business growth opportunities

(Faizan and Haque, 2016). There has been a slew of microfinancing organizations in Pakistan that provide funding for smaller projects. Although microfinancing institutions help some entrepreneurs, they are often criticized for not having adequate customer service and not always following regulations. Furthermore, the cost of borrowing informal loans (i.e., interest rates) is high, and these entrepreneurs do not have other options but accept those terms (Alam et al., 2023). In Brazil, local community loans and family financing are mostly used by entrepreneurs while accepting a high rate of interest (Borges et al., 2018). In Nigeria, rotating savings and credit associations (ROSCAs) play a critical role in funding small businesses and startups, providing support in the absence of formal financial support (Felicia and Ogunleye, 2024). Interestingly, crowdfunding is gaining popularity in Nigeria (Ogwu et al., 2022). In Vietnam, social capital and microfinance remain essential for business survival, although the cost is high (Pham et al., 2023).

In contrast, advanced economies such as Germany and the UK have well-established crowdfunding ecosystems. In Canada, Germany, and the UK, there are many emerging alternative financing models. These include crowdfunding platforms and peer-to-peer lending networks. These platforms leverage technology to connect investors with businesses seeking capital, democratizing access to funding and facilitating community-driven support for entrepreneurial ventures (Mollick, 2024).

5.6 Factors Contributing to Access Challenges

The following are the contributing factors to access funding:

5.6.1 Regulatory and Institutional Framework

The regulatory environment for financial institutions and businesses plays a crucial role in shaping access to capital in any economy. In Pakistan, complex regulatory requirements, bureaucratic inefficiencies, and legal ambiguities contribute to the challenges faced by entrepreneurs in navigating the formal financial system. Simplifying regulatory processes, enhancing transparency, and improving legal protection for lenders and borrowers are essential steps to facilitate greater access to capital. There is a clear need for implementing policy reforms that promote financial inclusion, such as credit guarantee schemes, tax incentives for venture capital investments, and streamlined business registration processes, which could improve the regulatory environment and institutional framework in Pakistan (Ahmed, 2007; Zahra et al., 2009; Aazim, 2021). In Vietnam, reforms are in process, and SMEs are benefiting from it. However, the challenges are still high because of the weak enforcement of legal protections and outdated financial systems (Nguyen and Research Team, 2016; Tran and Lo, 2024). In Brazil, bureaucratic inefficiency contributes to difficulties in capital access (Godke Veiga and McCahery, 2019).

In contrast, Canada, Japan, Germany, and the UK have well-established financial systems with strong regulatory frameworks, which support entrepreneurial activities and promote entrepreneurial ventures (Magerman, 2007; McKenzie et al., 2023; OECD, 2024). The Canadian government offers a range of support programs designed to increase access to capital for entrepreneurs. These include the BDC, which provides loans and venture capital to SMEs, and Export Development Canada (EDC), which offers financing and insurance solutions to facilitate international trade (Haq et al., 2024). Additionally, provincial and territorial governments administer various grants, tax incentives, and loan programs to support innovation and business growth.

5.6.2 Economic and Market Factors

Economic factors such as inflation, exchange rate volatility, and economic downturns impact the availability and cost of capital in Pakistan. Market conditions, including sector-specific risk and market integration, also influence investor confidence and the willingness to finance entrepreneurial ventures (Khan, 2007). Strengthening macroeconomic stability and promoting sector-specific growth strategies can enhance the overall investment climate and stimulate capital inflows. Although the IMF and World Bank have been working closely to improve fiscal policy, economic volatility remains a challenge for businesses in Pakistan (World Bank, 2022). In Nigeria, currency devaluation, high interest rates, and inflation pose challenges (Ogwu et al., 2022). In addition, corruption further intensifies challenges in accessing funding (Idris Zubair, 2014). Brazil has mixed market risks, as entrepreneurs face the challenge of fluctuating exchange rates and inflation affecting capital availability (Godke Veiga and McCahery, 2019). On the other hand, Germany has a stable economy and reliable financial system that are conducive to entrepreneurial activities. Similarly, Japan maintains a stable financial environment, which is favorable for businesses (IMF, 2024). The UK has a well-regulated financial market and a robust banking system (McKenzie et al., 2023). Canada also has a stable currency. There are world-class stock markets that promote Canadian business and industry worldwide.

5.6.3 Financial Literacy and Entrepreneurial Education

Limited financial literacy among entrepreneurs and a lack of awareness of available financing options contribute to access challenges in emerging economies. Many entrepreneurs in Pakistan lack formal education in financial management, which hinders their ability to prepare viable business plans, access funding needs, and effectively negotiate with lenders. Promoting financial literacy programs and entrepreneurial education initiatives can empower entrepreneurs with the knowledge and skills needed to access and manage capital effectively (Razzaq et al., 2024). In Vietnam, financial literacy is a challenge, particularly in rural areas, while the government is working toward improving financial literature through financial institutions (Nguyen and Research Team, 2016; Tran and Lo, 2024). Nigeria also has low levels of financial literacy, which limits entrepreneurs' ability to access formal capital (Idris Zubair, 2014). Nonetheless, Brazil is addressing these challenges by promoting financial literacy in schools and offering training programs for entrepreneurs (Godke Veiga and McCahery, 2019).

The Canadian education system is managed by provincial governments. Most Canadian provinces now include financial literacy in high school curricula. There are also colleges and universities that provide programs for new and aspiring entrepreneurs (Magerman, 2007). The Canadian education environment, which is still far from perfect, is relatively better than the system in Pakistan, Vietnam, Brazil, and Nigeria. Germany and the UK are leaders in financial literacy and entrepreneurial education (McKenzie et al., 2023; OECD, 2024).

5.7 Recommendations

Based on literature review, the following are the recommendations in the context of emerging and advanced economies context.

5.7.1 *Entrepreneurial Education*

We also believe that entrepreneurship should be taught to students during secondary school. In this way, these students will be able to understand the risks associated with entrepreneurial activities and learn how to mitigate these risks. In this way, these students will be ready to start their businesses when they have limited debt and family responsibilities. Thus, educational institutions should integrate entrepreneurship education into the school curriculum early. They should introduce modules on entrepreneurship, organize startup competitions, and invite successful entrepreneurs to share their experiences with students. The government can partner with private companies and educational institutions to provide aspiring entrepreneurs with skill development programs and training opportunities.

5.7.2 *Regulatory Framework*

The government should simplify paperwork, reduce bureaucratic hurdles, and ensure clear guidelines for local funds and investors. It should also offer tax breaks and incentives to local funds that invest in startup enterprises. They should offer exemptions on capital gains or dividends earned from startup investments. They should provide clarity and encourage more investors to support early-stage ventures.

5.7.3 *Access to Finance and Incentives*

The government should use digital platforms, workshops, and awareness campaigns to educate startups about the various funding sources and incentives they can access. They should establish entrepreneurship funds to provide early-stage capital to startups. This fund should be dedicated to supporting innovative and promising startups that may face challenges accessing traditional financing. Thus, the government can streamline registration and compliance requirements, reducing the time and effort needed to access loans or grants.

5.7.4 *Access to Markets*

The government should organize workshops, seminars, and trade shows to educate enterprises about market opportunities and export potential in diverse sectors. They should collaborate with industry stakeholders to develop effective policies promoting market access. Thus, the government can address regulatory barriers and facilitate market entry for startup enterprises.

5.7.5 *Information Technology and Innovation*

The government should create a conducive environment for startup enterprises by providing efficient and modernized infrastructure to support their operations. The development of

a user-friendly online business registration platform simplifies the process for entrepreneurs. The government can offer incentives and grants to startups that focus on developing innovative solutions and contributing to sustainable development.
The following are the recommendations based on our literature review in the context of advanced economies:

5.7.6 Government Support

Advanced economies have specific programs, such as the Canadian Government's Registered Retirement Savings Program (RRSP), the UK's Self-Invested Personal Pensions (SIPPs), Germany's Gesetzliche Rentenversicherung (GRV), and Japan's Individual-type Defined Contribution Pension Plan (iDeCo). They should allow startups to use these accounts. The money saved in these accounts is not used for startups and can only be used for specific purposes, such as education or first-time home buying opportunities, especially in the case of Canada. Both activities are valuable for our society; however, the benefits are far lower than the expected benefits from entrepreneurial activity. Investment in further education may lead to better employability, and buying a house indicates financial stability. However, research shows that most graduates in Canada need help in finding work in the field of their studies. Therefore, there is no direct relationship between further education and employability. For first-time house buyers, the result, in fact, is adding more debt to themselves rather than becoming financially independent. Thus, experience and observation, both of which are activities in which such funds withdrawals are currently allowed, do not compare to the potential benefits of starting one's own business. Therefore, the government should also allow these funds to be withdrawn to start their own businesses.

5.7.7 Grants

The governments of advanced economies should offer grants and enlarge innovation funds targeted at new entrepreneurs with more streamlined and straightforward application processes, particularly for early-stage and newly established businesses.

5.7.8 Access to Debt Financing

Most new entrepreneurs face financial barriers, making it impossible to seize opportunities. Governments can improve credit markets through initiatives to improve access to debt capital for those entrepreneurs. These could include regulation to improve the efficiency and competitiveness of credit markets by making debt capital cheaper and more accessible.

5.7.9 Income Tax Relief

High personal income tax levels currently reduce the potential financial benefits of starting a business, making it more challenging to reach the cost–benefit equilibrium. Therefore, policy initiatives lowering personal income taxes are likely to encourage many potential entrepreneurs to engage in entrepreneurial activities. The governments should establish a national policy of income tax deductibility for qualifying investments in early-stage companies. This policy will incentivize investment in early-stage companies and thus support entrepreneurial activities. Owing to the volatile nature of these investments, any return of capital takes several years, with investors likely to experience significant losses. Tax relief compensates for the high-risk nature of these investments while accelerating much-needed economic returns.

5.7.10 *Joint Public–Private Funding*

The governments should establish a collaborative public/private fund to match investments into early-stage companies supported by incubators and accelerators. This common fund will increase the capital available to new entrepreneurs and encourage regional ecosystems, creating jobs and economic growth.

5.7.11 *Community-based Programs*

Many entrepreneurial activities are community-based. Supporting local initiatives can be an effective way to produce initial results. Governments need to increase such activities to provide more resources and capital to emerging communities. In summary, governments should play an important role by reducing barriers, improving the reward of entrepreneurship through the tax system, and providing access to resources such as better information, mentorship, entrepreneurship education, and entrepreneurship centers. Policymakers' task is to encourage entrepreneurship and make it a rational and informed choice for new entrepreneurs.

5.8 Conclusion

Entrepreneurs encounter different challenges based on their geographic location. While some regions offer robust support systems and access to capital, others need help with political instability, limited funding options, and regulatory hurdles. However, these challenges also present opportunities for innovation and growth. Government policies and support are influential and crucial in shaping the entrepreneurial environment. Policies that foster innovation, provide funding opportunities, and establish a supportive regulatory framework can significantly enhance the entrepreneurial landscape.

Entrepreneurs in both emerging and advanced economies encounter multifaceted financial challenges influenced by distinct economic, regulatory, and sociocultural factors. This comparative literature review highlights key issues, including access to capital, financial management practices, risk management strategies, and the role of government policies. Addressing these challenges requires context-specific interventions that enhance access to financing, promote financial literacy, foster risk management capabilities, and optimize regulatory frameworks. By leveraging insights from comparative analysis, policymakers and stakeholders can devise targeted initiatives to support entrepreneurial endeavors and drive sustainable economic development.

Bibliography

Aazim, M. "How Effective is the New SME Policy?" *Business—DAWN.COM*, 2021. Accessed November 1, 2024. www.dawn.com/news/1665906.

Ahmed, S. M. "Amendments to the Microfinance Institutions Ordinance, 2001—Implications for the Sector." 2007. Accessed November 1, 2024. www.findevgateway.org/sites/default/files/publications/files/mfg-en-paper-amendments-to-the-microfinance-institutions-ordinance-2001-implications-for-the-sector-oct-2007.pdf; www.semanticscholar.org/paper/Amendments-to-the-Microfinance-Institutions-%2C-2001-Ahmed-Shah/59ee7d8e184ad6f96917a8983af1811e8fdc414a

Ajim Capital. "Problems Faced by Startups in Africa." 2023. Accessed November 1, 2024. www.ajimcapital.com/blog/problems-faced-by-startups-in-africa.

Akhtar, S., and Y. Liu. "SME Managers and Financial Literacy: Does Financial Literacy Really Matter?" *Journal of Public Administration and Governance* 8, no. 3 (2018): 353.

Alam, N., J. Shopovski, and A. El Alaoui. "Obstacles to Development of Entrepreneurship in Pakistan." *European Scientific Journal* 20, no. 4 (2024): 52. https://doi.org/10.19044/esj.2024.v20n4p52.

ApexBrasil. "Connect with Brazil through." 2021. Accessed August 21, 2023. https://apexbrasil.com.br/br/en.html

Bank of Canada. "Key Interest Rate." 2023. Accessed November 1, 2024. www.bankofcanada.ca.

Block, J. H., and P. G. Sandner. "What is the Effect of the Financial Crisis on Venture Capital Financing? Empirical Evidence from US Internet Start-Ups." *Venture Capital: An International Journal of Entrepreneurial Finance* 11, no. 4 (2009): 295–309.

Bokhari, A., and A. Syed. "Pakistan's Start-up Landscape: Three Ways to Energize Entrepreneurship." *McKinsey*, 2019.

Borges, C., É. D. Bezerra, G. Silva, and V. Ferreira. "Entrepreneurship Policy in Brazil: Its Focus and Gaps." *International Journal of Entrepreneurship and Small Business* 34, no. 2 (January 2018): 183. https://doi.org/10.1504/IJESB.2018.092026.

British Business Bank. *Alone Together: Entrepreneurship and Diversity in the UK*, 2020. Accessed November 1, 2024. www.british-business-bank.co.uk/about/research-and-publications/alone-together-entrepreneurship-diversity-uk.

Carter, N. M., W. B. Gartner, K. G. Shaver, and E. J. Gatewood. "The Career Reasons of Nascent Entrepreneurs." *Journal of Business Venturing* 18, no. 1 (2003): 13–39.

Cosgrove, A. L., Beaty, R. E., Diaz, M. T., and Kenett, Y. N. "Age differences in semantic network structure: Acquiring knowledge shapes semantic memory." *Psychology and Aging* 38, no. 2 (2023): 87–102.

Faizan, R., and A. U. Haque. "The Relationship between Societal Attributes, Feminine Leadership & Management Style: Responses from Pakistan's Urban Region Female-Owned Businesses." *European Journal of Business and Management* 8, no. 23 (2016): 171–191.

Farooq, M., A. Noor, and S. Ali. "Corporate Governance and Firm Performance: Empirical Evidence from Pakistan." *Corporate Governance: The International Journal of Business in Society* 22, no. 1 (2022): 42–66.

Felicia, A., and T. A. Ogunleye. "On Some Factors Contributing to Entrepreneurial Economic Success in South-West, Nigeria: An Empirical Approach." *WSEAS Transactions on Business and Economics* 21 (2024): 1167–1189. https://doi.org/10.37394/23207.2024.21.96.

Germany Trade and Invest. "Financing for Entrepreneurs in Germany." 2023. www.gtai.de.

Godke Veiga, M., and J. A. McCahery. "The Financing of Small and Medium-Sized Enterprises: An Analysis of the Financing Gap in Brazil." *European Business Organization Law Review* 20 (2019): 633–664. https://doi.org/10.1007/s40804-019-00167-7.

Government of Canada (2023). "Venture Capital Catalyst Initiative." Accessed November 1, 2024. https://ised-isde.canada.ca/site/sme-research-statistics/en/venture-capital-catalyst-initiative

Haq, I., A. U. Haque, and N. A. A. Rahim. "Entrepreneurial Stress and Mental Well-Being: Pre- and Post-COVID-19 Comparative Analysis of SMEs in Canada." *Forum Scientiae Oeconomia* 12, no. 1 (2024): 53–71.

Haq, I. U., A. U. Haque, H. Kaur, and N. A. A. A. Rahim. "Occupational Stress Affecting Innovative Capabilities and Innovative Work Behavior of Migrant Entrepreneurs." *Polish Journal of Management Studies* 9, no. 2 (2024): 238–253. https://doi.org/10.17512/pjms.2024.29.2.12.

Haque, A. U. "How Occupational Stress Impacts the Innovative Work Behaviour and Innovative Entrepreneurial Capabilities of Migrant Entrepreneurs in Contrasting Economies?" In *Migration and Entrepreneurship in the Global Context*, edited by D. Hyams-Ssekasi and E. Daskalaki, 15–30. Cham: Palgrave Macmillan, 2024. https://doi.org/10.1007/978-3-031-34067-3_2.

Idris Zubair, A. K. "Entrepreneurship and Economic Development in Nigeria: Evidence from Small and Medium Scale Enterprises (SMEs) Financing." *International Journal of Social Science and Business* 5, no. 11 (2014): 1–16.

International Monetary Fund. "*Asia and Pacific Dept.*" Volume 2024: Issue 119. International Monetary Fund, 2024. https://doi.org/10.5089/9798400276682.002.

Kerr, W. R., and R. Nanda. *Financing Constraints and Entrepreneurship.* Harvard Business School, 2009.

Khan, M. A. "Foreign Direct Investment and Economic Growth: The Role of Domestic Financial Sector." 2007.

Kushida. K. The People Powering Japan's Startup Ecosystem. Carnegie Endowment, 2023. Accessed November 1, 2024. https://carnegieendowment.org/research/2023/02/the-people-powering-japans-startup-ecosystem?lang=en.

Li, Y., and M. Rama. "Firm Dynamics, Productivity Growth, and Job Creation in Developing Countries: The Role of Micro- and Small Enterprises." *The World Bank Research Observer* 30, no. 1 (2015): 3–38. https://doi.org/10.1093/wbro/lkv002.

Magerman, C. "Entrepreneurship: Business and Government – Introduction." *Canada-United States Law Journal* 33, no. 1 (2007): 303. CanLIIDocs 588. https://canlii.ca/t/t97j.

Mangi, F. "Pakistan Hikes Rate to Record in Emergency Meet as IMF Looms. Bloomberg." 2023. Last access: September 30, 2024. Available at: www.bloomberg.com/news/articles/2023-06-26/pakistan-raises-key-rate-to-record-high-in-emergency-meeting?embedded-checkout=true

McKenzie, D., C. Woodruff, K. Bjorvatn, M. Bruhn, J. Cai, J. Gonzalez-Uribe, S. Quinn, T. Sonobe, and M. Valdivia. "Training Entrepreneurs." *VoxDevLit* 1, no. 3 (September 2023). Accessed November 01, 2024. https://voxdev.org/sites/default/files/2023-11/Training_Entrepreneurs_Issue_3.pdf

Mollick, E. "The Dynamics of Crowdfunding: An Exploratory Study." *Journal of Business Venturing* 29, no. 1 (2014): 1–16. https://doi.org/10.1016/j.jbusvent.2013.06.005.

Nguyen, V. H., and Research Team. "The Factors Affecting the Success of Vietnam Entrepreneurs and the Lessons for Developing Countries." *Journal of Economics, Business and Management* 4, no. 12 (December 2016): 660. https://doi.org/10.18178/joebm.2016.4.12.469.

OECD. Promoting Entrepreneurship and Private Sector Engagement. In *Regions in Industrial Transition*, 87–109. Paris: OECD, 2019. Accessed November 1, 2024. https://doi.org/10.1787/e3ffdc84-en.

OECD. Financing SME Growth in Germany. OECD SME and Entrepreneurship Papers No. 61, 2024. Accessed November 1, 2024. www.oecd.org/content/dam/oecd/en/publications/reports/2024/07/financing-sme-growth-in-germany_16c8ab23/8f9a90e9-en.pdf.

Ogwu, K., P. Hickey, O. J.-P. Okeke, A. U. Haque, E. Pimenidis, and E. Kozlovski. "An Integrated Online/Offline Social Network-Based Model for Crowdfunding Support in Developing Countries: The Case of Nigeria." *Sustainability* 14, no. 15 (2022): 9333. https://doi.org/10.3390/su14159333.

Petig, J., and Z. Shangjing. *Opportunity Recognition and Motivation in Entrepreneurship—A Comparative Study of Would-Be Entrepreneurs and Experienced Entrepreneurs.* Master's thesis, Linnaeus University, 2018.

Pham, V. M., T. V. Binh, and L. N. K. Duong. "How Social Capital Affects Innovation, Marketing, and Entrepreneurial Orientation: The Case of SMEs in Ho Chi Minh (Vietnam)."

Journal of Innovation and Entrepreneurship 12, no. 1 (2023). https://doi.org/10.1186/s13731-023-00350-8.

Raspotnik, A., R. Grønning, and V. Herrmann. "A Tale of Three Cities: The Concept of Smart Sustainable Cities for the Arctic." *Polar Geography* 43, no. 1 (2020): 64–87. https://doi.org/10.1080/1088937X.2020.1713546.

Raza, S. "Analysis of Startups - Scalable Business Models: A New Horizon for Pakistan. M.Phil Thesis. Pakatan Institute of Development Economics Islamabad (PIDE)." 2020. Last accessed: 30 September, 2024. Available at: https://file-thesis.pide.org.pk/pdf/mphil-public-policy-2017-sibtain-raza--analysis-of-startups-scalable-business-models-a-new-horizon-for-pakistan.pdf

Razzaq, A., S. Qin, Y. Zhou, et al. "Determinants of Financial Inclusion Gaps in Pakistan and Implications for Achieving SDGs." *Scientific Reports* 14 (2024): 13667. https://doi.org/10.1038/s41598-024-63445-6.

Tran, M.-L., and S. Lo. "Unlocking the Power of Entrepreneurship Activity in Vietnam's Regions: The Role of Formal Institution." *SAGE Open* 14, no. 1 (2024). https://doi.org/10.1177/21582440241233037.

Vietnam Country Climate and Development Report. "Vietnam Country Climate and Development Report." World Bank Group. 2022. Accessed November 1, 2024. https://documents1.worldbank.org/curated/en/099355507062229876/pdf/P17724103036ee07909701028a237b6d18b.pdf

World Bank. "Doing Business in Pakistan: Access to Credit and Financial Inclusion." 2022. Accessed November 1, 2024. www.worldbank.org.

Yousaf, H. "The Impact of Institutional Quality on Financial Inclusion." 2021.

Zahra, S. A., E. Gedajlovic, D. O. Neubaum, and J. M. Shulman. "A Typology of Social Entrepreneurs: Motives, Search Processes, and Ethical Challenges." *Journal of Business Venturing* 24, no. 5 (2009): 519–532.

Case Study: Access to Financing for Startups in Emerging vs. Advanced Economies

Harmandeep Kaur and Ali Sher

Background

One of the most crippling problems that would-be business owners experience in developing economies such as Nigeria, Vietnam, Pakistan, and Brazil is access to financial resources. This frequently happens under circumstances resulting from, but not limited to, political instability, regulatory deficiencies, unstable economic activities, and low levels of public financial education. Conversely, Germany, Japan, Canada, and the United Kingdom show a friendlier landscape for business with better offerings in venture finance, angel investors, and government support, among other subsidizing instruments.

Most entrepreneurs in emerging markets usually start their businesses through the available, less rigid informal sources of finance like personal savings or MFI institutions, only to realize the high cost of the finance they accessed and the limited scope of growth thereafter. On the contrary, the developed economies have various well-stipulated formal sources of finance, such as venture capital, commercial banks, and even government grants.

The funding disparity between developing and developed economies presents a critical challenge for entrepreneurs in most developing countries since it hinders their growth and scale.

Key Issues

Risk Aversion and Funding Challenges

In emerging markets, while the business environment is developing, investors tend to avoid risks and finance visually "safe" projects that are well established and have collateral. The traditional way of thinking does not support startup businesses, even though they make sense from a financial perspective, as they have the potential for growth and innovation despite their higher risks.

Government Support

Advanced economies offer more supportive government policies for the growth of entrepreneurship. This support can come in the form of tax rebates, financial awards, and programs tailored to startups and small-medium scale businesses.

Informal Capital

In such countries as Pakistan and Nigeria, using unstructured financing for startups like family savings and pawnbrokers is common. However, the majority of these funding sources are very expensive, limiting growth opportunities for developing businesses and restricting their access to capital.

Reflection Questions

- What major obstacles do venture founders in developing economies encounter during financial acquisition?
- In what regard do willingness to take risks and aspects of investment behavior differ in the context of the developed/advanced economy versus the emerging market?
- How significant are government interventions in terms of creating a supportive image for entrepreneurship and advancing the financial access of advanced nations?
- To what extent can the use of the equipment of unwanted mechanisms impact the development abilities of new businesses in less developed countries?
- In what ways can governments in emerging economies improve the political environment to enable the formulation of more startup-friendly policies?
- To what extent does education on financial matters impact entrepreneurs' access to capital in developing nations, and how can it be enhanced?
- How will the differences in venture capital systems in Canada versus Pakistan promote or inhibit entrepreneurial advancements?

Chapter 6

Strategic Segmentation and Environmental Adaptation in Business Planning for Entrepreneurial Success

Riffat Faizan and Oluchi E. Oti

6.0 Introduction to Entrepreneurial Business Planning

In the modern-day, business plans have evolved into a dynamic roadmap empowering entrepreneurs and corporations to navigate the complexities of the business environment while achieving sustainable growth. Traditional entrepreneurial training focuses on business plans, which are seen as essential guides for achieving business goals and objectives (Welter et al., 2021). Business plans enable entrepreneurs to take business initiatives that maximize stakeholders' (customers, partners, investors, employees, government, etc.) satisfaction while attaining business objectives (Kalane, 2015). Hence, a business plan is comprehensive strategic documentation that helps entrepreneurs attain their business objectives and increases the satisfaction of stakeholders. A poorly written business plan is a recipe for disaster. Byrd and Megginson (2009) famously reported that "a good business plan is written for a minimum of five months, but you need five minutes to convince the reader not to throw it in the trash" (Abdullah, 2020). This reflects the importance of business plans. Interestingly, a survey of the United States Bureau of Labor (Howarth, 2023) was conducted. Sixty-five percent of new startup businesses fail during the first ten years, whereas 34% fail due to a lack of proper product–market fit. In contrast, in Canada, 21.5% of small businesses fail during their first year (GOC, 2022). Approximately 50% of small businesses are able to survive the first five years (GOC, 2022).

One could argue that there could be several factors for failure and survival; however, the business plan could not be excluded from the list. A well-written business plan is critical for the strategic success of business (Saah, 2022). Moreover, it allows businesses to develop the ability to identify opportunities, satisfy customer demands, gain a competitive advantage, mitigate risks, foster innovation, and drive growth and investor confidence (Welter et al., 2021). Therefore, business plans play a pivotal role in enabling entrepreneurs to understand and respond to changing market needs and formulate a strategy for survival. A business plan is a powerful tool that goes beyond the traditional understanding of documentation and works as a blueprint for entrepreneurial empowerment, tackles market challenges, capitalizes opportunities, and attains sustainable growth in the long run. The next step is to assess the factors interlinked with the business plan.

6.1 Importance of Entrepreneurial Vision and Value Proposition in Business Plan

The entrepreneurial vision is a dynamic process of change and creation (Kamuri, 2022). In contrast, value proposition is often viewed as the firm's core marketing strategy for a

DOI: 10.4324/9781003504351-6

competitive edge in the market (Rosário, Raimundo, & Cruz, 2021). In other words, an entrepreneurial vision is a roadmap to enlighten life into an idea. Although entrepreneurial vision has often been viewed as a factor behind success in a competitive environment, vision transformation into value proposition is an equally important factor, which, if ignored, can cost the business. In other words, value propositions support entrepreneurial vision.

A strong value proposition allows brands to set themselves apart from other competing products/services. In addition, it effectively affects the minds of consumers, which is why they should prefer it over other products/services. Often, a strong value proposition stops consumers from switching to substitutes. In contemporary business, companies offer value propositions through various marketing and services strategies, whereas customers further increase value through purchases and preferences for a certain brand (Rosário, Raimundo, & Cruz, 2021). Therefore, understanding customer needs and catering to those needs are essential for entrepreneurs because they offer them a chance to fill the identified gaps and make most of the opportunities at hand.

However, value propositions embedded solely in customers can have a negative effect on businesses' market sharing, as they narrow the market focus, limiting it to the existing customer base. Moreover, overemphasizing current customer needs reduces innovation. The lack of opportunities to attract new market segments exposes businesses to competitive vulnerability while contributing to market saturation. Thus, a balanced approach must be considered for both existing and potential customers by creating a clear and comprehensive value proposition that resonates with the target audience and reaches out to potential customers (Camelleri, 2017).

The development of a strong value proposition is an iterative process that demands continuous refinement and adaptation of strategies in response to market dynamics and customer feedback. Consumers' attitudes and behavior are significantly shaped by the co-creation process of value proposition (Espejo and Dominici, 2016). Consequently, a value proposition must be viewed as an investment that operates simultaneously in the economic and social realms. Entrepreneurs must grasp the Value preposition's impact on innovation and its role in continuous change.

The value proposition serves as a yardstick to measure an organization's progress in navigating economic and social realms. Moreover, an organization's ability to embrace the significance of the value proposition demonstrates a profound alignment with the entrepreneurial vision that leads to business success. In developing business plans, it is important for entrepreneurs to commence rigorous research and identify the target market. The success of a business plan depends on the understanding of customer needs, wants, pain points, preferences, and aspirations. By doing so, entrepreneurs could create empathy maps to gain a deeper understanding of customers' thoughts, feelings, and motivations. By empathizing with customers' experiences, entrepreneurs can identify their pain points more effectively for value co-creation. Through a customer-centric approach, entrepreneurs inform customers about product development, marketing strategies, and overall operations management, leading to sustainable growth. Business plans enable entrepreneurs to be more proactive and responsive to market trends and customer feedback and to monitor changes in competitive environments.

6.2 The Art of Managing Market Dynamics to Gain Competitive Edge

Through a comprehensive business plan, rigorous market research, and securing investor support, entrepreneurs further strengthen their entrepreneurial ventures. In the context of the business plan, marketing plays an essential role by empowering businesses to assess the target market's needs and ensure that they stand apart from their competitors. By strategically deploying marketing strategies, businesses can not only identify market demands but also carry out distinctive identities that resonate with their audience, fostering a competitive edge in the marketplace. Marketing cannot be considered a separate function on its own (Camilleri, 2018). Hence, it is part of the business plan that must be used effectively by the entrepreneurs. Business success is measured through positive customer feedback by valuing the product/service, which is indirectly the result of many efforts carried out by different strategic marketing moves.

Overreliance only on listening to customers' complaints, needs, and feedback to alter the product or service could eventually cost the entrepreneurs their venture success (Christensen and Bower, 1996). This suggests that relying solely on customer feedback without validation through systematic research can lead to misguided decisions. Evidence-based decision-making is critical to business innovation and strategies. Nevertheless, customer feedback is important and thus should be corroborated with empirical evidence to ensure that decisions are well informed and effective. In the business plan, although market need is viewed as the business's desire, goal, or specific requirement to reach the target audience, it is vital to understand such needs in light of functional requirements (how the product or service can be used), emotional desires (how it makes the customer feel), and aspirational goals (what the customer aims to achieve by using the product or service).

6.3 Understanding Customer Persona

A driver of successful innovation is the process of discovering customer needs prior to product development (Narver, Slater & MacLachlan, 2004). However, this approach may not entirely align with innovation, as customer needs exist in two distinct forms: express needs, which customers are aware of, and latent needs, which customers are unaware of. Therefore, it is important for businesses to effectively identify market needs by understanding both the evident and concealed needs of their customers. Studying consumer behavior and conducting preference tests can help businesses tailor their products or services to align with their target audience's desires.

An effective way of identifying both evident and concealed needs of current and potential customers is through Personas. The emergence of Persona dates to 1999, when Alan Cooper introduced it as a design tool and rapidly grew in popularity in the software industry. Today, it is created to help the development team understand for whom they are designing a product. Personas have since been utilized beyond software as businesses begin to understand the importance of defining fictional generalized characters that encompass customer needs, goals, challenges and behavior patterns.

Cooper (1999) defines personas as "A precise description of our user and what he wishes to accomplish" (p. 123). Additionally, Calde et al. (2002) expand on this, defining personas as "fictional, detailed archetypical characters that represent distinct groupings of behaviors, goals and motivations observed and identified during the research phase." Revella (2015) further defines buyer persona as a detailed representation of an ideal customer based on research and data, encompassing demographics, behaviors, motivations, and goals.

While personas are visually depicted by a single individual, their characteristics are not defined by one individual user but rather a collection of similar patterns from various users. Understanding customer personas helps businesses inform and tailor their efforts more effectively. What is special about defining your customer persona is the focus on your business area as a lens to view your potential customers' attitudes and specific context as they relate with that domain, product or service. Personas help tell the story of what life is like for your customer today within your business domain and what they'd like it to be in the future, allowing you to explore possibilities.

Personas are developed by engaging in thorough market research and data collection leveraging customer interviews, customer insight tools and data analytics to present a visual representation of one's buyer, demographics, psychographics, motivations, needs, preferences, and challenges and behavior patterns.

When developed, they become the guiding principles that help illuminate user preferences and decision-making patterns, allowing organizations to map their the customer journey to see what is most commonly useful and what is one-off. When strategy or process design questions arise, through touchpoints and interaction channels along the customer journey, personas are a practical tool for making better decisions. Organizations that understand their customer personas can tailor specific customer journeys with targeted market campaigns, sales pitch messaging, and design authentic customer relationships. For example, Google creates personas through relational databases to target specific regions for specific advertisements.

6.4 Balancing Proactive and Reactive Approaches to Gain Competitive Advantage

In the business plan, it is important to note that, traditionally, businesses have utilized an active market orientation approach, focusing primarily on current market demands and needs. However, to better understand and respond to the preferences and needs of the intended market, businesses must adopt both reactive and proactive market orientations. A reactive market orientation allows businesses to respond to market demands and changes after they occur. This approach is effective for understanding customer feedback, monitoring competitors, and reacting to market trends. There is an expected relationship between reactive market orientation and business performance metrics such as sales growth, profitability, and new product success (Narver, Slater & MacLachlan, 2004). In a business plan, businesses with proactive market orientation can effectively identify opportunities and create demand for their products or services. Proactive market orientation distinguishes itself as market-driving behavior (Jaworski, Kohli, and Sahay, 2000). Therefore, proactive market orientation can be termed as a forward-thinking approach that leads businesses to initiate risks and capitalize on future opportunities.

A business adopting such an approach goes beyond simply reacting to current market needs; instead, it actively shapes and influences market demands. In today's competitive market, entrepreneurs have learned that to be effective at attaining a strong competitive edge, they must be excellent at discovering customer needs as well as being able to satisfy those needs. As Lew Platt, CEO of Hewlett-Packard, said, "If we don't eat our lunch, somebody else will" (Moore, 1995). Thus, businesses must use market research techniques to understand the norms of consumer behavior and use it as a guide to act in an entrepreneurial manner to create superior customer value. Market research methods are critical for businesses, as they assist in risk minimization and have become a standard practice for businesses to initiate decisions on their products or services.

6.5 The Market Research Method

There are several methods for conducting market research, each with its own advantages and limitations. The most important aspect of all these methods is the nature of the question asked. The approach of asking strategic questions enables businesses to attain the level of depth required to gain insight into their product or service and make an informed decision.

6.5.1 Surveys

Surveys involve gathering data from a sample respondent via an organized questionnaire. This is useful in attaining insight into a participant's preference, behavior and attitude. This quantitative technique is useful for data collection when a selected sample represents the population.

6.5.2 Focus Groups

The focus group method is useful for exploring in-depth insights to uncover the underlying motivation that drives consumer behavior. Small group discussions on specific topics enable participants to share their experiences, perceptions and opinions in the presence of a mediator. Therefore, businesses can understand how customers respond to different stimuli, develop effective marketing strategies, develop communication techniques and effectively position their products.

6.5.3 Interviews

Interviews, a qualitative method, aim to gather in-depth insights, opinions, perceptions, and experiences related to specific topics, products, services, or market trends. The interviews can be structured or unstructured and can be conducted in person, over the phone, or via video conferencing. Unlike surveys, interviews provide detailed insight into participants' thoughts, highlighting the underlying consumer motivation. Interviews are good tools for validating surveys or focus group findings.

6.5.4 Observational Research

This method allows businesses to study consumer behavior in real time. This method allows for systematic observation and recording of behavior, eliminating the need for self-imported data. This technique allows businesses to understand consumer interactions with a product and navigate the environment when making a purchase decision.

6.5.5 Secondary Research

This method is used to gather and analyze existing data collected through other sources. This method provides valuable context for understanding industry trends and their impact on consumers and markets. However, it may lack relevance to a specific topic for comprehensive understanding and therefore should be complemented with primary research methods.

6.5.6 Ethnographic Research

Ethnographic research involves immersing researchers in the natural environment of the target audience to observe and understand their behavior, beliefs, and cultural practices. Ethnographic research offers a powerful approach for gaining deep insights into the complexities of human behavior and culture. Ethnographic research often involves long-term engagement and participant observation, interviews and cultural analysis to gain deep insights into consumer lifestyles, habits, and social dynamics.

6.5.7 Experiments

It is a method for investigating cause–and–effect relationships and testing theoretical hypotheses. It involves systematically manipulating variables and controlling for extraneous factors. Experiments provide valuable insights into understanding the underlying effects on consumer behaviors.

6.5.8 Online Analytics

This method involves analyzing collected data from a digital source, such as social media engagement, website traffic or online sales data. This method provides real-time insight into consumers' online behavior, preferences and trends to optimize digital marketing efforts and launch online campaigns to reach the target market.

6.6 Analyzing Market Segmentation

A process of subdividing a market into various subsets of customers that have similar behavior or needs is defined as market segmentation (Kwak and Lee, 2009). Businesses perceive the market environment as a reliable indicator of market activity analysis, allowing for the prioritization of customer taste and need, leading to new product development. An important aspect of business to reach from the present state into a desired state is attained through various elements, one of which is market segmentation. Moreover, organizations view market segmentation as a strategic tool for allocating sources to increase the likelihood of success. Market segmentation is not a uniform approach and can be a cluster of multiple approaches to meet market objectives (Assael and Roscoe, 1976). Defining an overall market that the organization wants to analyze and segment is critical to leveraging itself in the market. Moreover, dividing the market into segments based on demographics, psychographics, and behavior involves understanding different aspects of consumer behavior and characteristics to create targeted marketing strategies.

Demographic segmentation involves dividing the market based on demographic variables such as age, gender, income, education, occupation, marital status, family size, and ethnicity. The business identifies relevant demographic variables on the basis of the product or service offered to the target market.

Psychographic segmentation involves dividing the market on the basis of lifestyle, personality traits, values, interests, attitudes, opinions, and behavior. These techniques use a cluster approach to group consumers with similar psychographic profiles reflecting various consumer preferences and motivations.

Behavioral segmentation involves dividing the market based on consumers' purchasing behavior, usage patterns, brand loyalty, benefits sought, and other behavioral variables. This method allows analysis of customer purchase history, buying frequency, product usage, loyalty programs, and other behavioral data.

Profile segmentation allows the development of detailed profiles for each segment, describing their characteristics, preferences, needs, and behaviors. This helps businesses understand the unique requirements of each segment and tailor marketing strategies accordingly.

Targeted marketing allows businesses to evaluate the attractiveness of each segment and select the segments that align with the organization's objectives and capabilities. For many companies, target market selection is one of the most important marketing decisions (Aghdaie, 2015). Business can decide which segments to target based on factors such as size, growth potential, competition, and compatibility with one's brand and resources. Moreover, through market segmentation, businesses can develop a unique positioning strategy for each targeted segment to differentiate its products or services and create a compelling value proposition. Decision-making criteria significantly impact the choice of selecting the target market segment (Aghdaie, 2015). This involves crafting messages and marketing initiatives that resonate with the specific needs and preferences of each segment. In addition, businesses must implement marketing strategies and strategies targeted at each segment and continuously monitor performance and feedback to refine segmentation approaches and adapt to changing market dynamics.

6.7 Embracing Changes in the Dynamic Business Environment

Environmental scanning is a proactive tool for entrepreneurs to understand the broader context in which their businesses operate and navigate the complex and ever-changing business landscape. One of the key resources for fostering competitive advantage is the creation of new knowledge (Inkpen, 1998). For entrepreneurs, environmental scanning goes beyond the context of identifying opportunities and threats that may arise from external shifts. In essence, environmental scanning provides the foundational data and insights needed to create a realistic, strategic, and adaptive business plan that aligns with the current and future external business environment. Environmental scanning is one of the critical components of any business plan, enabling entrepreneurs to acquire the knowledge needed to bridge the gap between available information and its relevance to the current business environment. An organization's ability to plan and act strategically enables it to adapt creatively to changing circumstances (Saah, 2022). Furthermore, it assists entrepreneurs in making informed decisions by leveraging the most up-to-date information sourced from outside the organization. However, it is essential to recognize that the ever-evolving business landscape can significantly influence both environmental scanning processes and the motivation and performance levels of entrepreneurs.

There is a correlation between strategic planning and business success (Weiss, 2014). Mitigating the risk of failure relies on adeptly monitoring the evolving business landscape through environmental scanning. Serving as a vital source of external insight, environmental scanning shapes and enriches every aspect of the business plan, ensuring its robustness, strategic alignment, and ability to adapt to changing business conditions. Business environmental scanning allows the identification of factors such as task, external, and internal environmental dynamics that impact business activities as a part of strategic management (Cheng et al., 2014). Although environmental scanning is valuable, it has certain limitations that can hinder organizational direction and impact entrepreneurial vision. The extensive information acquired through environmental scanning can lead to indecisiveness in decision-making, resulting in delayed decisions due to a cautious approach. Therefore, it is crucial for businesses to strategically utilize the insights gained from environmental scanning to develop robust strategies for effective market navigation.

In addition, the unreliability of environmental scanning in future forecasts and its inability to eliminate uncertainties leave an organization more volatile to the changing business landscape. Therefore, environmental scanning is more of a strategic approach that enables entrepreneurs to strategically plan market navigation and product development. New opportunities and threats both emerge with increasing uncertainty and increasing speed of change (Shane and Venkataraman, 2007). Relying solely on the analysis of information acquired through environmental scanning without proper data verification can pose a significant challenge in accurately interpreting data for new business initiatives. Therefore, environmental scanning should be integrated into the business plan as a deliberate tool, enabling a timely approach to identifying emerging trends, market shifts, and customer needs that present potential business opportunities. Strategic planning ensures that the business is equipped to respond proactively to change and shape its market presence accordingly. Furthermore, insights learned from environmental scanning should aid entrepreneurs in contextualizing business plans, emphasizing effective business strategies and goals. Effective environmental scanning methods should be applied by an organization to measure its market strength and positioning. PEST, SWOT, ETOP and QUEST are significant methods for conducting environmental scanning.

6.7.1 PEST Analysis

PEST analysis assists organizations in gaining insight into external factors by analyzing political, economic, social, and technological trends. Through this external macro environment, organizations can determine the factors that shape their operating environment. PEST analysis allows the entrepreneurial vision to assess political regulatory developments and anticipate how changes may impact customers, industries, and markets. Businesses should focus on analyzing trade rules, tax regulations, and environmental legislation. Economic evaluations facilitate the identification of how customers and suppliers are impacted by changes in interest rates, currency exchange, economic growth, and inflation. This enables organizations to identify market opportunities and mitigate threats that may impede growth. Evaluating shifts in social and cultural dynamics can be beneficial in creating customer profiles and observing attitudinal changes in a broader context. Technological analysis allows us to understand the constant shift in modern technology and its impact on potential opportunities. Organizations can use technological analysis to create innovative products, remain competitive through research and development, or understand potential market threats.

6.7.2 SWOT

The growing industrialization, urbanization and social legislation have enabled entrepreneurs to become a significant part of the global economy. The use of SWOT analysis allows strategic environmental scanning through the consideration of strengths, opportunities, weaknesses and threats. The entrepreneurship process assumes risk and combines necessary resources to pursue profitability in an uncertain and ambiguous environment (Abdullah et al., 2020).

SWOT analysis allows entrepreneurs and organizations alike to research sectors, evaluate resources, and assess risks prior to decision making. In addition, SWOT analysis serves as a valuable tool within a business plan to evaluate the feasibility of advancing in an evolving business landscape. Nonetheless, the reliance on assumption-based data inherent in SWOT analysis can yield adverse outcomes. Moreover, the perpetual pace of change presents a challenge for organizations striving to anticipate future developments accurately within their business plans.

Conducting a strengths and weaknesses analysis enables businesses to assess external activities highlighting their distinguishing unique market advantages while identifying areas for improvement to gain a competitive edge. Moreover, exploring external opportunities and threats empowers entrepreneurial visionaries to seize innovative ideas amidst market fluctuations. Recognizing threats aids in understanding a business's ability to maintain competitiveness. However, a vigilant approach must be initiated to avoid the risk of vast data collection, which may lead to paralysis via the analysis approach.

6.7.3 ETOP

To survive amidst evolving business dynamics, organizations must adapt their strategies to be aligned with environmental changes and be prepared to make strategic decisions. Strategic analysis largely comprises making subjective decisions on the basis of objective information, requiring careful analysis to identify and implement the most suitable choices within the business plan. One outcome of this strategic analysis is the Environmental Threat Opportunity Profile (ETOP), which provides entrepreneurs with a comprehensive understanding of the sector and its various influencing factors. By segmenting the environment into sectors and subsectors, ETOP offers insight into the relative impact of market opportunities and threats. This understanding is vital for businesses, as they formulate strategies to capitalize on opportunities and mitigate environmental threats through purposeful decision-making within their business plans.

The ETOP profile employs forecasting techniques to predict future events that may impact current organizational plans, leveraging these forecasts to formulate business plans and strategies. Information is gathered from verbal and written sources such as journals, articles, newsletters, and media outlets to stay abreast of environmental changes, enabling businesses to incorporate these changes into their plans and strategies. The management information system facilitates the timely utilization of this information, empowering management to make proactive decisions. This systematic approach enables entrepreneurs to effectively organize, plan, control, and operate functions within their organizations. However, while ETOP can identify key opportunities and threats to create a profile, it lacks the ability to demonstrate the interaction between these factors. As a subjective tool, it may not fully capture the dynamic nature of the business environment.

6.7.4 QUEST

The Quick Environmental Scanning Technique (Quest) serves as a valuable tool within the business plan, offering organizations a cost-effective means to analyze the environment quickly. This tool enables businesses to prioritize critical issues that require immediate attention, ensuring a focused approach within short timeframes. Quest empowers entrepreneurs to distinguish between external and internal factors and assess their impact on business operations. An interaction matrix is often utilized as part of the QUEST process. By utilizing an interaction matrix, organizations can identify initial opportunities and threats, gaining clarity on their consequences. This matrix helps organizations visualize the relationships between different environmental factors and their potential impact on business operations. It encourages careful analysis and prioritization of critical factors for strategic decision-making. The interaction matrix further facilitates a systematic analysis, prioritizing critical and high-priority factors for strategic adjustment while allowing for the observation of other factors.

6.8 Navigating Business Uncertainties

The emergence of the entrepreneurial concept has empowered individuals to leverage market opportunities through avenues such as corporate organizations, new ventures, or startup businesses. However, the unique entrepreneurial journey is branded by distinct phases, starting with conceptualization, transitioning into the startup phase, and eventually reaching a steady operational phase. Throughout each phase, entrepreneurs encounter evolving requirements and challenges, reflecting the dynamic nature of their journey. For entrepreneurs, the desire to embrace these shifts and excel in a dynamic environment comes from the notion of adaptation. Incorporating this adaptive mindset into the business plan allows entrepreneurs to envision strategies that not only address current challenges but also anticipate and respond to future shifts in the market landscape, aligning with their entrepreneurial vision. For entrepreneurs, adaptation is a critical skill in navigating the journey from conception to success. It reflects the willingness and ability to adjust the business concept as a venture evolves from an initial idea into a business plan, transitions into an operational organization, and ultimately achieves success. The ability of entrepreneurs to leverage market opportunities comes from adapting to and embracing the changing business environment. The art of entrepreneurship's rapid increase consists of mastering chaos and ensuring that dimensional advances are cohesive and timely (Marmer et al., 2011). Furthermore, the adaptive approach contributes to understanding and filling market gaps, enabling entrepreneurs to respond effectively to market needs within their business plan.

There is no doubt that an entrepreneurial feeling of success can be highly rewarding; however, it does come with its own set of challenges. Therefore, gaining a deep understanding of the various elements of market dynamics, risks, and the level of threats they pose is crucial for a business' overall success and market sustainability. Integrating this understanding into the business plan ensures that strategies are formed by market realities, enhancing the organization's ability to thrive amidst challenges and capitalize on opportunities. Embracing uncertainties requires a significant mindset and operational shift. This requires a core focus on business functions while strategically altering and developing business plans, defining timelines and goals and setting up metrics for measuring business success. Moreover, strategic investment in marketing, personal and technological investment is needed to remain competitive and focus on core business functions. The existence of external environmental opportunities is defined by demographics, new knowledge, and changes in industry structure. Entrepreneurial ventures come to life in uncertain and altering environments. Entrepreneurs viewing challenges as opportunities tend to highlight growth and learning. The experience of successes and failures in the business landscape contributes to the resilience, creativity, and adaptability necessary for entrepreneurial success. Incorporating this understanding into the business plan fosters a mindset of continuous improvement and innovation, enabling the organization to navigate uncertainties effectively and capitalize on opportunities for growth. Entrepreneurship inherently involves understanding that taking calculated risks is necessary for growth and innovation. In addition, adaptation to an evolving business environment is key to staying relevant and competitive in the long run. However, embracing market uncertainties can be a game changer for a venture's success and growth. Embracing market uncertainties embodies the entrepreneurial vision of seizing opportunities and challenging the status quo to achieve transformative outcomes.

6.9 Entrepreneurial Triumph – Integration into the Business Plan

The incorporation of entrepreneurial triumphs into business plans demonstrates the achievements and success of entrepreneurs, highlighting their business credibility and appeal. Sections of business plans, such as executive summaries, company descriptions, and management teams, allow us to showcase quantifiable achievements, such as revenue millions, awards, and percentage growth. To increase business plan reliability and utility, the integration of triumphs will support direct relevance to business culture while avoiding the risk of overshadowing core business plan details.

6.9.1 Executive Summary

Should highlight key accomplishments or begin with a compelling story to set the tone for the rest of the business plan. This could consist of prior successful ventures, major milestones, or recognition. For example, the executive summary for ABC Corporation is as follows:

6.9.1.1 Who

OORF Corporation, founded by Oluchi E. Oti and Riffat Faizan, is a leading provider of renewable energy solutions headquartered in Toronto City.

6.9.1.2 What

The OORF Corporation specializes in developing and implementing innovative renewable energy technologies, including solar panels, wind turbines, and energy storage systems, to address climate change and promote sustainability.

6.9.1.3 When

Since its establishment in 2003, OORF Corporation has been at the forefront of the renewable energy industry, pioneering new technologies and solutions.

6.9.1.4 Where

Operating globally, OORF Corporation has offices and projects in major cities worldwide, facilitating the transition to clean energy on a global scale.

6.9.1.5 Why

OORF Corporation is committed to combating climate change, promoting environmental sustainability, driving innovation in the renewable energy sector, and contributing to a greener future for generations to come.

6.9.1.6 How

OORF Corporation achieves its goals through strategic partnerships, research and development, investment in cutting-edge technologies, and a dedicated team of experts who are passionate about making a positive impact on the planet.

6.9.2 Company Description

This section highlights the entrepreneurial journey through the narrative of entrepreneurs' previous experiences and successes with the current business idea. It should demonstrate how past achievements have equipped the entrepreneur with unique insights and skills. For example, the company summary for OORF Corporation is as follows:

6.9.2.1 Company Overview

OORF is a pioneering renewable energy company focused on providing sustainable energy solutions through innovative technologies and services. In 2003, OORF Corporation aimed to reduce the carbon footprint and promote environmental sustainability by offering a range of products and services, including solar panel installations, wind turbine systems, and energy-efficient consulting.

Table 6.1 Company Summary

Business Type: Limited Liability Company (LLC)
Location: Toronto, Ontario
Founders: Oluchi E. Oti and Riffat Faizan
Industry: Renewable Energy

Source: *Own illustration*

6.9.2.2 *Mission Statement*

Our mission is to revolutionize the energy sector by delivering clean, affordable, and reliable renewable energy solutions, empowering communities and businesses to achieve energy independence and sustainability.

6.9.2.3 *Vision Statement*

To become a global leader in renewable energy, driving the transition to a greener, more sustainable future through cutting-edge technology and unparalleled customer service.

6.9.2.4 *Core Values*

- Sustainability – Committed to reducing environmental impact and promoting green practices.
- Innovation – Continuously developing and implementing the latest renewable energy technologies.
- Integrity – Upholding the highest standards of transparency, honesty, and ethical practices.
- Customer Focus – Providing exceptional service and tailored solutions to meet our customers' unique energy needs.
- Collaboration – Fostering partnerships with stakeholders, communities, and industry leaders to drive collective progress.

<u>Products and Services</u>

- Solar Panel Installation: Customized solar solutions for residential, commercial, and industrial properties.
- Wind turbine systems – Design and installation of wind energy systems for various applications.
- Energy Storage Solutions – Advanced battery storage systems to ensure a reliable and uninterrupted power supply.
- Consulting Services – Energy audits, efficiency assessments, and sustainability planning for businesses and communities.
- Maintenance and Support – Comprehensive maintenance services to ensure the optimal performance and longevity of renewable energy systems.

6.9.2.5 *Management Team*

Elaborates on the detailed individual achievements of each key team member, including specific accomplishments, awards, and recognitions that highlight their ability to drive the business to success.

6.9.2.6 *Market Analysis*

Integrating past successes leverages credibility, significantly reassuring stakeholders and investors that the business plan is supported by proven experience. For example:

Table 6.2 Market Analysis

Market Analysis *The demand for renewable energy is rapidly increasing as governments, businesses, and individuals seek sustainable alternatives to traditional energy sources. With favorable regulatory policies and technological advancements, the renewable energy market presents significant growth opportunities.* OORF *is well-positioned to capitalize on these trends, offering innovative solutions that meet the evolving needs of the market.*
Competitive Advantage • *Expert Team: A highly skilled and experienced team of engineers, technicians, and sustainability experts.* • *Innovative Technology: Utilizing the latest advancements in renewable energy to deliver efficient and cost-effective solutions.* • *Customer-Centric Approach: Tailored solutions and exceptional customer service to build long-term relationships and ensure customer satisfaction.* • *Strong Partnerships: Collaborations with leading technology providers and industry stakeholders to enhance service offerings and expand market reach.*

Source: *Own illustration*

Table 6.3 Financial Projection

Financial Projections OORF *Corporation anticipates steady growth in revenue and profitability over the next five years, driven by increasing demand for renewable energy solutions and strategic market expansion. Detailed financial projections, including sales forecasts, expense estimates, and profitability analysis, are provided in the financial plan section.*

Source: *Own illustration*

6.9.2.7 Strategy and Implementation

In this segment, incorporating the detailed lessons learned assists in revealing how past experiences have shaped the current strategy and implementation plans. This demonstrates a pragmatic and informed approach to business planning.

6.9.2.8 Financial Plan

To demonstrate financial insight, past financial achievements that highlight the entrepreneur's ability to manage and grow financial resources effectively should be shared. These include financial milestones such as fundraising successes or profitable exits. For example, the financial projection of a company is as follows:

6.10 Conclusion

In the continuously transforming market, it is important for entrepreneurs to ensure that the strategic responsiveness and adaptation of strategies are carried out through adequate environmental scanning. Moreover, market segmentation helps businesses reach potential customers and develop products by assessing their buying patterns, demographic analysis, and psychographic dimensions. The fundamentals of business plans play an important role in achieving scalability and sustainability. It helps with strategic planning, risk mitigation, and capitalizing on market opportunities.

Bibliography

Abdullah, R. "Importance and Contents of Business Plan: A Case-Based Approach." *Jurnal Manajemen Indonesia* 20, no. 2 (2020): 164. https://doi.org/10.25124/jmi.v20i2.3204.

Abdullah, N. H. N., A. Harjito, and J. Said. The role of strategic management accounting on heterogeneity of human capital, information technology capabilities and value creation. *International Journal of Innovation, Creativity and Change* 10, no. 11 (2020): 653–673.

Aghdaie, M. H., and M. Alimardani. "Target Market Selection Based on Market Segment Evaluation: A Multiple Attribute Decision Making Approach." *International Journal of Operational Research* 24, no. 3 (2015): 262. https://doi.org/10.1504/ijor.2015.072231.

Assael, H., and A. M. Roscoe. Approaches to market segmentation analysis. *Journal of Marketing* 40, no. 4 (1976): 67–76. https://doi.org/10.1177/002224297604000408

Byrd, M. J., and L. C. Megginson. *Small Business Management: An Entrepreneur's Guidebook.* New York, USA: McGraw-Hill Irwin, 2009.

Calde, S., K. Goodwin, and R. Reimann. *SHS Orcas: The First Integrated Information System for Long-Term Healthcare Facility Management.* Conference on Human Factors and Computing Systems, Case Studies of the CHI2002/AIGA Experience Design Forum. New York: ACM Press, 2002.

Camilleri, M. A. Corporate sustainability and responsibility: Creating value for business, society and the environment. *Asian Journal of Sustainability and Social Responsibility* 2 (2017): 59–74. https://doi.org/10.1186/s41180-017-0016-5

Cheng, B., I. Ioannou, and G. Serafeim. Corporate social responsibility and access to finance. *Strategic Management Journal* 35 (2014): 1–23. https://doi.org/10.1002/smj.2131

Christensen, C. M., and J. M. Bower. Customer power, strategic investment and the failure of leading firms. *Strategic Management Journal* 17 (1996): 197-218. https://doi.org/10.1002/(SICI)1097-0266(199603)17:3<197::AID-SMJ804>3.0.CO;2-U

Espejo, R. and G. Dominici. Cybernetics of value cocreation for product development. *Systems Research and Behavioral Science* 34, no. 1 (2016): 24–40. https://doi.org/10.1002/sres.2392

Camilleri, M. A. "Market Segmentation, Targeting and Positioning." In *Travel Marketing, Tourism Economics and the Airline Product*, 69–83. Cham, Switzerland: Springer, 2018. https://doi.org/10.1007/978-3-319-49849-2_4

Cooper, A. *The Inmates Are Running the Asylum.* Indianapolis, IA: SAMS/Macmillan, 1999.

Government of Canada (GOC). "Language Selection – Innovation, Science and Economic Development Canada Main Site." Innovation, Science and Economic Development Canada, January 11, 2022. Accessed November 1, 2024. https://ised-isde.canada.ca/site/sme-research-statistics/en/key-small-business-statistics/key-small-business-statistics-2022.

Howarth, J. "Startup Failure Rate Statistics (2024)." *Exploding Topics*, November 3, 2023. https://explodingtopics.com/blog/startup-failure-stats.

Inkpen, A. C. Learning, knowledge acquisition, strategic alliances. *European Management Journal* 16 (1998): 223–229. http://dx.doi.org/10.1016/S0263-2373(97)00090-X

Kalane, L. *Reasons for failure of SMEs in the Free State.* Master dissertation, University of the Free State, Bloemfontein, 2015.

Kamuri, S. "Understanding entrepreneurial vision for growth, innovation and performance in Kenya's leather industry." *Journal of Global Entrepreneurship Research* 12 (2022): 119–130. https://doi.org/10.1007/s40497-022-00308-2

Kwak, J., and E. Lee. "An empirical study of "fringe benefits" and performance of the Korean firms." *International Journal of Business and Management* 4, no 2 (2009): 3–3.DOI:10.5539/ijbm.v4n2p3

Marmer, M., B. L. Herrmann, E. Dogrultan, R. Berman, C. Eesley, and S. Blank Startup genome report extra: Premature scaling. *Startup Genome* 10 (2011): 1–56.

Moore, M. H. *Creating Public Value: Strategic Management in Government.* Harvard University Press, London, 1995.

Narver, J. C., S. F. Slater, and D. L. MacLachlan. "Responsive and proactive market orientation and new-product success." *Journal of Product Innovation Management* 21 (2004): 334–347. http://dx.doi.org/10.1111/j.0737-6782.2004.00086.x

Revella, A. *Buyer Personas: How to Gain Insight into Your Customer's Expectations, Align Your Marketing Strategies, and Win More Business.* Hoboken, NJ: Wiley, 2015.

Rosário, A. T., R. J. Raimundo, and S. P. Cruz. (2022). "Sustainable entrepreneurship: A literature review." *Sustainability* 14 no. 9 (2022): 5556. https://doi.org/10.3390/su14095556

Saah, P. "Critical factors for the successful implementation of a strategic business plan among small and medium size enterprises." *International Review of Management and Marketing* 12, no.4 (2022): 19–28.

Shane, S., and S. Venkataraman. The Promise of Entrepreneurship as a Field of Research*. In: Cuervo, Á., Ribeiro, D., Roig, S. (eds) Entrepreneurship. Springer, Berlin, Heidelberg, 2007. https://doi.org/10.1007/978-3-540-48543-8_8

Weiss, A. Guest Column: Execution IS the Strategy, 2014. Available at: https://alanweiss.com/guest-column-execution-is-the-strategy/ (Last access: 04 November, 2014).

Welter, C., A. Scrimpshire, D. Tolonen, and E. Obrimah. "The road to entrepreneurial success: business plans, lean startup, or both?" *New England Journal of Entrepreneurship* 24, no. 1 (2021): 21–42. https://doi.org/10.1108/NEJE-08-2020-0031

Case Study: Seniorpreneur's SMART Plan for an Aging-In-Place Services

Diya Nitinbhai Patel

Background

An individual whose preference is to live independently at home rather than in a senior housing facility, 60-year-old retired executive Jack decided to pursue his entrepreneurial plan only after witnessing a brief stay in aging-in-place services. He started his venture by focusing on aging-in-place services. He immediately recognized a business opportunity in the aging-in-place market due to the growing elderly population and increasing demand for in- home care.

SMART Objectives for Business Plan Development

Understanding that actionable and clear goals would help Jack respond effectively to evolving market demands, he used SMART objectives that would guide his business planning process. Below are the SMART objectives he set:

Specific

Tailored to the elderly client's needs, His business provided home modification services such as handrails, wheelchair ramps, and monitoring systems through tech support to ensure there were medical alerts and fall detection. Within a year, his target was to provide 100 home modifications in his vicinity, which was the target he set for himself.

Measurable

Jack tracked customer satisfaction using surveys, striving for a 90% satisfaction rate, and set a milestone to obtain 50 new customers within the first six months in order to gauge success. This reflects the component of measurability.

Achievable

With his support network and experience, Jack knew he could accomplish his objective. He collaborated with neighborhood contractors to modify homes and health tech firms to install monitoring systems. Jack ensured that his venture could fulfil its commitments on time by establishing strategic alliances.

Relevant

Due to demographic shifts like the aging population and rising in-home care preferences, the market demand for aging-in-place services was expanding. These trends aligned with Jack's business, so his plan was extremely pertinent to the demands of the market today. Thus, this reflects the element of relevance.

Time-bound

Within three months after availing funds, Jack's plan was supposed to be completely functional. By this deadline, he wanted to finish all the fundamental business setup tasks such as establishing strategic alliances, launching a website, and reaching out to customers so the company could react quickly to cater to market demands.

Comprehensive Business Plan

SMART goals enabled Jack to develop his comprehensive business plan:

Executive Summary

A simplistic overview of his experience along with the rising need for aging-in-place services, and the solutions his company would provide.

Market Research and Analysis

To validate market gaps and identify competitors, he carried out market research on the care industry, focusing on senior care. He identified the limited regional home modification services.

Marketing Strategy

He intended to target adult children of elderly people through digital marketing, senior living community advertising, and market himself to form partnerships with healthcare providers.

Operations Plan

Jack laid out the procedures his team followed, including giving tech assistance for monitoring systems and outsourcing home modifications contracts to professional certified contractors.

Financial Projections

By the end of the first year, Jack projected a break-even point and expected his revenue to rise steadily in the upcoming year, as anticipated increases in clients.

Customer Discovery Process

Interviewing senior citizens and their families to learn about their needs was the first step in Jack's customer discovery process. His service offerings were improved as a result of these discussions; responding to feedback, he introduced optional monthly monitoring subscriptions and customizable safety packages.

Outcome

Jack created a business plan that addressed the increasing demands of senior care in a practical and comprehensive manner by employing SMART objectives. His methodical strategy enabled him to gain capital, launch successfully, and attain his market objectives on schedule.

Reflection Questions

- In what ways did Jack employ SMART goals to ensure the business plan remains realistic, feasible, and flexible enough to cater to changing market demands?
- How did Jack's entrepreneurial venture meet the rising need for aging-in-place services?
- How was Jack's service offering improved by the customer discovery process?
- Explain how the customer discovery process enabled Jack in improving his service offering?
- Reflect on key features of the business plan that helped Jack in addressing effectively customer demands and market trends?

Chapter 7

Essential Considerations

Controllable and Uncontrollable Factors

Negar Sohaee and Rokhsareh Farsad

7.0 Introduction

Entrepreneurship is a complex and dynamic endeavor that involves navigating several factors that affect the success or failure of new businesses. There is a thin line between the success or failure of a startup business due to controllable or uncontrollable factors (Pan et al., 2022). To build resilient businesses, entrepreneurs need to understand and manage these elements effectively. Some essential factors, such as entrepreneurs' personal motivation, learning ability in the face of failure, and family and peer support, encourage entrepreneurs to perform better and be willing to keep trying even though they might face some challenges (Pan et al., 2022).

The controllable factors include business planning, management, leadership, marketing strategies, financial management, human resources, operational efficiency, technological utilization, and customer relations. On the one hand, a business's success depends on managing these factors strategically and optimizing production (Guerola-Navarro et al., 2022). As a result of these factors, startup ventures can increase their success probability in the market (Sevilla-Bernardo et al., 2022). On the other hand, other factors outside of a company's control, known as uncontrollable factors, can also impact a business. These factors include market conditions, the regulatory environment, competitors, global events, legal and political conditions, and societal trends. Consequently, entrepreneurs can develop strategies to mitigate risks and adopt changes by considering these influential factors (Popescu, 2014).

The success rate for SMEs in the first few years is low. Many startup businesses fail in their first few years of operation due to specific challenges that they faced, and they have not been ready for those challenges (McCartan-Quinn et al., 2003). Most of these challenges are predictable and prohibitable. In fact, ventures' failure can be minimized by developing accurate market research and designing a business. Entrepreneurs must maximize their business potential by leveraging controllable factors while preparing for and adapting to uncontrollable factors. By combining these two approaches, entrepreneurs can develop businesses that can thrive in diverse environments.

7.1 Controllable Factors

7.1.1 Business Plan

A business plan is the most controllable factor in businesses; a business plan shows what you intend to do with your business and how it will be done. The process of writing

DOI: 10.4324/9781003504351-7

a business plan involves bringing your idea to reality, which requires dealing with why, where, when, and how much your venture is (Botha and Robertson, 2014). Additionally, it provides structure to your thoughts and helps you create a step-by-step plan to reach your goals. The business plan typically includes the following:

7.1.1.1 *Business Description*

Entrepreneurs form their business plans because doing so helps them provide direction by discussing where they want to take the venture and what they want out of it. Ghezzi and Cavallo (2020) emphasized the importance of the business plan for the objectives of the venture and its identification of the target market through comprehensive market analysis.

7.1.1.2 *Market Analysis*

Who will be your end users, and what do they want from your business? Understanding market needs and demands is crucial for adjusting the final products and services that meet market demands (Ghezzi and Cavallo, 2020).

7.1.1.3 *Competitor Assessment*

Who will be your competitors, and how can you compete with them? Assessing competitors' strengths and weaknesses enables entrepreneurs to establish and develop competitive strategies that distinguish their competitive advantages in the market (Bortolini et al., 2018).

7.1.1.4 *Marketing Plan*

How will you approach your customers? A detailed marketing plan focuses more on brand awareness and consumer loyalty, and these elements position the business position in the market (Bortolini et al., 2018).

7.1.1.5 *Operation Plan*

How do you plan to implement your idea? Brinckmann et al. (2010) argue that a business plan provides a step-by-step blueprint for implementing new ideas in the market, operation processes, resources (financial, human and technological resources) and timelines that should be considered in this process.

7.1.1.6 *Financial Plan*

How much does it cost to establish and run the business, and what are the financial sources? The financial plan outlines the cost of expenditure for establishing a business and running and performing the business in the market. Financial forecasting helps anticipate crises and challenges, and it considers budget planning for establishing and growing the venture in the market (Brinckmann et al., 2010).

7.1.1.7 Executive Summary

What is the fundamental aspect of the venture that stakeholders should know? Executive summaries communicate entrepreneurs' mission and vision along with strategic goals to stakeholders (financiers, employees, potential employees, suppliers and customers) (Richbell et al., 2006; Scarborough, and Cornwall, 2016). Entrepreneurs must tailor their business plans based on whether they are seeking funding from a bank, venture capital funds, or business angles. A business plan will help founders have greater chances of obtaining equity investors. An effective business plan not only provides a road map for decision-making but also enhances credibility among stakeholders, including investors, partners, and customers (Mason and Stark, 2004).

7.1.2 Management and Leadership

According to Utoyo et al. (2020), if entrepreneurs want to succeed in delivering the greatest value, they should be effectively innovative. The purpose of a supportive leader in a business is to hunt for opportunities by taking risks and implementing creativity and innovation (Suriawaty Bahkia et al., 2020). This important addition to a team in a business can lead employees and stakeholders to progress and be actively productive by considering the business's development conditions. To indicate the importance of supportive leadership in the success of entrepreneurs, Hussein et al. (2023) proved that for construction-based renewable energy projects in Pakistan, supportive leadership intervenes between the entrepreneurial success and critical success factors that cause an entrepreneur to succeed. In fact, the results showed that supportive leadership has both a direct and considerable positive effect on the success of entrepreneurs (Hussein et al., 2023).

7.1.2.1 Marketing Strategy

Marketing strategies are patterns of managerial initiatives and actions that relate an organization to its customers and markets. Entrepreneurs should develop their marketing strategy as their first step before allocating funds or committing time to marketing. In their industry, they need to know who their target audience is, what their business is about, and how they differ from other businesses (Cham et al., 2022). For entrepreneurs to succeed, they must develop a proper marketing strategy that provides them with the necessary tools for understanding their target market, building brand awareness, driving long-term growth and revenue, creating a successful marketing strategy, building customer loyalty, adapting to market changes, and utilizing digital marketing channels (Khandare et al., 2022). Although designing a flawless marketing strategy for entrepreneurs is essential, creative ideas always revitalize a business in addition to the marketing strategy.

7.1.2.2 Technology Utilization

In this fast-paced, changing environment, the integration of artificial intelligence (AI) has already merged and transformed businesses. AI can be used by entrepreneurs to increase customer reactions and establish a strong competitive advantage over competitors in the market. AI also has a considerable impact on market analysis, and it can analyze advanced data and predict modeling to contribute to decision making and market forecasting (Usman, 2024).

7.1.2.3 Financial Management

Effective financial planning, innovative funding mechanisms such as cash flow management, crowdfunding, and accurate financial and cost forecasting are essential to start a venture's growth and stability. Optimal resource allocation, budgeting, and capital structuring reduce financial risk. Using crowdfunding to raise capital and validate markets facilitates community engagement and economic stabilization. Liquidity and operational continuity depend on effective cash flow management. Furthermore, advanced financial forecasting enables startups to adapt to volatile market conditions. Startups benefit from tailored financial management (Idris, 2024).

7.1.3 Innovation and Product Development

The term "entrepreneur" was first used by an economist called Richard Cantillon in the 18th century. It was attributed to a person who is a risk taker and innovator (Cantillon, 1755). Schumpeter (1934) focuses on how innovation can cause economic advancement by implementing the process of "creative destruction". This process replaces existing technology and resources with new technologies and resources. Schumpeter (1934) also called this replacement the "innovative function", which is associated with entrepreneurship. All these coined terms and their relationships show how closely entrepreneurship and innovation are interrelated and are considered motives for economic growth and competitiveness. Entrepreneurs can create value by introducing new products or processes, which are called product innovation or process innovation.

Researchers have shown the multidisciplinarity and diversity of entrepreneurship and innovation (Faizan and Haque, 2016; Haq et al., 2024; Haq et al., 2024; Haque, 2024). New entrepreneurship opportunities create solutions and possibilities for innovation, such as artificial intelligence, through digitalization and technology. Collaborative consumption, which allows millions of people to have access to products without ownership, and co-creation, which creates values in which several stakeholders obtain mutual benefits, are new trends and opportunities for entrepreneurship (Cohen and Kietzmann, 2014). Therefore, entrepreneurs can consider innovation as a controllable factor that can improve both their own business and the country's economy.

7.1.4 Human Resource Practices and Organizational Performance

In "The relationship between HR practices and firm performance" and "The impact of HR practices on the performance of business units" Wright et al. (2004, 2003) highlighted that employees are rare and valuable blessings who are considered sources of competitive advantage for organizations. This is what Barney (1991) called the resource-based view. Human resource management is in charge of employees' motivation, acquisition and development. If HRM practices positively affect the performance of employees, organizational performance will also improve considerably. HRM, by recruiting the right people who have appropriate experience and skills, can have a significant influence on organizational performance (Ogunyomi and Bruning, 2016).

Various models, such as Michigan, Harvard and Warwick, categorize the relationships between HR practices and how an organization performs. Each model analyses the effect of practices on performance and outcomes. They also provide different variations to check how the performance and outcomes have changed. Factors such as employee selection, training, and their appraisals are considered in the Michigan Model, whereas more criteria such as manpower flow, socialization, work systems and employee relations and well-being are examined in other models such as Guest's Model (2002) and the Warwick Model (Henry and Pettigrew, 1992). The greater the use of these practices is, the greater the organization's productivity and profitability. After implementing different practices in hospitality industries, researchers have realized that some practices can have a tremendous impact on the financial performance of organizations as well as reduce employees' rate of replacement. These practices include incentive plans, preemployment tests and labor management participation.

Although all previous scholars have indicated the significance of HRM for organizational outcomes in large firms, the SME sector has been ignored. Therefore, these results might not be exact and identical for SMEs (Huselid, 2003; Purcell and Kinnie, 2007); however, according to Wapshott and Mallett (2015), a lack of formal HRM and experts is clearly observable. In SMEs, founders and proprietors manage human resources, and they are not experts in this regard; mostly SMEs encounter the issue of employee turnover (Pingle, 2014). What can be concluded is that wherever effective human resources do not control employee performance, regardless of the size of the enterprise, the organization is entitled to failure. Thus, this problem in organizational performance can be avoided and controlled by human resource practices.

7.1.5 Customer Relations

Relationship marketing has always been clearly associated with customer loyalty. Enterprises have always been obliged to first know the market, product and their customers to attain a great customer–company bond. This bond can cause positive word-of-mouth (WOM) that, in return, can not only retain customers but also bring new customers (Sarioglu, 2023). Viral marketing is a popular strategy to encourage customers to talk about their shopping experience to other potential customers; in fact, it is e-WOM (Sarioglu, 2023). The advancement of technology has increased the use of viral marketing tools such as social networking sites, blogs and company websites (Choshaly and Mirabolghasemi, 2022). Although online branding studies indicate customers' decision to purchase a product, the effect of WOM seems more significant than that of e-WOM (Baker et al., 2016). People prefer to discuss their satisfaction with their purchases face-to-face in traditional ways rather than writing reviews on social networking sites or shopping websites; they might face social risks by conveying their marketing experiences. Conversely, the fast pace and broad size area of viral marketing have led to rapid expansion in brand awareness and improved measurability at minimum cost (Kaplan and Haelein, 2011; Baker et al., 2016).

7.1.6 Operational Efficiency

Advanced digital solutions such as automation software, cloud computing, big data, blockchain technology, and AI can simplify operations, reduce costs, and increase the productivity of startups. Modern technology has made data management, customer service management (CRM), and other administrative chores more precise and effective. Startups can easily adapt to market demands using modular and scalable technology. Adaptability enables them to maintain competitiveness despite constantly changing market conditions. Modern technologies allow business owners to reach a broader audience and maximize their growth potential. It allows them to interact with clients, access global markets, and work more efficiently with partners (Muley et al., 2024).

Davenport and Ronanki (2018) examine AI's practical applications in the business world. On the basis of their research, AI can support three important needs of businesses: process automation, cognitive insight, and cognitive engagement. They emphasize the importance of a clear AI strategy, substantial data management investments, and a commitment to change management. Although intelligent machines are likely to replace some jobs, AI should enhance human capabilities rather than replace them. Davenport and Ronanki (2018) recommend that businesses start small, build expertise, and scale AI initiatives thoughtfully.

7.2 Uncontrollable Factors

7.2.1 Market Conditions

In today's fast-paced competitive environment, market conditions are crucial, and businesses should be extremely adaptive (Ireland and Webb, 2007). Market demand, customer behavior, and economic trends all have significant effects on firms, although they are largely unpredictable. Inflation, unemployment, economic growth, and demographic changes are some of the economic factors that affect consumer behavior, purchasing power, and overall businesses. Since these patterns can offer predictions about the future and insights into how the economy is going, entrepreneurs should be aware of them. The decline in consumer spending during financial downturns may have a negative effect on revenues and sales. However, economic booms may present opportunities for market expansion and growth. To successfully predict market changes, business owners must examine these patterns (Blanchard and Johnson, 2013; Mankiw, 2020).

Entrepreneurs must conduct extensive market research to assess consumer demand and understand how the market can be used to bring about upcoming products or services in the future (Venkataraman, 2019). Perloff (2016) says that companies may be constantly forced to adapt and innovate to satisfy customer demands as demand for sustainable products grows. As these trends evolve, entrepreneurs must continue collecting data from customers and evaluating them. Entrepreneurs have a great advantage through market research, strategic planning, and flexible business models, which can lessen the impact of these unpredictable elements (Solomon, 2017; Hoyer et al., 2018).

7.2.2 Regulatory Environment

National governments often establish complex and broad regulatory frameworks to protect their goals. Several methods can be used to achieve this, including legislative changes, administrative reporting requirements, and financial incentives such as subsidies and fines. The regulatory environment has a significant effect on entrepreneurship (Saltman and Busse, 2002). Respecting legal and ethical requirements is necessary to act morally and lawfully. Canada's federal, provincial, and local laws govern many aspects of an entrepreneur's business operations. These include tax regulations, health and safety standards, environmental limitations, and employment legislation. To ensure transparency, accountability, and equity, the Canadian Business Corporations Act (CBCA) established legal standards for forming and operating corporations in Canada in 1985. The Canadian Environmental Protection Act (CEPA) also imposes strict environmental regulations on companies to safeguard the environment and public health (Canadian Environmental Protection Act, 1999).

Globalization places business owners in an even more challenging regulatory environment. In 2016, the European Union's General Data Protection Regulation (GDPR) required businesses that handle the personal data of EU residents to adhere to strict data protection and privacy standards. A violation of international standards can lead to severe fines and adverse legal consequences; thus, understanding and adhering to them are essential. A trade agreement also affects market access, tariffs, and trade regulations, allowing businesses operating in multiple countries to compete smoothly, such as the United States-Mexico-Canada Agreement or USMCA and NAFTA (United States-Mexico-Canada Agreement, 2020). Being aware of these restrictions will prevent legal problems and preserve their reputation in the international market. Complying with the law requires proactive measures.

Entrepreneurs can overcome regulatory obstacles by investing in legal skills and compliance methods. Maintaining a regular auditing schedule, providing employee training, and keeping up with new laws can help businesses navigate the regulatory landscape more effectively. A high level of compliance can reduce risks, build confidence among stakeholders, and prepare entrepreneurs for long-term, sustainable growth.

7.2.3 Competition

The business world is rife with competition, and it is imperative to learn and adapt to the strategies of competitors to stay ahead and prosper. There are many types of competitive strategies, such as pricing, innovation, marketing, distribution, and customer service, that aim to satisfy financial objectives, increase market share, and retain customers.

The business world is filled with competition, and it is imperative to learn and adapt to the strategies of competitors to stay ahead and prosper. There are many types of competitive strategies, such as pricing, innovation, marketing, distribution, and customer service, that aim to satisfy financial objectives, increase market share, and retain customers.

Three analytical methods should be used to identify, appraise, and place entrepreneurs in the market to compete effectively:

- SWOT analysis (strengths, weaknesses, opportunities, and threats)
- Porter's Five Forces
- PEST model (political, economic, social, and technological)

SWOT analysis enables entrepreneurs to identify internal strengths and weaknesses and external opportunities and threats in the organization's environment. Porter's five forces framework provides insight into the competitive aspect of businesses by evaluating competition in an industry by considering industry dynamics and structure. Based on the five forces determined in this model, the shape of the industry will be formed: competitive rivalry, supplier power, buyer power, threat of substitution, and threat of new entry. The last framework, the PEST model, is used to analyze the general environment. On the basis of the results of these three analyses, the organization's vision, mission, and strategic plans are determined (Sammut-Bonnici and Galea, 2015; Waworuntu et al., 2024).

Innovative companies can gain a significant market share and set higher quality and functionality standards if they consistently introduce new and improved products. Entrepreneurs need to stay updated on industry trends and invest in research and development (R&D). As a result, not only are customers satisfied, but the business also stands out from its competitors. In today's highly competitive environment, organizations aim to overcome competition and win new or innovative products or services (Schilling, 2020).

To build awareness and attract customers, competitors may use a variety of marketing channels, such as digital marketing, social media, traditional advertising, and public relations. The development of responsive marketing strategies that highlight their unique selling proposition is crucial for entrepreneurs. Engaging customers through personalized marketing efforts and maintaining a strong online presence can counteract competitors' marketing strategies (Kotler and Keller, 2016). In addition, competitors may use e-commerce platforms, partnerships with retailers, or direct-to-consumer channels to reach a broader audience. Entrepreneurs need to assess their distribution strategies so that they can reach their target customers efficiently and effectively. As consumers and market conditions change, businesses can adapt to distribution flexibility.

Finally, outstanding customer service can control competition in the market. Competitors, who provide superior customer service, set high standards for others to strive to meet, leading to retaining customers and generating positive word-of-mouth referrals. To compete effectively, entrepreneurs should develop strong customer relationships, resolve issues promptly, respect service quality and continuously improve customer satisfaction (Zeithaml et al., 2018).

By comprehensively analyzing their competitors' actions and strategies, entrepreneurs can improve their competitive position. This involves reacting to competitors' moves, anticipating market trends, and setting industry standards. Entrepreneurs must remain agile during intense competition, maintain innovative business models, and adapt to the demanding environment, as Ghezzi and Cavallo (2020) noted. Implementing an agile methodology allows organizations to respond quickly to market changes, and it can shorten the development time of products and services and reduce costs (Nurdiani et al., 2019; Xu and Koivumäki, 2019).

7.2.4 Technological Changes

Brynjolfsson and McAfee claim that rapid advances in computer power, artificial intelligence, and the internet are causing a second industrial revolution. This latest revolution has transformed cognitive work and human–machine interactions compared with the previous industrial revolution, which mechanized manual labor. Technology rapidly transforms businesses, economies, and society. Automation and AI are likely to replace occupations, causing labor market shifts. Indeed, they believe that these technologies will boost innovation, productivity, and economic growth. The organization promotes innovation, entrepreneurship, technological advancements, and equity (Brynjolfsson and McAfee, 2014).

Blockchain technology is a significant development for entrepreneurs since it provides secure, transparent data management and transactions that are appealing to both customers and investors (Zheng et al., 2018). The use of these technologies reduces fraud, improves traceability and enhances security in finance, supply chain management, and healthcare. Additionally, the Internet of Things (IoT) is changing business operations. Real-time data collection and exchange from IoT devices improves operational efficiency and product innovation (Agarwal et al., 2022).

Smart devices can optimize supply chain logistics, equipment health, and energy efficiency. With the help of the IoT, entrepreneurs can create new business models and value-added services to meet the growing demand for connected solutions. Augmented reality (AR) and virtual reality (VR), which are used in different industries, such as retail, real estate, education, health care and entertainment, immerse consumers. AR and VR allow entrepreneurs to differentiate their businesses with virtual try-ons in fashion retail and real estate tours (Flavián et al., 2021). Rapid technological advances include improving decision-making, securing transactions, optimizing operations, creating immersive customer experiences, and reshaping the entrepreneurial landscape. In an increasingly digital world, entrepreneurs who adopt these technologies can innovate, increase productivity, and grow sustainably (Fleming et al., 2019).

7.2.5 Global Events

Economic recessions, pandemics, and geopolitical crises present business challenges and possibilities. The external variables affect companies, supply networks, and customer behavior. Understanding and adapting to these events help entrepreneurs decrease risks and take advantage of opportunities.

When revenues and profitability decrease, credit tightens, consumer spending decreases, uncertainty increases during recessions, and businesses struggle to survive. Despite decreasing purchasing power, businesses must maintain positive cash flow, lower expenditures, and engage customers. Flexible pricing, focusing on key goods and services, and diversifying income sources can help companies weather economic storms. Companies can gain an edge by recovering quickly (Mankiw and Taylor, 2020).

Pandemics such as the COVID-19 pandemic affect all industries. Businesses must be flexible in response to remote work, consumer behavior shifts, and global supply chain interruptions. Entrepreneurs should modify business structures, improve their digital skills, and find new distribution methods to attract customers. Retailers need e-commerce and contactless delivery during pandemics such as the COVID-19 pandemic (Donthu and Gustafsson, 2020).

The impact of global events can be felt by businesses, trade policy changes, currency exchange rate fluctuations, and political instability. Entrepreneurs can reduce global problems through diverse supply chains, local contacts, and risk management, as diverse supply chains keep operations stable during the US–China trade war (Hanson, 2020).

7.3 Balancing Controllable and Uncontrollable Factors

Entrepreneurs need to control risk to reduce uncontrollable circumstances, including market swings, regulatory changes, and global events. When business conditions change, entrepreneurs need to have a strong financial plan as well as liquidity to cope with economic downturns. Regular market research helps entrepreneurs anticipate and plan for changes (Ghezzi and Cavallo, 2020; Mankiw, 2020).

In unpredictable environments, firms need flexibility and resilience to survive. Resilience can be created by encouraging employees to accept change and seek improvement. In addition, by investing in technology and digital transformation, corporations can adapt more quickly to market changes and consumer needs. The structure and procedures of an organization can make it easier to recover faster from recessions or global events such as pandemics (Donthu and Gustafsson, 2020; Pan et al., 2022).

Business owners can prepare for future opportunities by using strategic scenario planning; identifying and planning events that could affect the firm; simulating recessions, regulatory changes, and technological revolutions; and identifying and preparing for alternative outcomes. Scenario planning enables firms to take advantage of new market circumstances by identifying transformational opportunities (Blanchard and Johnson, 2013; Schilling, 2017).

It is important to reduce uncertainty through controllable factors, such as strong leadership, business planning, and unique marketing strategies. IoT and AI facilitate operations and decision-making. To maintain financial stability and attract investors, forecasting and budget preparation are critical. A focus on controllable elements can help entrepreneurs achieve long-term success (Kotler et al., 2016; Guerola-Navarro et al., 2022).

A business succeeds when it balances controlled and uncontrollable circumstances and uses risk management techniques, encourages flexibility and resilience, develops scenario plans, and utilizes controllable factors to succeed in varied and demanding situations. An entrepreneur needs to learn and plan constantly.

7.4 Conclusion

Establishing a new business is a marathon and not a sprint. The entrepreneurial journey of establishing a successful and thriving business is not easy, and this process requires understanding both controlled and uncontrollable aspects of the market. The purpose of this chapter is to demonstrate how entrepreneurs should design and develop business planning, leadership and marketing strategies; financial management; human resources; operational efficiency; technological identification and implementation; and customer interactions. These characteristics can increase an entrepreneur's success and market competitiveness. However, uncontrollable factors such as market conditions, the regulatory environment, competition, technological advancements, and global events require adaptability and resilience.

An entrepreneur who uses controllable aspects and adapts to unpredictable conditions may build a strong and resilient company. By taking advantage of global events and market and regulatory changes, entrepreneurs can survive and grow in volatile circumstances.

Entrepreneurship will continue to develop through innovation improvements, market adjustments, and societal changes. To remain competitive, entrepreneurs must innovate and follow trends. Artificial intelligence, blockchain, augmented reality, and virtual reality will continue to be important technological advancements. These technologies allow entrepreneurs to improve their consumer experience, manage operations, and create new business models. If entrepreneurs would like to remain successful in the competitive market, investment in technology and digital transformation is necessary.

Globalization and market expansion create new opportunities for businesses to increase profit by expanding their market and allowing them to gain access to wider resources.

Additionally, it requires entrepreneurs to negotiate complex and challenging markets. Growing a business requires understanding foreign legal frameworks, adjusting to cultural norms, and using global supply networks.

Entrepreneurs must also consider environmental and social factors when developing models for sustainability and ethical business practices. This strategy can help entrepreneurs differentiate themselves from competitors in the market and increase their market share by being innovative and creative. Companies are often caught unprepared and unable to react rapidly and effectively to global disruptions such as recessions and pandemics. Businesses that are more resilient and adaptable react quicker to those changes, survive in the market and have a greater chance of success.

To conclude, the future of entrepreneurship depends on the strategic management of controllable elements, adaptive reactions to uncontrollable effects, and resilience to adapt to uncontrollable forces. Entrepreneurs can expand sustainable business practices if they follow these guidelines. Constant learning and development in start-up companies are essential. Entrepreneurs should maintain this aspect by monitoring industry development, personal development, and innovation.

Bibliography

Agarwal, D., M. Dixit, N. Kumar Dixit, and M. Agarwal. "Dry Sliding Wear Performance of Semi-Solid Al/LM6 Cast Composite: Effect of Silicon Particles on Worn Surfaces." *Materials Today: Proceedings* 56 (2022): 2227–2231.

Baker, A. M., N. Donthu, and V. Kumar, "Investigating How Word-of-Mouth Conversations About Brands Influence Purchase and Retransmission Intentions." *Journal of Marketing Research* 53, no. 2 (2016): 225–239.

Barney, J. B. "Firm Resources and Sustained Competitive Advantage." *Journal of Management* 17 (1991): 99–120.

Blanchard, O. J., and D. R. Johnson, *Macroeconomics*. Pearson, 2013.

Bortolini, R. F., M. N. Cortimiglia, A. D. M. F. Danilevicz, and A. Ghezzi. "Lean Startup: A Comprehensive Historical Review." *Management Decision* 59, no. 8 (2021): 1765–1783.

Botha, M., and C. L. Robertson. "Potential Entrepreneurs' Assessment of Opportunities Through the Rendering of a Business Plan." *South African Journal of Economic and Management Sciences* 17, no. 3 (2014): 249–265.

Brinckmann, J., D. Grichnik, and D. Kapsa. "Should Entrepreneurs Plan or Just Storm the Castle? A Meta-Analysis on Contextual Factors Impacting the Business Planning–Performance Relationship in Small Firms." *Journal of Business Venturing* 25, no. 1 (2010): 24–40.

Brynjolfsson, E., and A. McAfee. *The Second Machine Age: Work, Progress, and Prosperity in a Time of Brilliant Technologies*. WW Norton & Company, 2014.

Canada Business Corporations Act, R.S.C. 1985, c. C-44. Accessed November 1, 2024. https://laws-lois.justice.gc.ca/eng/acts/c-44/.

Canadian Environmental Protection Act, S.C. 1999, c. 33. Accessed November 1, 2024. https://laws-lois.justice.gc.ca/eng/acts/C-15.31/.

Cantillon, R. *An Essay on Commerce in General*. McMaster University, 1755.

Cham, T. H., J. H. Cheah, M. A. Memon, K. S. Fam, and J. László. "Digitalization and Its Impact on Contemporary Marketing Strategies and Practices." *Journal of Marketing Analytics* 10 (2022): 103–105. https://doi.org/10.1057/s41270-022-00167-6.

Choshaly, S. H., and M. Mirabolghasemi. "The Role of Viral Marketing Strategies in Predicting Purchasing Intention of Eco-Labelled Products." *Journal of Islamic Marketing* 19(2),

(2020): 1759–083.Cohen, B., and J. Kietzmann. "Ride On! Mobility Business Models for the Sharing Economy." *Organization & Environment* 27 (2014): 279–96.

Davenport, T. H., and Ronanki, R. "Artificial Intelligence for the Real World." *Harvard Business Review (HBR)*. (2018, January 9). www.bizjournals.com/boston/news/2018/01/09/hbr-artificial-intelligence-for-the-real-world.html

Donthu, N., and A. Gustafsson. "Effects of COVID-19 on Business and Research." *Journal of Business Research* 117 (2020): 284–289.

Faizan, R., and A. U. Haque. "The Relationship between Societal Attributes, Feminine Leadership & Management Style: Responses from Pakistan's Urban Region Female-Owned Businesses." *European Journal of Business and Management* 8, no. 23 (2016): 171–191.

Flavián, C., S. Ibáñez-Sánchez, and C. Orús, "Integrating Virtual Reality Devices Into the Body: Effects of Technological Embodiment on Customer Engagement and Behavioral Intentions." *Journal of Business Research* 122 (2021): 5–16. https://doi.org/10.1016/j.jbusres.2020.08.034.

Fleming, M., W. Clarke, S. Das, P. Phongthiengtham, and P. Reddy. "The Future of Work: How New Technologies are Transforming Tasks." *MIT-IBM Watson AI Lab*, 2019.

Ghezzi, A., and A. Cavallo. "Agile Business Model Innovation in Digital Entrepreneurship: Lean Startup Approaches." *Journal of Business Research* 110 (2020): 519–537. https://doi.org/10.1016/j.jbusres.2018.06.013.

Guerola-Navarro, V., H. Gil-Gomez, R. Oltra-Badenes, and P. Soto-Acosta. "Customer Relationship Management and its Impact on Entrepreneurial Marketing: A Literature Review." *International Entrepreneurship and Management Journal* (2022). https://doi.org/10.1007/s11365-022-00800-x.

Guest, D. "Human Resource Management, Corporate Performance and Employee Wellbeing: Building the Worker into HRM." *Journal of Industrial Relations* 44 (2002): 335–358. https://doi.org/10.1111/1472-9296.00053

Hanson, G. H. "The Impacts of the US–China Trade War." *Business Economics* 55, no. 2 (2020): 69–72.

Haq, I., A. U. Haque, and N. A. A. Rahim. "Entrepreneurial Stress and Mental Well-Being: Pre- and Post-COVID-19 Comparative Analysis of SMEs in Canada." *Forum Scientiae Oeconomia* 12, no. 1 (2024): 53–71.

Haq, I. U., A. U. Haque, H. Kaur, and N. A. A. A. Rahim. "Occupational Stress Affecting Innovative Capabilities and Innovative Work Behavior of Migrant Entrepreneurs." *Polish Journal of Management Studies* 9, no. 2 (2024): 238–253. https://doi.org/10.17512/pjms.2024.29.2.12.

Haque, A. U. "How Occupational Stress Impacts the Innovative Work Behaviour and Innovative Entrepreneurial Capabilities of Migrant Entrepreneurs in Contrasting Economies?" In *Migration and Entrepreneurship in the Global Context*, edited by D. Hyams-Ssekasi and E. Daskalaki, 15–30. Palgrave Macmillan, 2024. https://doi.org/10.1007/978-3-031-34067-3_2.

Hendry, C., and A. Pettigrew. "Patterns of Strategic Change in the Development of Human Resource Management." *British Journal of Management* 3, no. 3 (1992): 137–156.

Hoyer, W. D., D. J. MacInnis, and R. Pieters. *Consumer Behavior*. 7th ed. Cengage Learning, 2018.

Huselid, M. A. "Editor's Note: Special Issue on Small and Medium-Sized Enterprises: A Call for More Research." *Human Resource Management* 42, no. 4 (2003): 297.

Hussain, M., S. F. Rasool, W. Xuetong, M. Z. Asghar, & A. S. A. Alalshiekh. "Investigating the Nexus Between Critical Success Factors, Supportive Leadership, and Entrepreneurial Success: Evidence from the Renewable Energy Projects." *Environmental Science and Pollution Research* 30, no. 17 (2023): 49255–49269. https://doi.org/10.1007/s11356-023-25743-w.

Idris, M. M. R. "Strategic Financial Management in Entrepreneurial Ventures: A Comprehensive Qualitative Review of Financial Practices and Their Impact on Startup Growth and Stability." *Atestasi: Jurnal Ilmiah Akuntansi* 7, no. 2 (2024): 742–761.

Ireland, R. D., and J. W. Webb. "Strategic Entrepreneurship: Creating Competitive Advantage Through Streams of Innovation." *Business Horizons* 50, no. 1 (2007): 49–59.

Kaplan, A. M., and M. Haenlein. "Two Hearts in Three-Quarter Time: How to Waltz the Social Media/Viral Marketing Dance." *Business Horizons* 54, no. 3 (2011): 253–263.

Khandare, A. U., R. K. Srinivasa, and S. N. Ingle. "How to Be a Successful Entrepreneur Using Marketing Skills." *NeuroQuantology* 20, no. 19 (2022): 4168–4176. https://doi.org/10.48047/NQ.2022.20.19.NQ99379.

Kotler, P., K. L. Keller, M. Brady, M. Goodman, and T. Hansen. *Marketing Management.* 3rd ed. Pearson Higher Ed, 2016.

Mankiw, N. G. *Principles of Economics.* 9th ed. Cengage Learning, 2020.

Mankiw, N. G., and M. P. Taylor. *Economics.* Cengage Learning EMEA, 2020.

Mason, C., and M. Stark. "What do Investors Look for in a Business Plan? A Comparison of the Investment Criteria of Bankers, Venture Capitalists and Business Angels." *International Small Business Journal* 22, no. 3 (2004): 227–248. https://doi.org/10.1177/0266242604042377.

McCartan-Quinn, D., and D. Carson. "Issues Which Impact Upon Marketing in the Small Firm." *Small Business Economics* 21, no. 2 (2003): 201–213. https://doi.org/10.1023/A:1025070107609.

Muley, A., L. K. Sharma, S. Kumar, and D. Sarkar. "Role of New Technology and Atomization of Business Operations on Efficiency of Startup Entrepreneurs in India: An Empirical Study." *Journal of Informatics Education and Research* 4, no. 2 (2024): 199–206.

Nurdiani, I., J. Börstler, S. Fricker, K. Petersen, and P. Chatzipetrou. "Understanding the Order of Agile Practice Introduction: Comparing Agile Maturity Models and Practitioners' Experience." *Journal of Systems and Software* 156 (2019): 1–20. https://doi.org/10.1016/j.jss.2019.05.035.

Ogunyomi, P., and N. S. Bruning. "Human Resource Management and Organizational Performance of Small and Medium Enterprises (SMEs) in Nigeria." *International Journal of Human Resource Management* 27, no. 6 (2016): 612–634. https://doi.org/10.1080/09585192.2015.1033640.

Pan, L. Y., I. C. Tsai, S. H. Popan, and S. C. Chang. "Entrepreneurial Business Start-Ups and Entrepreneurial Failure: How to Stand Up After a Fall?" *Frontiers in Psychology* 13 (2022): 943328. https://doi.org/10.3389/fpsyg.2022.943328.

Perloff, J. M. *Microeconomics: Theory and Applications with Calculus.* 4th ed. Pearson Education, 2016.

Pingle, S. S. "A Comparative Study of the HRM Practices in Small and Medium Enterprises." *IUP Journal of Management Research* 13, no. 1 (2014): 55.

Popescu, S. "Controllable and Uncontrollable Variables in the Study of Entrepreneurship, in Small and Medium Business." *International Review of Management and Business Research* 3, no. 2 (2014): 762.

Purcell, J., and N. Kinnie. "HRM and Business Performance." In *The Oxford Handbook of Human Resource Management,* edited by P. F. Boxall, J. Purcell, and P. Wright. Oxford University Press, 2007.

Richbell, S. M., H. D. Watts, and P. Wardle. "Owner-Managers and Business Planning in the Small Firm." *International Small Business Journal* 24, no. 5 (2006): 496–514.

Saltman, R. B., and R. Busse. *Balancing Regulation and Entrepreneurialism in Europe's Health Sector: Theory and Practice.* European Observatory on Health Systems and Policies Series, 2002.

Sammut-Bonnici, T., and Galea, D. "SWOT Analysis." In *Wiley Encyclopedia of Management,* edited by C. L. Cooper. Wiley, 2015, 1–8.

Sarıoğlu, C. İ. "The Effect of Customer Perceptions Concerning Online Shopping, Viral Marketing and Customer Loyalty on Purchasing Behaviour." *International Journal of Management Economics & Business* 19, no. 2 (2023): 348–370. https://doi.org/10.17130/ijmeb.1210803.

Scarborough, N. M., and J. R. Cornwall. *Essentials of Entrepreneurship and Small Business Management.* Pearson, 2016.

Schilling, M. A. *Strategic Management of Technological Innovation.* McGraw-Hill, 2017.

Schilling M. A. *Strategic Management of Technology Innovation* (6th Edition). Mc–Graw Hill Education, 2020. Electronic Version: ISBN–13.

Schumpeter, J. *The Theory of Economic Development*. Oxford University Press, 1934.

Sevilla-Bernardo, J., B. Sanchez-Robles, and T. C. Herrador-Alcaide. "Success Factors of Startups in Research Literature." *Journal of Business Research* 12, no. 3 (2022): 102.

Solomon, M. R. *Consumer Behavior: Buying, Having, and Being*. 12th ed. Pearson Education, 2017.

Suriawaty B. A., Z. Awang, N. A. Rahlin, and M. Z. A. Rahim. "The Importance of Supportive Leadership in the Sewerage Operation Industry in Malaysia: A Case of Indah Water Konsortium Private Limited (Iwk)." *Humanities and Social Sciences Reviews* 8, no. 3 (2020): 149–162. https://doi.org/10.18510/hssr.2020.8317.

United States-Mexico-Canada Agreement. "United States-Mexico-Canada Agreement. Office of the United Stated of Trade Representative." 2020. Retrieved from: https://ustr.gov/trade-agreements/free-trade-agreements/united-states-mexico-canada-agreement.

United States-Mexico-Canada Agreement. "United States-Mexico-Canada Agreement." Accessed November 1, 2024. https://ustr.gov/trade-agreements/free-trade-agreements/united-states-mexico-canada-agreement.

Usman, F. O., N. L. Eyo-Udo, E. A. Etukudoh, B. Odonkor, C. V. Ibeh, and A. Adegbol. "A Critical Review of AI-Driven Strategies for Entrepreneurial Success." *International Journal of Management & Entrepreneurship Research* 6, no. 1 (2024): 200–215.

Utoyo, I., A. Fontana, and A. Satrya. "The Role of Entrepreneurial Leadership and Configuring Core Innovation Capabilities to Enhance Innovation Performance in a Disruptive Environment." *International Journal of Innovation Management* 24, no. 6 (2020). https://doi.org/10.1142/s1363919620500607.

Venkataraman, S. "The Distinctive Domain of Entrepreneurship Research." In *Seminal Ideas for the Next Twenty-Five Years of Advances,* edited by M. Morris, 5–20. Emerald Publishing Limited, 2019.

Wapshott, R., and O. Mallett. *Managing Human Resources in Small and Medium-Sized Enterprises*. Routledge, 2015.

Waworuntu, E. C., M. Yasuwito, and E. Sumanti. "Analyzing Global Industry Dynamics Using Porter's Five Forces and Ratio Analysis Model." *Jurnal Ekonomi* 13, no. 2 (2024): 745–760.

Wright, P. M., T. M. Gardner, and L. M. Moynihan. "The Impact of HR Practices on the Performance of Business Units." *Human Resource Management Journal* 13, no. 3 (2003): 21–36.

Wright, P. M., T. M. Gardner, L. M. Moynihan, and M. R. Allen. "The Relationship Between HR Practices and Firm Performance: Examining Causal Order." *CAHRS Working Paper #04-06.* Cornell University, School of Industrial and Labor Relations, Center for Advanced Human Resource Studies, 2004. http://digitalcommons.ilr.cornell.edu/cahrswp/13.

Xu, Y., and T. Koivumäki. "Digital Business Model Effectuation: An Agile Approach." *Computers in Human Behavior* 95 (2019): 307–314. https://doi.org/10.1016/j.chb.2018.10.021.

Zeithaml, V. A., M. J. Bitner, and D. D. Gremler. *Services Marketing: Integrating Customer Focus Across the Firm*. McGraw-Hill, 2018.

Zheng, Z., S. Xie, H. N. Dai, X. Chen, and H. Wang. "Blockchain Challenges and Opportunities: A Survey." *International Journal of Web and Grid Services* 14, no. 4 (2018): 352–375.

Case Study: Navigating VUCA Challenges in Franchise Entrepreneurship

Anuraj Sangha, Adnan ul Haque and Negar Sohaee

A modern-day entrepreneur – Alwin wants to start his own entrepreneurial venture in the food industry. He has substantial ideas about the VUCA – volatile, uncertain, complex, and ambiguous – environments, where various challenges emerge due to unpredictable economic situations (aka economic fluctuations), consumer preferences shift, and quickly changing market conditions. After detailed and comprehensive analysis of the environment, he opted for a strategic approach: the franchise business model. This model allows him to tackle the challenges emerging in the VUCA environment.

Financing Considerations

Alwin's decision-making in a VUCA environment heavily relies on securing adequate funding, making financing a pivotal role in his decision-making. He carefully weighs his options between debt financing and equity financing.

Debt Financing

The biggest advantage of debt financing is that no profit sharing thus retains full ownership and control in decision-making. Moreover, higher potential of tax benefits due to interest payments subject to tax deduction. However, the drawback is that in volatile and uncertain markets, there is a higher risk due to cash flow repayments being made on a regular mode. The mode of payment is consistent while the market is uncertain. Additionally, possibility of higher stress in recession as the financial obligation burden increases.

Equity Financing

The absence of repayment obligations eases financial strain in economically constraining times is the biggest advantage of equity financing. Furthermore, investors offer networks and expertise that might increase business growth and opportunities. However, the disadvantage is that sharing equity may lead to reduction in business ownership and control. In addition to that, individual proprietors might lose invaluable profits due to sharing money with investors.

After detailed consideration, Alwin decides to use a hybrid financing strategy that combines both debt and equity financing. His strategy entails securing a small business loan to finance the preliminary costs related to the enterprise. At the same time, he is seeking investors to endorse his franchise. This strategy allows him to mitigate risks while utilizing external support to expand his business.

Labour Market and Globalization Impact

Challenges as well as opportunities are presented by the labour market. Alwin observes that the food service sector exhibits trends of employability rates rising, indicating substantial potential for attracting skilful workers. Nonetheless, globalization exposes the food industry to a stiff competition from multinational franchises that can adversely impact the dynamics of the local market.

Alwin has opted to leverage the franchise model to thrive in this competitive environment. This approach offers him recognized brand identity, a solid and constructive business framework, and access to extensive training programs for his workforce. He strategically positions himself to compete efficiently and effectively with big global brands while also attracting a local workforce keen to join a reputable franchise.

Conclusion

The approach of Alwin regarding the franchise model is a tactical response to the challenges the VUCA environment posed. He assesses carefully his financing alternatives as well as understands the globalization and labour market's overall impact. This deliberate consideration enables him to strategically position himself for success in a fiercely competitive environment. In other words, to stay resilient and flexible in the face of change, Alwin uses the franchise model not only to navigate uncertainty, but also seize opportunities.

Reflection Questions

- Which franchise financing factors should Alwin highly focus on when deciding between debt and equity financing?
- What distinct types of risks are involved while operating in a VUCA environment?
- How can the franchise model help in dealing with those risks?
- Explain the approaches Alwin should consider in attracting and retaining talented workers while operating in the competitive food service industry?
- How does globalization impact the abilities of Alwin's to launch a profitable franchise in his domestic market?
- Explain how franchise leveraging resources can help Alwin to tackle the VUCA environment posed challenges?

Chapter 8

Operations Management and Entrepreneurship

Adnan ul Haque, Pavlos Gkasis and Harmandeep Kaur

8.0 Introduction

This chapter aims to analyze operations management from the perspective of both manufacturing and service industries in the context of entrepreneurship. It explores how the principles of operations management and entrepreneurial strategies can reduce costs, increase workflows, and increase profitability. One key focus of the chapter is the process of choosing customers in the service industry. The following sections delve into detail into how interactions with other external stakeholders, such as operations employees, suppliers, the government, and the public, impact the success of entrepreneurs.

8.1 Understanding Operations Management in Entrepreneurship

The term "operations management" describes the process by which companies that produce and distribute goods and services create value for customers. According to Heizer, Render and Munson (2016), operations management refers to a systematic process that formulates, designs, coordinates, and controls the operations involved in the production of goods and services; it seeks to do this at the optimal possible levels of efficiency and effectiveness. Operations management serves as the backbone for the growth, development, and expansion of successful companies. To better address this, the present analysis distinguishes between operations management in the manufacturing sector and that in the services sector.

8.1.1 Manufacturing Sector

In manufacturing, operations management generally focuses on issues such as production planning, inventory control, quality control, and efficiency in supply chain activities. This focus is necessary because manufacturing is one of the most competitive sectors and a significant driver of growth. The most important goal, therefore, is to attain the highest possible manufacturing quality at the lowest reasonable cost. For example, Toyota was able to innovate and transform the automotive manufacturing industry through the implementation of the Toyota Production System (TPS), which began with the notion of total quality control (TQC), then transformed to total quality management (TQM), and paved the way for lean manufacturing techniques that reduce waste, maximize resources, minimize defects, and result in quality products (Ohno, 1988).

DOI: 10.4324/9781003504351-8

8.1.2 Services Sector

However, considerable attention is given to engaging clients so that the delivered quality is unparalleled and client expectations are fully realized (Fitzsimmons and Fitzsimmons, 2013). This is not what characterizes manufacturing operations management. Usually, the services created are consumed simultaneously. In such cases, the holistic experience that a consumer enjoys should be the primary focus. Starbucks has sustained quality across its store chain around the world and pays close attention to how consumers interact by training their staff on the overall customer service experience to create a brand to which people will remain loyal. Although Starbucks has been franchising as a strategy for many years, each of its stores must ensure specific levels of quality (Michelli, 2007).

8.2 Strategic Management for Entrepreneurs in Operations

Through the process of aligning operational procedures with future objectives, strategic management acts as the basis for attaining sustainable growth. For many company owners, this typically comprises employing innovative and flexible schemes and strategies to keep their businesses competitive. According to the work of David and David (2017), strategic management provides the basis on which resources can be allocated, risks managed, and products or services differentiated, either in the industrial or the services sectors.

8.2.1 Manufacturing Strategy

Lean production and agile procedures are two popular strategies that manufacturers employ to retain their agility and responsiveness to the needs of their customers. In this context, Tesla has been able to apply its strategic management capability to achieve rapid growth through a focus on internal production and high-technology automation to sustain quality. In this way, Tesla not only meets but also satisfies the rising demand for electric automobiles (Mangram, 2012). Tesla desires to accelerate the world's transition to sustainable energy sources, and its strategy clearly reflects its coherent strategic intent toward this end.

8.2.2 Services Strategy

In service sectors, strategic management may also involve developing and sustaining relationships with customers. One prominent example is Airbnb, whose strategic management has disrupted the traditional hotel and hospitality industry with the competitive advantage it created toward offering affordable and high-quality experiences to its clientele. According to Guttentag (2015), a competitive advantage has been maintained by Airbnb through the careful control of a host network and the leveraging of technology such that a scalable compatible business model has been created.

8.3 The Role of External Stakeholders in Entrepreneurial Operations

Entrepreneurs are supposed to handle different external stakeholders by influencing their operations. These external stakeholders include customers, investors, regulators, and suppliers. According to the work of Freeman et al. (2010), effective stakeholder management in operations management can improve not only resources but also brand reputation and operational effectiveness.

8.3.1 Suppliers

The competitive advantage an entrepreneur has in the industry depends on the suppliers they deal with, as suppliers have a say in delivery schedules, quality issues, and pricing strategies. In other words, relationships with suppliers play a vital role in gaining a competitive advantage. Walmart's just-in-time (JIT) inventory system, which is highly effective in trimming down warehousing costs and can supply inventories on a routine basis to meet customers' demands in a timely manner, has been made possible largely by the strong connections that the company maintains with its suppliers (Chopra and Meindl, 2016).

8.3.2 Investors

Investors usually expect efficient and profitable business operations in return for the investment (capital) they have provided. Venture capitalists and business angels provide funds to online businesses such as Uber and Airbnb and demand high and fast growth and thrift in business operations so that the return of their investment can be maximized. A requirement of this type affects the goals of operations and the choice of strategies undertaken (Davila, Foster, and Gupta, 2003).

8.3.3 Regulators

Regulatory bodies that have an impact on operations through the assurance of safety, environmental, and ethical standards also play a key role in how entrepreneurs manage their operations. Tesla has been able to reap benefits by adhering to government clean energy regulations, a factor that is in line with regulatory compliance and the environmental objectives of businesses (Mangram, 2012). Following standards set by regulators in various countries and markets around the world can be significantly challenging for firms, especially multinational enterprises (MNEs). MNEs need to adjust and customize their operations strategies on the basis of the intricacies of each regulatory setting in the respective countries in which they operate.

8.4 Client Selection in Service Industry

The strategic selection and management of clients are likely to provide even more long-term growth with lower or minimal expenditure and greater profitability for entrepreneurs within the service industry. According to Zeithaml, Bitner, and Gremler (2017), key processes include identifying invaluable consumers, meeting expectations set forth by those clients, and fostering loyalty.

8.4.1 Targeting Niche Markets

Firms operating in the service sector have a significant advantage since their focus is usually on areas in which they are likely to establish their presence, exhibit their potential, and demonstrate expertise as well as professionalism. In this context, Square targeted small businesses since the financial technology startup company provided them with an easy and accessible method of processing payments. According to Kim and Mauborgne (2014), Square was able to achieve this rapid growth in its target market because of the unmatched strategy it employed in customer selection.

8.4.2 Client Relationship

In addition, the long-term development of customer relationships can increase profitability further by encouraging repeat business and referrals. Payne and Frow (2013) have argued that consulting firms typically target high-budget customers whose needs are complex. This, they explain, is because such partnerships provide service development opportunities as well as reliable streams of revenue.

8.4.3 Customer Lifetime Value (CLV)

Customer lifetime value (CLV) is an important indicator that aids business owners in carefully assessing their customers regarding the revenue they will generate during the time they will be with them. Analytics is a tool utilized by companies such as Netflix to gain an understanding of their customer tastes and preferences to effectively maximize CLV through offering personalized recommendations of content, thus increasing customer satisfaction and loyalty. Zhang, Watson, and Palmatier (2017) support this notion through their research on personalized content. Their study shows that companies enrich customer experiences and cater to their demands by offering and recommending personalized content.

Indeed, enterprise operations management fills the gap between vision and execution; it is an essential element of successful entrepreneurship. Waste should be minimized, and the maximization of resources should be realized for owners to manage their companies in the manufacturing or services sectors so that their output meets the expectations of consumers. Strategic management enables companies to cope with crises and maintain their adaptiveness in uncertain and turbulent times by organizing their operational process while remaining focused on their long-term goals.

Through prudent customer selection and the effective and efficient management of external stakeholders, companies can retain long-term relationships, increase financing, and stay within the rules and regulations. Real-life examples of a differentiated service proposition by Airbnb and a game-changing manufacturing strategy by Tesla showcase how effective operations management can trigger growth and build a sustainable competitive advantage. By mastering these operational strategies, entrepreneurs can create highly lucrative businesses that also benefit customers, investors, and society in general. Operations management is constantly changing due to ever-changing technological advancements and market trends. Therefore, a flexible, customer-oriented strategy can lead to long-term success in entrepreneurship.

8.5 Conclusion

The main conclusion drawn from the above discussion is that effective and efficient operations management plays a vital role in bridging the strategic vision of an organization with its operational execution. Entrepreneurial success relies heavily on an alignment between strategic vision and operational execution, which results from effective and efficient operations management. In both the manufacturing and service sectors, operations management efficiency and effectiveness are measured through the optimal utilization of resources, reduction in waste, and the degree to which consumers' needs and demands are met. In other words, entrepreneurs use operations management to strategize their approach to meet and exceed the expectations of customers, reduce waste, and achieve optimal utilization of resources. The ability of companies to adapt according to the constantly changing market, as well as deal with future contingencies or crises in an adequate manner, depends on the degree of alignment between strategic vision and on-going operational processes.

Finally, effective stakeholder management, especially that of external stakeholders, helps entrepreneurs keep operations on track. Thus, proactive management of external stakeholders is an important aspect of effective operations management. Moreover, the selection of potential customers in a detailed and thorough manner also helps entrepreneurs achieve operational excellence. It helps entrepreneurs strengthen relationships, ensure funds, secure investments, and adhere to compliance and regulatory standards. The innovative manufacturing strategies of Tesla and the differentiated service proposition of Airbnb are prime examples of operations management transforming industries and helping businesses attain a sustainable competitive advantage in a constantly changing business environment. Entrepreneurs who exhibit flexibility and are able to develop operational strategies that are customer-centric are likely to sustain long-term success, especially in an era of rapidly changing market trends and technological advancements. Flexibility and customer-centric approaches help businesses as well as investors, customers, and communities.

Bibliography

Chopra, S., and P. Meindl. *Supply Chain Management: Strategy, Planning, and Operation*. 6th ed. Upper Saddle River, NJ: Pearson Education, 2016.

David, F. R., and F. R. David. *Strategic Management: A Competitive Advantage Approach, Concepts*. 16th ed. Upper Saddle River, NJ: Pearson Education, 2017.

Davila, A., G. Foster, and M. Gupta. "Venture Capital Financing and the Growth of Startup Firms." *Journal of Business Venturing* 18 (2003): 689–708. https://doi.org/10.1016/S0883-9026(02)00127-1

Fitzsimmons, J. A., and M. J. Fitzsimmons. *Service Management: Operations, Strategy, Information Technology*. 9th ed. New York: McGraw-Hill Education, 2013.

Freeman, R. E., A. C. J. Harrison, Wicks, B. L. Parmar, and S. De Colle. *Stakeholder Theory: The State of the Art*. Cambridge: Cambridge University Press, 2010.

Guttentag, D. "Airbnb: Disruption or Disturbance?" *Tourism Management* 54 (2015): 167–177. https://doi.org/10.1016/j.tourman.2015.02.014.

Heizer, J., B. Render, and C. Munson. *Operations Management*. 11th ed. Upper Saddle River, NJ: Pearson Education, 2016.

Kim, W. C., and R. Mauborgne. *Blue Ocean Strategy*. Expanded ed. Boston, MA: Harvard Business Review Press, 2014.

Mangram, M. E. "The Toyota Production System: A Historical Perspective." *Journal of Business & Economics Research* 10, no. 3 (2012): 183–188.

Michelli, J. A. *The Starbucks Experience: 5 Principles for Turning Ordinary into Extraordinary*. New York: McGraw-Hill, 2007.

Ohno, T. *Toyota Production System: Beyond Large-Scale Production*. New York: Productivity Press, 1988.

Payne, A., and P. Frow. "Strategic Customer Management: Integrating Relationship Marketing and CRM." *Journal of the Academy of Marketing Science* 41, no. 3 (2013): 392–406. https://dokumen.pub/strategic-customer-management-integrating-relationship-marketing-and-crm.html

Zeithaml, V. A., M. J. Bitner, and D. D. Gremler. Services Marketing: Integrating Customer Focus across the Firm. Boston, MA: McGraw-Hill/Irwin, (2017). www.amazon.ca/Services-Marketing-Integrating-Customer-Across/dp/0078112109

Zhang, J., D. Watson, and R. Palmatier. "Customer Lifetime Value: A Review and Future Directions." *Journal of Marketing* 81, no. 2 (2017): 122–146.

Case Study: Strategic Operations Management in a Growing Service Startup

Pardeep Singh Malhi and Adnan ul Haque

Background

Crystal-Clean Spark was recently launched by Zoe. The focus of the cleaning service company was to ensure cleaning solutions are non-toxic and eco-friendly. With the expansion of her venture, she encountered many different operations management challenges, which are common in the service industry. Handling client relationships in a strategic manner, effective and efficient supply chain management, and maintaining a balance between cost-efficiency and quality were some of the notable challenges. Zoe was quick to recognize that to maintain not only profitability but also stay competitive in the market, she must need efficient operational management, as it was the key to success.

Challenges interlinked with Operations Management

By using a customer booking app, she schedules her team based on peak demand periods, thus maximizing resource utilization.

Timeline and quality are both critical aspects closely linked to the service industry. Zoe decided to invest aggressively into a training program for her team because this not only provides the best services to the customers but also maintains the high-quality standards. Additionally, to differentiate her brand from others, she needed to adopt non-toxic cleaning supplies, however, it could increase overhead costs. Moreover, lean management techniques were adopted by Zoe to utilize time efficiently, reduce waste, and lower overall expenses. In pursuit of maximizing resource utilization, she also uses the customer booking app to schedule her team during peak seasons.

Stakeholder Management

Various external stakeholders influence operational decisions of Zoe.

Suppliers and distributors play a vital role. A difficult task for Zoe was finding authentic and reliable distributors for eco-friendly solutions. For this purpose, she negotiates and builds contracts with suppliers who are committed to providing sustainable products without sacrificing quality while ensuring timely deliveries.

Zoe's target audience includes both commercial and residential customers. Her strategic move was to target the consumers who are more conscious about the environment and prefer green cleaning solutions. Interestingly, they are willing to pay extra for eco-friendly products. Her niche market remained focused on high-end consumers, who are willing to spend more for her premium services, further increasing profitability.

Green Organisations and communities represent another stakeholder group affecting her operations. Sustainable practices are part of Crystal-CleanSpark's operations. She frequently engages with ecological societies on a regular basis to seek their support for not only promoting her brand, but also targeting new customers whose preferences were in line with the values of the company.

Strategic Decision-Making

Zoe needed to follow a balanced approach to maintain both quality and cost efficiency, which would help sustain profitability. She determines that her services packages range from basic to premium services, allowing customers to choose services according to their budget. Furthermore, she could maintain a supply chain for green cleaning products by stabilizing and working closely with suppliers.

Overall, operational management decisions played an imperative role in the success of Zoe's business. Additionally, she strategically managed each process in her business, ensuring her plans were implemented in a sustainable manner, allowing her growth to reach new heights.

Reflection Questions

- Explain Zoe's approach to incorporating operations management practices to ensure her brand can sustain and thrive in the competitive service sector?
- Explain the roles of customers and suppliers in Zoe's operations and how her strategic decisions are influenced by these roles?
- In your view, how can Zoe achieve cost-efficiency while ensuring the quality and timelines are not compromised?
- Explain how Zoe's focus on environmentally friendly practices affected her relationship with clients and suppliers?
- Recommend additional strategies that could help Zoe improve operational efficiency and increase profitability?

Chapter 9

Marketing Strategies, Tools, and Entrepreneurship

Tahmina Akhter, Harmandeep Kaur and Adnan ul Haque

9.0 Introduction

The process of developing, promoting, providing, and trading offerings that are valuable to partners, consumers, clients, and society is known as marketing. It involves recognizing the needs of the consumer, creating goods or services to satisfy those requirements, and skillfully marketing those goods or services to increase sales and promote customer loyalty (Mariadoss, 2015). An essential component of entrepreneurship is a marketing strategy, which acts as a road map for how a company will accomplish its objectives and engage with its target market. A strong marketing plan can mean the difference between an entrepreneur's success and failure since it offers a defined course for expansion, client acquisition, and brand building (Laverty and Littel, 2020). A company's plan for promoting its goods or services to draw in and keep consumers is called a marketing strategy. It includes the following: brand positioning, target audience identification, market research, and the marketing mix (product, price, place, and promotion). This is a crucial approach for entrepreneurs for several reasons (Mariadoss, 2015).

9.0.1 Market Understanding

Gaining a detailed understanding of the market is the first step in developing a comprehensive marketing plan. By doing so, business owners can better grasp market trends, client demands, and rivalry dynamics. To find chances for distinction and to make well-informed business decisions, this knowledge is key (Kaur, 2023).

9.0.2 Target Audience Identification

For any organization, understanding the target audience is essential. On the basis of behavior, psychographics, and demographics, a marketing plan helps business owners identify their target clientele (Sarkheil and Hosseini, 2024). As a result, engagement and communication are improved.

9.0.3 Brand Positioning

A company can set itself out from the competition with strong brand positioning. A marketing plan helps business owners define their own value offer and distribute it consistently

DOI: 10.4324/9781003504351-9

through all channels. As a result, customers become more loyal to the brand (Rane, Achari, and Choudhary, 2023).

9.0.4 *Resource Allocation*

New businesses frequently have a small budget. By concentrating on high-impact initiatives that spur growth, a marketing strategy ensures that these resources are used effectively. This involves deciding on appropriate marketing strategies and channels (Mariadoss, 2015).

9.1 Entrepreneurship and Marketing

The marketing function is not only a department within the context of entrepreneurship but also an activity that is necessary to establish, develop, and maintain an enterprise. For entrepreneurship to successfully address the difficulties it is usually confronted with, such as scarce resources, uncontrollable market fluctuations, and tough competition, it needs to have a successful marketing strategy. For business proprietors, in terms of advertising, the following are the highlights of the most important highlights:

9.1.1 *Knowledge of the Market in Terms of Entrepreneurship*

Organizations must gain deep insight into industry so that opportunities can be grasped and critical mistakes in the field can be avoided. Through market research, an entrepreneur can also determine where consumer wants are not being satisfied or when the competition is weak. For example, during Airbnb's early days, its founders perceived a market niche: guests needed unique, moderately priced accommodations that were not supplied by traditional hotels (Guttentag, 2015). By identifying this specific target market segment, Airbnb was able to create a business model that turned out to be tremendously successful.

9.1.2 *Locating the Right Customers for Start-ups*

Because they usually operate with limited resources, entrepreneurs must select and focus their marketing efforts. By using tools such as demographic data and psychographic segmentation, enterprises can position their products in a way that specifically appeals to the most relevant customers. According to Matzler, Friedrich von den Eichen, Anschober, and Kohler (2018), Dollar Shave Club constructed an entire brand around its target market, comprising men who were concerned with shaving expenses and were looking for uncomplicated grooming solutions. The company also used focused web-based marketing strategies to scale up fast but required only a minimal amount of initial investment.

9.1.3 *Brand Positioning for New Businesses*

Brand positioning, which is important in immensely competitive markets, is used to enable a businessperson to differentiate his or her ventures from those of competitors. The identity of a strong brand can help a new business be both distinct and different from its direct and indirect competitors. For example, Warby Parker entered the eyewear industry with unique differentiation from traditional brick-and-mortar firms, which are positioned as firms that can provide stylish glasses at affordable prices directly to clients via the internet. Although the resources were minimal, the strategic positioning of the brand in the market led to the ability of the company to spread quickly and attract customers.

9.1.4 The Distribution of Resources Within the Projects of Entrepreneurs

Profit-based businesses are often forced to exercise extra prudence in the way they make use of the few finances that are available to them for marketing purposes. A marketing plan ensures that every dollar spent increases the probability of growth. For instance, startups commonly invest in digital marketing strategies, such as SEO and social media, rather than putting a large portion into commercials on television or print. Business owners can generate the highest return on investment by funneling efforts and resources into low-cost, high-impact channels. Nevertheless, in its infancy, Dropbox created a referral marketing campaign in which clients were rewarded with increased storage space to refer people to utilize their services. For Dropbox, this allowed them to amass a customer base quickly and at a relatively low financial cost of acquisition (Reichheld, 2003).

9.1.5 The Role of Innovation in the Entrepreneurial Marketing

As innate innovators, entrepreneurs must have their marketing strategies customized accordingly. It's not about playing by the rules and regulations of marketing; rather, it's about creating new avenues to communicate with the customers. For example, Tesla has been able to prosper without relying on conventional advertising campaigns because the power of word-of-mouth marketing has been amplified through the personal branding of its founder, Elon Musk, on social media outlets (Li, 2023). This has given Tesla the ability to reach success without relying on traditional forms of advertising.

9.2 Marketing Strategies and Types of Marketing Strategies (Entrepreneurship Perspective)

Marketing strategies are structured plans of action designed to promote and sell a product or service. They focus on identifying target audiences, understanding their needs, and delivering value through tailored messaging and channels (Camps, 2023). The aim is to achieve specific business objectives, such as increasing sales, building brand awareness, or entering new markets. Creative marketing is an effective way for firms to make long-lasting impacts with minimal financial resources. From the viewpoint of an entrepreneur, different market techniques relevant for business development are used. Because they lay a sound foundation for development, customer acquisition, and competitive advantage, marketing strategies play an important role for business owners when starting their own ventures. These strategies are planned courses of action designed to promote and sell a product and/or service. They are realized through the identification of target consumers, determination of their needs, and delivery of value through personalized messaging and channels. Such marketing strategies are implemented by an entrepreneur in pursuit of specific objectives, such as generating and increasing revenue, spreading brand awareness, or entering new markets.

9.2.1 Product Differentiation and Evaluation

Product differentiation, which involves creating distinctive features, qualities, designs, or services to stand out in the market, is a crucial entrepreneurship tactic (Kopp, 2024). Differentiation is a tool used by entrepreneurs to craft a unique value proposition that appeals to clientele and gives them a competitive advantage. Entrepreneurs may better address client demands, foster brand loyalty, and support premium pricing by providing something exceptional or distinctive (Griva, Bardak, Pramatari, and Doukidis, 2022). To sustain the product's distinctive position, effective differentiation necessitates comprehension of market expectations, creative thinking, and ongoing improvement. This tactic aids in the establishment of a solid market presence and promotes long-term expansion for startups (Mabilard, Pasquier, and Vuignier, 2023).

Product differentiation is one of the major strategies for entrepreneurs, and it refers to a process of developing unique traits, designs, features, or services that help distinguish themselves from their competitors in the market. For any new business, it is crucial to have differentiation attributes that create a unique value proposition to attract customers and give them an edge over their competitors. By using creativity and invention, entrepreneurs aim to utilize opportunities emerging from identified gaps in the market. For example, a new company producing green packaging has an advantage in a competitive packaging market by attracting ecologically aware consumers, building brand loyalty, and justifying higher prices.

9.2.2 Digital Marketing

Since digital marketing offers scalable and affordable ways to connect and interact with target audiences, it is crucial for entrepreneurs (Zahay, 2021). To market their goods and services, entrepreneurs use digital platforms, including email, social media, search engines, and content marketing. This strategy improves client acquisition and retention by enabling accurate targeting and tailored communication (Desai, 2019). Entrepreneurs can analyze the efficacy of campaigns and optimize real-time strategies with the use of tools such as analytics and A/B testing (Zahay, 2021). The development of a strong online presence and brand identity is another benefit of digital marketing, which is essential for drawing in clients and earning trust (Desai, 2019). By using digital marketing, business owners may effectively reach a wider audience, adjust to changing market conditions, and see steady growth in their company.

In recent years, digital marketing has become increasingly important for businesses because of the growing importance of e-commerce. This growth is attributed to digital marketing's scalable and affordable options for both reaching and engaging target audiences. Comparatively, large businesses that spend millions of money on marketing can be outperformed by startups in terms of brand awareness and customer acquisition through leveraging digital channels such as email, social media, and content marketing at a fraction of the cost of traditional marketing. In addition, entrepreneurs can also introduce real-time changes in their marketing, on the basis of the data and feedback from customers.

Thus, ensuring that every dollar spent by the marketing department is utilized to its fullest potential. One classic example of this might be an online fashion company that uses influencer partnerships and Instagram marketing to achieve exponential followership.

9.2.3 Content Marketing

Content marketing is an inexpensive way for businesses to build credibility and earn trust in industry. Startups can create and publish content that is not only useful to their audience but also relevant and consistent, enabling them to build and maintain a clearly defined audience for their brand. This leads, in the words of Desai (2019), "profitable ways of behaving" by customers. Content marketing allows companies with fewer resources to build strong, lasting relationships with their customers, increase brand awareness, and build organic traffic. To attract and keep a clearly defined audience and ultimately drive profitable consumer action, content marketing is a strategic approach that focuses on producing and delivering valuable, relevant, and consistent information (Desai, 2019). The material created for their target market includes bloggers, filmmakers, infographic creators, social media marketers, and other content creators. Strong brand awareness, authority and trust establishment, and consumer engagement are all facilitated by effective content marketing (Bhargava and Ojha, 2019). For example, a technology company might release regular blog posts or video lectures that educate its customers on the benefits of using its platform to better nurture leads over time.

9.2.4 Influencer Marketing

Influencer marketing is an effective approach for business owners working toward rapid brand awareness (Mathews, 2018). This approach draws on the trust and influence that social media stars command. In other words, influencer marketing promotes goods and services by teaming up with well-liked online celebrities. This tactic helps business owners increase their brand's visibility and reputation by taking advantage of the audience's faith in influencers (Desai, 2019). Entrepreneurs can attain targeted reach and increased conversion rates by carefully choosing influencers whose followers are similar to their target market. Identifying proper influencers, developing sincere connections, and coordinating content with company values are all necessary for successful influencer marketing (Beichert, Bayerl, Goldenberg, and Lanz, 2024). By leveraging established, active communities, this strategy enables business owners to swiftly increase their influence, broaden their sphere of influence, and stimulate economic expansion (Bhargava and Ojha, 2019). Hence, a business in its early phase can reach new markets and earn a reputation without necessarily using many funds for advertisements. Businesses may nurture leaders, assist them in the buyer's journey, and establish enduring partnerships by giving them insightful information. In addition to increasing organic traffic and visibility, this strategy also increases search engine ranks (Desai, 2019). Understanding the target audience, establishing specific objectives, producing excellent content, and utilizing analytics to gauge progress and improve tactics are all crucial components. In addition to setting themselves apart from rivals, businesses may create a devoted clientele and foster long-term business growth by regularly producing insightful content (Haan, 2024). Businesses may choose to partner with such influencers who relate well to the target market to maximize reach and conversion. For example, a beauty company might want to partner with a prominent beauty influencer so that it is able to promote its product. This would involve taking advantage of the influencer's preset list of followers and using it to promote the brand. In other words, it increases brand visibility by reaching the fanbase of the beauty influencer.

9.2.5 *Experiential Marketing*

According to Gomez (2024), a marketing toolkit is one of the most important additions that business owners must have in their plans and operations. Customers are fully immersed in interactive brand encounters through experiential marketing, which forges deep, emotional ties. Offering distinctive, hands-on experiences that connect with their target audience helps entrepreneurs stand out in a crowded market, increasing engagement, fostering brand loyalty, and promoting their business through word-of-mouth (Li, 2023). With the help of experiential marketing, which is characterized by the creation of interactive brand experiences, entrepreneurs can distinguish themselves in highly competitive markets. Startups provide unique, hands-on experiences and build emotional connections with their customers. This will not only help in customer engagement but also in developing customer loyalty. For example, a food company might organize cooking events either in person or pop-up that allow consumers to experience products firsthand. Later, they share it on social media or through word-of-mouth, enhancing engagement as well as brand visibility.

9.2.6 *Direct Marketing*

Direct marketing involves contacting potential clients by telemarketing, direct mail, or email that is tailored to their needs. Directly addressing the requirements and preferences of each individual client fosters relationships, facilitates customized messaging, and increases conversion rates and marketing efficiency for business owners (Kenton, 2024). It allows business owners to reach out and communicate with prospective customers directly through various communication channels, including telemarketing, direct mail, or personalized emails. According to Kenton (2024), it can offer businesses with minimal marketing resources more focused and measurable responses at lower costs. This is illustrated by a new subscription box service that uses email marketing to reach out to potential subscribers, providing personalized offers to encourage them to subscribe to the service.

9.2.7 *Guerrilla Marketing*

To create memorable and lasting brand experiences, guerilla marketing depends on low-cost activities and unconventional approaches. This makes guerilla marketing an ideal strategy for entrepreneurs. Start-ups can emerge in a highly competitive enterprise through creative and bold activities that generate buzz (Hall, 2023). For example, a small city coffee shop uses flash mobs or sidewalk chalk art to attract the attention of pedestrians and promote their business (Hall, 2023).

9.3 Relationships in Marketing

The success of businesses depends on the nourishment of long-term relationships with customers through the provision of excellent service and personal contact (Rosario and Casaca, 2024). Relationship marketing moves business from one-time sales to promote repeat business and customer satisfaction. According to Rosario and Casaca (2024), this method is vital for businesses that intend to sustain their growth and increase positive image through word-of-mouth. For example, a small e-commerce firm may prioritize excellent customer service and follow-up emails tailored to each consumer as a strategy to build trust and ensure repeat purchases.

9.3.1 B2B (Business-to-Business) Marketing

Business-to-business, or B2B, marketing involves advertising goods and services to other companies as opposed to individual customers. This approach necessitates that business owners concentrate on developing connections, proving their worth, and attending to the requirements of corporate clients (Chen, 2024). Targeted content, networking, and customized sales techniques are frequently used in effective B2B marketing to build trust, provide leads, and create enduring relationships. Crafting attractive value offers and promoting effective business growth in the B2B sector require a thorough understanding of the decision-making processes and pain areas of business clients (Rane, Achari, and Choudhary, 2023). Entrepreneurs have a greater focus on building trust with corporate clients and ensuring that solutions are provided to the specific problems that arise from their interaction. Compared with business-to-consumer marketing, business-to-business marketing involves deeper relationship-building activities, developing customized value propositions for targeted segments (Panday et al., 2020). Moreover, it helps in understanding a complex organizational decision-making process (Panday et al., 2020). For example, a software company that specializes in providing services to businesses may attend industry events or use LinkedIn to network and connect with decision-makers so they can generate leads.

9.3.2 Consumers-Directed Advertising (B2C)

Business-to-consumer, or B2C, marketing focuses on appealing to the requirements and preferences of specific customers. To increase brand awareness and increase sales, businesses should create interesting content, make use of social media, and use direct promotion (Mazhar, 2024). Good business-to-consumer (B2C) marketing improves customer satisfaction and builds brand loyalty. Finally, effective marketing strategies often involve a combination of these approaches to maximize reach and impact. Entrepreneurs engaged in business-to-consumer (B2C) marketing concentrate on communicating with potential customers by gauging their preferences, needs, and purchase habits. As Mazhar (2024) explains, startups employ strategies such as social media engagement or providing personalized offers to rapidly increase brand awareness and loyalty. For example, a gym business can utilize Instagram to share training tip posts and customer testimonials to increase interaction and sales.

9.4 Multi-Channel Marketing

For any successful launch of goods or services, entrepreneurs must strategize and carefully plan the marketing channels they will use. A distribution channel, also known as a marketing channel, refers to the route or path that products and services undertake from manufacturing or vending to the end consumer. This travel path constitutes a distribution channel. Sometimes, businesses must analyze the best distribution techniques that ensure that goods reach their intended market. Middlemen, such as wholesalers, retailers, distributors, and even online channels, can play a significant role in this process (Stoyanov, 2021).

As Mabilard et al. (2023) noted, the major functions of marketing channels are increasing the availability of products and services to target customers, assisting in the transfer of ownership, and providing relevant logistical support. The chosen marketing channel often determines whether entrepreneurs' enterprises will succeed or fail. Additionally, Jehanne (2024) indicates that there are four primary types of marketing channels available for physical products that are outlined as follows:

9.4.1 Direct selling

It is a method involving the promotion and sale of items directly to consumers without requiring a physical storefront. Business owners can build personal relationships with their clients through direct sales tactics and by leveraging social media platforms and online platforms (Jenanne, 2024).

9.4.2 Selling Through Middlemen

The products manufactured at their site of production are then sold to customers through intermediaries, such as wholesalers, retailers, brokers, and agents. All these intermediaries act as middlemen selling products and/or services (Jenanne, 2024). This can be helpful for the owners of the firm when they want quick expansion in terms of the distribution of their products, as it does not require a large infrastructure (Jenanne, 2024).

9.4.3 Dual Distribution

In dual distribution, manufacturers sell directly to the clients and, at the same time, through wholesalers and retailers. Hybrid approaches such as these allow firms to reach larger markets and expand their distribution channels (Jenanne, 2024).

9.4.4 Reverse Marketing

It refers to the process of returning products from the consumer back to the manufacturer, frequently seen in product recalls and recycling initiatives. Businesses can gain customer loyalty and even display their concern about environmental sustainability by adopting this strategy (Jenanne, 2024).

9.5 STP – Segmentation, targeting, and positioning

Abdullah and Ampauleng (2024) argued that STP or segmentation, targeting, and positioning are regarded as critical for companies aiming to be differentiated in a competitive market by building a relationship with an intended audience.

9.5.1 Market Segmentation

Segmentation involves the division of a large market into smaller and more manageable subgroups based on common characteristics among members. Entrepreneurs can use psychographics (such as lifestyle and values), geography (such as a place of residence), behavior (such as buying patterns), and demographics (such as age, gender, and income) to segment their market (Hanlon, 2024). For instance, manufacturers of green products may segment the market based on urban dwellers, young working professionals, and environmentally conscious consumers (Mabilard et al., 2023). Segmentation involves tailoring products or services according to the identified groups' needs and preferences.

Being able to identify and target customer groups improves product relevance and marketing efficiency, which is why market segmentation is so important to entrepreneurs. Market segmentation is a strategy approach that involves breaking down a large, diverse population into smaller, more comparable groups based on some shared observable features. Businesses can customize their offers to match the unique demands of each sector of the market by segmenting the market based on behavioral, psychographic, geographic, and demographic variables (Sawtooth Software, 2024).

Based on factors such as age, gender, income, education, and occupation, demographic segmentation separates the market. This strategy increases customer satisfaction and boosts marketing effectiveness by enabling firms to customize their offerings and marketing campaigns to meet the unique requirements and preferences of various demographic groups (Camps, 2023). Geographic segmentation, as the name implies, is the process of splitting the market according to geographical limits. This could apply to entire nations, regions, or even individual cities or neighborhoods. Businesses whose goods or services are impacted by regional variables such as climate, customs, or laws profit from geographic segmentation. For example, a clothing company may specialize in swimwear in coastal areas and sell bulkier coats and jackets in colder climates (Griva, Bardak, Pramatari, and Doukidis, 2022). The focus of psychographic segmentation is on the psychographic profiles of the clients, which comprise their values, beliefs, attitudes, interests, and lifestyle choices in addition to personality features. By using this type of segmentation, organizations can comprehend the underlying goals and motives that influence consumer behavior (Camps, 2023). Customers' actions or behaviors, such as their purchasing patterns, brand loyalty, and frequency of product usage, are the main emphasis of behavioral segmentation (Griva et al., 2022). In regard to customizing marketing tactics such as loyalty programs or customer retention initiatives, this type of segmentation can be very useful. For example, to increase user engagement and lower attrition, a streaming service may provide exclusive deals to loyal subscribers or binge watchers (Sawtooth Software, 2024).

9.5.2 Targeting

Targeting begins once segments are identified, the attractiveness of each segment is assessed, and one or more focused segments are selected. An entrepreneur would consider factors such as the size of the market, growth potential, competition, and alignment with the competencies of his organization. For example, a technology-based organization might only target the millennial generation, who are more engaged in technology and eager to explore new technologies, even those willing to adopt newer technologies. Here, concentrating on this target market (tech-savvy millennials), businesses can optimize resource utilization and even develop marketing strategies that effectively appeal to their audience (Carpenter, 2024).

9.5.3 Positioning

The reason behind positioning any product or service is to create a unique image and identity for a product or service in the minds of the targeted market. The aim is to satisfy them, and thus, the objective is to position the product in such a way that key characteristics of the product or service are highlighted as distinct from those of the other competitors. According to Abdullah and Ampauleng (2024), it is necessary that entrepreneurs develop a value proposition that communicates the competitive advantage of their offering. Consistent messaging across all marketing channels is necessary for effective positioning because it guarantees that the brand image is upheld at every point of contact with the customer (Hanlon, 2024). For example, a coffee shop might position itself as the finest coffee in terms of quality and offer organic coffee because the beans are sourced through ethical practices and fair-trade policies. The position will be a sustainable product in the market, and it will use all marketing channels to convey consistently the same message. Interestingly, this also creates emotional appeal among consumers because they perceive the brand as an ethical brand.

By putting the STP marketing approach into practice, entrepreneurs may optimize their marketing efforts, more effectively target their desired consumer base, and create a strong, distinctive brand in the market (Zahay, 2021). In other words, businesspersons executing an STP marketing strategy will ensure that one realizes the full benefits of their marketing efforts, effectively reaches the targeted consumer segment, and builds a strong, unique brand in the marketplace.

9.6 SEO – Search Engine Optimization

SEO refers to the process of improving an organization's online visibility through methods other than paid advertisements, such as organic visits. An effective SEO can have a massive effect on the growth and development of a successful startup. Entrepreneurship requires SEO for firms to become more visible online, draw in organic traffic, and build a solid online presence. The development and success of a startup can be greatly impacted by effective SEO tactics and resources (Desjardins, 2024). *The* SEO strategies for entrepreneurs are as follows:

9.6.1 Keywords Selection

Selecting the appropriate keywords is essential. Entrepreneurs should concentrate on keywords that are pertinent to their target market and business. Long-tail keywords might draw in more targeted traffic because they frequently face less competition (Verschueren, 2024). This must be done through careful research to ensure that the best keywords are chosen. In other words, entrepreneurs should focus their attention on the keywords associated with their firm and the market they are trying to reach. Owing to lower competition, long-tail keywords have the potential to yield more targeted traffic.

9.6.2 Content Creation

High-quality and relevant content must be created for engaging audiences and achieving positive and favorable results in search engines. Coleman (2024) stated that web content such as blogs, articles, and multimedia needs more than keyword optimization does; it should provide genuine value to users.

9.6.3 *On-page Optimization*

This refers to the process of making certain web pages more search-friendlier to search engines. This includes optimizing meta tags, header tags, all text for images, and URL structures, which are essential components (Sahani, 2024). In addition, it should also include website loading speed and mobile responsiveness (Nicholson, 2024).

9.6.4 *Off-page Optimization*

It refers to the ability to acquire backlinks from reputable websites to increase the authority of a website. Entrepreneurs can improve the backlink profile through social media marketing, collaboration with influencers, and guest blogging (Silva, 2024).

9.6.5 *Local SEO*

It is crucial for companies that either serve a specific geographic region or have a type of brick-and-mortar model. The most important tasks include setting up a Google My business listing, increasing customer review counts, and maintaining consistent names, addresses, and phones (NAPs) across multiple directories and listings (Siebert, 2024).

9.7 Important SEO Tools for Entrepreneurs

The following are some of the important SEO tools for entrepreneurs:

9.7.1 *Google Keyword Planner*

It is a free and helpful tool for determining potential keywords, assessing competition, and evaluating search traffic. This tool is in high demand when entrepreneurs carry out keyword research and planning marketing (Greene, 2019).

9.7.2 *SEMrush*

Cachon (2014) described SEMrush as an all-rounded SEO tool that empowers organizations to capitalize on SEMrush offerings, such as backlink analysis, site audits, rival appraisals, and keyword research, to help them create and refine their SEO strategy.

9.7.3 *Ahrefs*

It has gained considerable popularity because of its in-depth backlink analysis and because it provides content and keyword research insights. These insights enable entrepreneurs to find link-building opportunities and analyze competitors' backlink profiles.

9.7.4 *Moz Pro*

Reyes-Lillo et al. (2023) explained that Moz Pro contributes to rank monitoring, site audits, keyword analysis, and link-building opportunities. In addition, it offers an extension in Chrome to review mobile websites and pages.

9.7.5 *Yoast SEO Plugin*

It is one of the most popular WordPress plugins for making on-page SEO easier and simpler. It analyzes the content in real time and provides suggestions on how to improve the performance of SEO.

9.7.6 *SimpleLearn Reports (Google Analytics)*

Google Analytics is the perfect tool used in tracking the behavior of visitors on a website. This tool provides insight into the level of user engagement, the sources of traffic, and the conversion rates.

9.7.7 *Google Search Console*

A free service that keeps track and maintains the appearance of a website in Google search results. It provides information about data on search traffic and indexing status and ensures that website visibility remains in search results.

9.8 Conclusion

In conclusion, entrepreneurs benefit from effective marketing strategies, as they help in the efficient use of limited resources, building customer engagement, and differentiating and promoting their brands in competitive environments. Entrepreneurs increase their reach and create positive impacts through the adoption of multiple channels and marketing approaches. Moreover, the STP framework is highly useful for reaching out to target audiences in an adequate manner. In the modern era, SEO offers leverage to entrepreneurs to operate in a digital environment. An innovative approach, strengthened relationships, and strong brand positioning help in attaining long-term success. Undoubtedly, a well-crafted marketing strategy helps businesses attain competitive advantage.

Bibliography

Abdullah, S., and A. Ampauleng. "The Micro-Influencers Effect on the Business Sustainability of Small Medium Enterprise: The Marketing Strategy Approach." *General Management* 25 (January 1, 2024). doi:10.47750/QAS/25.199.35.

Beichert, M., A. Bayerl, J. Goldenberg, and A. Lanz. "Revenue Generation Through Influencer Marketing." *Journal of Marketing* 88, no. 4 (2024): 40–63. doi:10.1177/00222429231217471.

Bhargava, P., and S. C. Ojha. "Impact and Experience of Social Media Marketing on Customer Engagement." *International Journal of Research in Engineering, Science and Management* 2, no. 2 (2019): 2581–5792. www.ijresm.com/.

Cachon, M. "How To Perform a Quick SEO Audit with Semrush." Semrush Blog, December 1, 2014. Accessed November 1, 2024. www.semrush.com/blog/perform-quick-seo-audit-semrush/.

Camps, L. "An In-Depth Overview of Market Segmentation." DesignCloud, September 1, 2023. Accessed November 1, 2024. https://designcloud.app/blog/an-in-depth-overview-of-market-segmentation#:~:text=Market%20segmentation%20is%20the%20division,to%20meet%20their%20specific%20needs.

Carpenter, A. "What is Market Segmentation?" Qualtrics, 2024. Accessed November 1, 2024. www.qualtrics.com/experience-management/brand/what-is-market-segmentation/.

Chen, J. "B2B." Investopedia, Accessed May 10, 2024. www.investopedia.com/terms/b/btob.asp.

Coleman, B. "Blog SEO: How to Search Engine Optimize Your Blog Content." HubSpot, Accessed June 6, 2024. https://blog.hubspot.com/marketing/blog-search-engine-optimization.

Desai, V. "Digital Marketing: A Review." *International Journal of Trend in Scientific Research and Development* Conference Issue, 5 (2019): 196–200.

Desjardins, P. "SEO Basics for Entrepreneurs: Easy Tips for Optimizing Your Website." BDC, 2024. Accessed November 1, 2024. www.bdc.ca/en/articles-tools/blog/seo-basics-entrepreneurs-easy-tips-optimizing-website.

Gomez, M. "Using Experiential Marketing When Building or Growing Your Brand." Forbes, August 21, 2024. Accessed November 1, 2024. www.forbes.com/councils/forbesbusinesscouncil/2024/08/21/using-experiential-marketing-when-building-or-growing-your-brand/.

Greene, J. "How to Use Google Keyword Planner." Databox, March 5, 2019. Accessed November 1, 2024. https://databox.com/how-to-use-google-keyword-planner.

Griva, A., C. Bardak, K. Pramatari, and G. Doukidis. "Factors Affecting Customer Analytics: Evidence from Three Retail Cases." *Information Systems Frontiers* (2022): 493–516. https://doi.org/10.1007/s10796-020-10098-1.

Guttentag, D. "Airbnb: Disruptive Innovation and the Rise of an Informal Tourism Accommodation Sector." *Current Issues in Tourism*, 18 (2015): 1192–1217. https://doi.org/10.1080/13683500.2013.827159

Haan, K. "Content Marketing Statistics." Forbes, 2024. Accessed November 1, 2024. www.forbes.com/advisor/business/software/content-marketing-statistics/.

Hall, B. "6 Types of Guerrilla Marketing: Affordable But Persuasive Marketing Tactics." ReferralCandy Blog, March 23, 2023. Accessed November 1, 2024. www.referralcandy.com/blog/guerrilla-marketing-tactics.

Hanlon, A. "Segmentation, Targeting, and Positioning." Smart Insights, Accessed January 24, 2024. www.smartinsights.com/digital-marketing-strategy/customer-segmentation-targeting/segmentation-targeting-and-positioning/.

Jehanne, M. "Marketing Channels: Key Definitions, Types, and Effective Strategies." ContentSquare, Accessed March 18, 2024. https://contentsquare.com/blog/marketing-channels/.

Kaur, H. "The Impact of Occupational Stress on the Performance of Employees: Systematic Review." *International Journal of Applied Business and Management Studies* 8, no. 2 (2023): 19–34.

Kenton, W. "Direct Marketing." Investopedia, Accessed April 30, 2024. www.investopedia.com/terms/d/direct-marketing.asp.

Kopp, C. M. "Product Differentiation." Investopedia, Accessed June 18, 2024. www.investopedia.com/terms/p/product_differentiation.asp.

Laverty, M., and C. Littel. "Entrepreneurship." OpenStax, Accessed January 16, 2020. https://openstax.org/details/books/entrepreneurship.

Li, N. "Experiential Marketing: Bridging the Gap Between Digital & IRL." NoGood Blog, September 1, 2023. Accessed November 1, 2024. https://nogood.io/2023/09/01/experiential-marketing/.

Li, Y. "Analysis of Tesla's marketing Strategy Model." *Advances in Economics Management and Political Sciences* 54 no. 1 (2023): 33–29. https://doi.org/10.54254/2754-1169/54/20230873

Mabilard, V., M. Pasquier, and R. Vuignier. *Place Branding and Marketing from a Policy Perspective.* London, 2023. https://doi.org/10.4324/9781003286189.

Mariadoss, B. J. "Core Principles of Marketing." Washington State University Open Textbook, 2015. Accessed November 1, 2024. https://opentext.wsu.edu/marketing/.

Mathew, J. "Understanding Influencer Marketing and Why it is So Effective." Forbes, July 30, 2018. Accessed November 1, 2024. www.forbes.com/sites/theyec/2018/07/30/understanding-influencer-marketing-and-why-it-is-so-effective/.

Matzler, K., S. Friedrich von den Eichen, M. Anschober, and T. Kohler. "The Crusade of Digital Disruption." *Journal of Business Strategy* (2018). https://doi.org/10.1108/JBS-12-2017-0187

Mazhar, A. "B2B vs. B2C Marketing: Difference Every Marketer Needs to Know." MailMunch Blog, Accessed May 20, 2024. www.mailmunch.com/blog/b2b-vs-b2c-marketing.

Nicholson, R. "The Ultimate Guide to SEO in 2024." HubSpot, 2024. Accessed November 1, 2024. https://blog.hubspot.com/marketing/seo.

Pandey, N., P. Nayal, and A. S. Rathore. "Digital Marketing for B2B Organizations: Structured Literature Review and Future Research Directions." *Journal of Business & Industrial Marketing* 35, no. 7 (2020): 1191–1204. https://doi.org/10.1108/JBIM-06-2019-0283.

Rane, N. L., A. Achari, and S. P. Choudhary. "Enhancing Customer Loyalty through Quality of Service: Effective Strategies to Improve Customer Satisfaction Experience, Relationship, and Engagement." *International Research Journal of Modernization in Engineering Technology and Science* (2023): May. doi:10.56726/IRJMETS38104.

Reichheld, F. F. "The One Number You Need to Grow." *Harvard Business Review* 81 (2003): 46–55.

Reyes-Lillo, D., A. Morales-Vargas, and C. Rovira. "Reliability of Domain Authority Scores Calculated by Moz, Semrush, and Ahrefs." *International Political Communication* 32 (2023). https://doi.org/10.3145/epi.2023.jul.03.

Rosário, A., and J. A. Casaca. "Relationship Marketing and Customer Retention – A Systematic Literature Review." *Studies in Business and Economics* 18 (January 2024): 44–66. doi:10.2478/sbe-2023-0044.

Sahani, V. "What is SEO – A Comprehensive Guide to Search Engine Optimization." LinkedIn Pulse, 2024. Accessed November 1, 2024. www.linkedin.com/pulse/what-seo-comprehensive-guide-search-engine-vishal-sahani-wc1kf/.

Sarkheil, H., and M. H. Hosseini. "Heuristic Simulated Annealing Modeling to Optimum Target Audience Identification in Digital Marketing: A Case Study of a Mining Industry Training Service Company." *International Journal of Supply and Operations Management* 11 (2024): 188–202. doi:10.22034/IJSOM.2023.109997.2805.

Sawtooth Software. "Market Segmentation Best Practices: Tips for Accurate Audience Identification." Accessed February 13, 2024. https://sawtoothsoftware.com/resources/blog/posts/market-segmentation-best-practices#types-of-segmentation.

Siebert, L. "Why Local SEO Is Important for Multi-Location Businesses." Uberall Blog, Accessed June 5, 2024. https://uberall.com/en-us/resources/blog/why-local-seo-is-important.

Silva, C. "What Is Off-Page SEO? A Guide to Off-Page SEO Strategy." Semrush Blog, Accessed February 16, 2024. www.semrush.com/blog/off-page-seo/.

Stoyanov, D. "The Role of Vending Channels in Marketing: A Systematic Review and Taxonomy of Studies." *Journal of Consumer Affairs* 55, no. 2 (January 2, 2021): 654–679. doi:10.1111/joca.12362.

Verschueren, B. "Best 10 Long-Tail Keywords Software for eCommerce." Verbolia Blog, 2024. Accessed November 1, 2024. www.verbolia.com/best-long-tail-keyword-research-tools/.

Zahay, D. "Advancing Research in Digital and Social Media Marketing." *Journal of Marketing Theory and Practice* 29 (2021): 125–139. https://doi.org/10.1080/10696679.2021.1882865.

Case Study: Crafting Success – Modern Marketing Strategies for Entrepreneurs

Manjot Kaur Brar, Adnan ul Haque and Tahmina Akhter

Distinguishing a unique brand identity from an established brand while meeting customers' preferences and expectations is one of the most significant challenges faced by entrepreneurs in today's constantly changing marketplace.

Celine, the owner of a small-scale entrepreneurial venture, launched an eco-friendly and sustainable skincare line named "EcoGlobeGlow." Her entrepreneurial journey demonstrates that modern-day businesspersons can benefit from establishing unique marketing strategies – such as digital platforms and data-driven information – to excel in the competitive business environment.

At the time of EcoGlobeGlow launch, Celine realized that connecting with her eco-conscious consumers required more than conventional methods. She opted for a purpose-driven marketing style over traditional product-based advertisement. As an entrepreneur, she immediately realised the significance of building trust with customers by being transparent, using environmentally friendly methods, sustainable, and sourcing materials ethically. These elements were essential for her not only the brand's message but also for her brand image. With this approach, the customers seeking genuine products and organic processes, endorsed EcoGlobeGlow that helped in establishing and strengthening its unique position in a highly competitive market.

Social media played a significantly important role in connecting her with a large number of audiences and enhancing her brand's presence in the market. In other words, social media acted as an essential factor in increasing the visibility of her brand. Platforms like Instagram and TikTok provided an opportunity to not only to promote sustainable and eco-friendly image of EcoGlobeGlow but also exhibited transparency by showing contextual content to consumers. Celine effectively transformed her audience into enthusiastic brand advocates, by concentrating on content marketing and utilized user-generated content, including tips for an eco-friendly lifestyle and customer testimonial. This approach enabled in building trust as well as increased her organic visibility via word-of-mouth (WoM).

In addition to that, by leveraging big data analytics, Celine acquired invaluable understanding about buying behaviour and preferences of the consumers, their habits and purchasing trends. Data-driven analysis empowered her to further refine the features of her products based on customer's preferences and feedback. Data-driven strategy enabled her to customize advertising and marketing campaigns to meet the individual consumer's preferences and expectations. Additionally, she improved her product line according to the actual demand of the customers. For instance, after observing the trends and patterns of purchases, she launched a new collection of sustainable and eco-friendly travel kits because she identified growing awareness and interest in eco-friendly travel products.

Celine further improved her marketing strategy through adopting segmentation, targeting, and positioning (STP). She segmented her target audience based on interests, identifying groups such as health-conscious, millennials, and eco-friendly individuals. The product offerings and messaging were customized according to the target consumers, reflecting the targeting approach. Finally, the brand was positioned as a sustainable alternative at an affordable price. This strategy helped in forming a loyal customer base while leading the competitive race in a dynamic environment.

The story of Celine showed how modern-day entrepreneurship excels by combining different marketing strategies including social media engagement, purpose-driven messaging, data-driven analysis, and STP. Additionally, the right marketing tools enable businesses, irrespective of their size, to target their potential customers effectively and refine their products or services to align with the needs and values of customers.

Reflection Questions

- Explain how the user-generated content and social media usage contributed towards Celine's entrepreneurial venture's growth?
- Explain the ways in which Celine used big data analytics to improve her product offerings and marketing strategy?
- Why segmentation, targeting, and positioning (STP) model is critical for businesses in competitive landscape?

Chapter 10

Risk Management and the Future of Evolving Entrepreneurship

Adnan ul Haque, Harmandeep Kaur and Abdul Naveed Tariq

10.0 Introduction

For entrepreneurial success and business growth, managing risk in an effective and efficient manner is essential. It is one of the most important and decisive factors considered when starting and managing entrepreneurship. Throughout the course of business, entrepreneurs face several distinct types of risk, ranging from the development of new products to the expansion of existing products. Strategic, operational, market, legal, and financial risks are some of the prominent types of risk commonly associated with entrepreneurship. This chapter explores the process of identifying and managing these distinct risks faced by entrepreneurs, with a particular emphasis on the strategic and psychological responses to such uncertainties. In addition, "futurepreneurs" approaches are taken into consideration to determine how modern entrepreneurs can adapt to a constantly evolving and complex environment in a smarter manner. Furthermore, the future of entrepreneurship in a dynamic and uncertain environment has been considered to assess the adaptation of modern-day entrepreneurs or future entrepreneurs (i.e., futurepreneurs).

10.1 Entrepreneurs Facing Various Risks

Different types of risk are taken by entrepreneurs, and these risks have the potential to influence not only the trajectory but also their firm's overall success. The ability of an individual to adequately recognize, analyze, and address these risks is highly important for the growth and sustenance of entrepreneurial determination and effort. The following are the primary types of uncertainties explained with examples:

10.1.1 Market Risk

Market risk occurs when there is a lack of knowledge regarding customer demand and preferences for a certain product and/or service. Most of the time, business owners misinterpret the needs of the market or fail to anticipate changes in the behavior of their customers. If the market is not accurately evaluated, it might lead a business into making products that are not sold, services that are not used, and ultimately the failure of the company.

The collapse of Blockbuster is widely acknowledged as one of the most well-known examples of market risk. Although Blockbuster was the dominant player in the movie rental business, the company failed to recognize the changing preferences of its customers

DOI: 10.4324/9781003504351-10

about digital streaming services. The rigorous business approach of Blockbuster, which was built on physical stores and DVD rentals, quickly became obsolete as companies such as Netflix and other online platforms gained prominence. By the time they attempted to adjust, the market had already changed. Blockbuster's demise might be attributed to the company's inability to accurately forecast the future course of the industry, which shifted from traditional video rentals to streaming services on the internet. Another example of this is Segway, a personal transporter that is two-wheeled and is anticipated to revolutionize transportation in urban areas. The Segway misjudged the demand in the market, despite the excitement around its introduction, which resulted in sales that were lower than anticipated (Tidd and Bessant, 2013). The commercial failure of the device was caused by the perception that it was expensive and that it was not practical for daily use.

10.1.2 Financial Risk

It is common for startups to operate with limited resources; hence, fundraising, managing cash flow, and maintaining solvency throughout the various stages of growth all involve a significant amount of risk. Even when their firm is experiencing a negative cash flow, entrepreneurs often find it challenging to acquire adequate funds to keep their business afloat. This is especially true in the early phases of growth.

An excellent example of financial risk may be seen in Tesla's early years at the company. Although Tesla is now one of the most successful automobile manufacturers in the world, the company has faced many financial difficulties. It was necessary for Elon Musk to continually look for substantial funding to sustain the company's research, production, and market development endeavors, in addition to other operations. A few occasions, throughout the process of ramping up production of Model 3, Tesla came dangerously close to running out of funding, which put significant pressure on the company's finances (Vance, 2015). Musk's ability to limit financial risk by assuring continuous investment from private investors to public markets; this investment came from both inside his firm and from outside sources. This was essential to Tesla's continued existence.

On the other hand, WeWork is a classic example of poor performance in terms of managing financial risk. Despite the quick expansion of the coworking space company, which was funded by venture capital, the company did not generate a profit. The attempt of WeWork to go public resulted in a decline in the company's valuation, which revealed unsustainable business methods, an improper allocation of money, and significant financial losses. Its initial public offering (IPO) tragedy is now regarded as a cautionary tale about the dangers of overreliance on venture capital without a clear path to profitability.

10.1.3 Operations Risk

When there are issues with internal organizational structures, processes, or human resources, operational risks are the outcome. The inefficiency of management, mismatched people, mismatched personnel, and disruptions in supply chains are all factors that have the potential to destroy even a well-funded and well-positioned organization. The case of the blood-testing company Theranos is a great example of how operational risk may go wrong and have disastrous consequences. Under the leadership of its founder, Elizabeth Holmes, the company boasted of its innovative technology, which could perform a variety of medical tests with only a single drop of blood. Nevertheless, the company was constrained by operational errors, the majority of which were consequences of insufficient core technology. According to Carreyrou (2018), the organization fell apart because of internal mismanagement, unrealistic timelines, and business practices that were not transparent. At this point, Theranos has become a symbol of how operational inefficiencies, weak leadership, and overpromising can all contribute to tragic tragedy. A further example of the difficulty of Boeing is that its 737 MAX is the consequence of operational errors in testing and quality control. Two terrible incidents occurred because of poor testing of the new software system—the Maneuvering Characteristics Augmentation System (MCAS), which was caused by the push to compete with Airbus. According to Schiavo's research from 2020, Boeing had devastating financial, legal, and reputational ramifications because of this operational failure.

10.1.4 Legal and Regulatory Risk

The ever-evolving framework of laws, regulations, and compliance requirements that businesses must operate within gives rise to the possibility of legal and regulatory hazards. Among them are regulations pertaining to labor, environmental laws, intellectual property rights, and regulations that specialize in a particular sector. To avoid financial penalties, legal action, or damage to reputation, business owners must be aware of these risks from the beginning and ensure that they comply with regulatory requirements.

To provide just one example, Uber has encountered several legal and regulatory challenges in a variety of places throughout the globe. The business model of the firm, which involves hiring drivers as independent contractors rather than employees, has led to legal problems related to the rights of workers, safety regulations, and local transportation legislation. Owing to concerns surrounding safety regulations, Uber was temporarily unable to maintain its operating license in London, which put the company's whole business in jeopardy (Stone, 2017). Legal threats have also been significant for Facebook, primarily in relation to data privacy. Facebook's exploitation of user data was brought to light by the Cambridge Analytica incident, which resulted in widespread outrage, an inquiry by the government, and significant legal repercussions. This case highlights the severity of the penalties and reputational harm that may arise from complying with data security regulations such as the General Data Protection Regulation (GDPR) in Europe (Zuboff, 2019).

10.1.5 Technology Risk

Companies run the danger of technological risk when they fail to keep up with rapidly advancing technology or when they execute concepts that, in the future, become obsolete. Entrepreneurs need to be constantly inventive, make investments in research and development, and stay ahead of the trends in their sector to prevent technology from becoming obsolete.

Kodak, which was once a giant in the photography industry, is a well-known example of a renowned case study of technological risk. Even though it was the company that created the first digital camera in 1975, Kodak was hesitant to switch its business strategy from film-based photography to digital photography. According to Lucas and Goh (2009), the demise of the firm in 2012 was ultimately the consequence of its refusal to embrace the emerging digital photography sector. The failure of Kodak demonstrates the dangers of prioritizing outdated technology above current advancements in the industry.

More recently, BlackBerry achieved a dominant position in the smartphone sector throughout the early 2000s. However, the company's rapid decline was due to its failure to develop innovative solutions and adapt to the touch-screen interface of the iPhone. According to McNish and Silcoff (2015), BlackBerry's once-dominant market share vanished because of increased competition from Apple and Android devices.

10.1.6 Strategic Risk

The act of making significant decisions on the future path of the company, such as entering new markets, expanding activities, or forming partnerships, is what constitutes strategic risk. Because of these options, company owners are required to forecast consumer trends, assess the dynamics of competition, and allocate resources in an appropriate manner. There is a possibility that strategic errors contributed to the calamity that occurred at Nokia. The company Nokia, which was once the largest mobile phone manufacturer in the world, failed to recognize the value of software and applications in the age of smartphones. Instead of converting to Android, it decided to stick with its Symbian operating system, which turned out to be a miscalculation that brought about severe consequences. This purposeful blunder, in conjunction with the introduction of smartphones manufactured by Apple and Android, was the primary factor that led to Nokia's precipitous decline in the market for mobile phones (Vuori and Huy, 2016).

On the other hand, the acquisition of Whole Foods by Amazon in 2017 is a dazzling illustration of how strategic risk-taking may be executed successfully. Amazon expanded its operations into the retail industry after seeing the growing demand for organic and health-conscious food products. According to Stone (2013), the acquisition was a strategic success for Amazon since it enabled the company to create a foothold in physical retail and revolutionize food delivery networks. This was even though it was a significant deviation from Amazon's traditional approach to e-commerce.

10.2 Risk Management and Entrepreneurial Mindset (Entrepreneurial Thinking)

Even though business is characterized by risk and uncertainty, many entrepreneurs often have a particular mindset that enables them to overcome challenges. This mindset of entrepreneurship is characterized by a combination of traits, including resilience, risk tolerance, adaptability, and the ability to make decisions in challenging situations. The ability to limit risks and exploit opportunities requires entrepreneurs to continuously strike a balance between rational and intuitive thinking.

10.2.1 The Dual Process of Decision-Making: Intuition Versus Logic

Logic and intuition are often used in the decision-making process by entrepreneurs, who frequently use dual techniques. This is System 1 thinking, which is based on intuition, and System 2 thinking, which is based on logic, according to Daniel Kahneman (2011), a psychologist. Every way of thinking is extremely significant in regard to making choices, particularly in regard to managing the risks that are associated with being an entrepreneur.

System 1 thinking, often known as intuition, is characterized by speed, automaticity, and reliance on emotions and previous experiences. It helps company owners move quickly, typically led by their gut feelings. This kind of thinking is often effective in situations in which people are required to make decisions within a limited amount of time or when there is a shortage of information.

Logic, which is part of System 2 thinking, is analytical, slower, and more deliberate. It demands critical thinking and a comprehensive study of the facts that are presented, and because of this, it often results in more balanced judgments. This kind of thinking is used by entrepreneurs when they are faced with challenging financial decisions, as well as when they are assessing long-term goals and calculating risks.

Those individuals who can effectively mix both types of thinking are better equipped to address the significant amounts of uncertainty that are associated with activities related to entrepreneurship. One of the most well-known examples of an entrepreneur who relied most heavily on their intuition was Steve Jobs, who was one of the cofounders of Apple. Jobs listened to his instincts when it came to considering the preferences of customers and the design of products. His legendary refusal to participate in market research stemmed from his conviction that consumers did not always know what they wanted until they actually saw it. According to Isaacson (2011), his innate capacity for decision-making resulted in the creation of innovative products such as the MacBook, iPod, and iPhone, all of which have become ubiquitous in popular culture. Although Steve Jobs' innovative approach was essential to Apple's success, his dependence on traditional market research was called into doubt by several individuals.

During the development of the first iPhone, for example, Steve Jobs made the obvious decision to skip the use of a physical keyboard, which was the norm for mobile devices such as smartphones at the time. Instead, he believed that a touch screen would provide a more inventive and user-friendly interface than is now available. Although it was first met with skepticism, this decision ultimately proved to be a game changer that completely reworked the smartphone industry.

On the other hand, Elon Musk is well known for his ability to combine intuition with precise data analysis, particularly in high-stakes initiatives such as Tesla and SpaceX. The intuitive vision that Musk has allowed him to establish lofty goals, such as human habitation on Mars or the acceleration of the transition to renewable energy on a global scale. On the other hand, he does improve this vision by doing extensive research in the fields of science and technology, which guarantees that these goals have a basis (Vance, 2015).

At first, the decision that Musk made to bet on electric cars with Tesla was seen as risky because of the prevalence of gasoline-powered automobiles and the fact that electric vehicles had not yet been put through their paces. Although his intuition led him to believe that electric cars would be the dominant mode of transportation in the future, he backed his decision with extensive scientific research and data on battery technology, production scalability, and market potential. Musk has shown a pragmatic approach to risk management and has pushed the boundaries of what is possible by combining gut instincts and rational thought.

10.2.2 Management of Uncertainty Through the Use of Contingent Strategies

The business environment in which entrepreneurs operate is in a state of perpetual change and is characterized by unpredictability. Business owners who are interested in effectively managing uncertainty may choose to use contingent methods, which emphasize adaptability and flexibility rather than rigid planning. Because of this, they are able to respond quickly to unforeseen occurrences, make adjustments to their plans, and reverse course if it is needed.

10.3 Effectuation Theory

The effectiveness theory proposed by Sarasvathy (2001) asserts that successful businesses do not begin with a well-defined and predetermined goal. As an alternative, they begin with the tools that are available to them and continually adjust their goals in response to new opportunities and feedback from existing stakeholders. One of the fundamental principles of effectuation is the ability to be flexible and experiment with a variety of methods, therefore acknowledging that failure is an unavoidable component of the process.

Effectiveness encourages company leaders to collaborate with partners in the creation of opportunities and to make use of whatever resources are available to them, whether they are financial, human, or social capital. Because of this, there is less of a need for long-term planning, which allows company leaders to focus on what is within their sphere of control and develop creative solutions to solve new problems. Consider, for example, the effectuation path of Airbnb.

Airbnb, which is a firm that allows people to share their homes, is a well-known example of effectuation. In the midst of the financial crisis that occurred in 2008, founders Brian Chesky and Joe Gebbia started Airbnb. Initially, they rented out air mattresses in their apartment to clients who were attending a design conference. It was clear from the beginning that they did not have a clear plan for disrupting the hotel operation. Instead, they put their idea to the test and relied on feedback from customers to make ongoing adjustments while working with the few resources they had available. According to Stone (2017), they changed the premise of the firm, initiated several different versions of the website, and gradually expanded the range of services their platform provided.

Rather than adhering to a rigid timetable, the founders of Airbnb made use of their resources and adapted their strategy in accordance with the information they gained from doing trial runs. Because of their adaptability and willingness to try new things, they were able to overcome early challenges and eventually become multibillion-dollar companies when they ultimately succeeded.

10.4 Lean Startups Principles

The Lean Start-up methodology used by Eric Ries, which was first introduced in 2011, is yet another reliable technique for managing uncertainty. The rapid development, testing, and learning capabilities of this technique are emphasized. In the process of developing a minimum viable product (MVP), which is the lowest version of a product that can be placed on the market, entrepreneurs iteratively improve the product by leveraging feedback from early adopters or customers (Ries, 2011). It is possible for entrepreneurs to lessen the likelihood of making significant investments in a product that does not meet the needs of the market if they emphasize learning and flexibility. As an example, the Lean Start-up Method used by Dropbox.

Dropbox, which is a cloud storage provider, is a brilliant illustration of how Lean Startup principles can be utilized to manage uncertainty. The founder of Dropbox, Drew Houston, decided against constructing the whole program from the beginning and instead made a brief explainer video that demonstrated how the system would function. This minimum viable product (MVP) allowed him to evaluate the level of interest in the market before he began writing a single line of code. The proposal was validated by the substantial amount of positive feedback received from prospective consumers, which gave Houston the assurance it needed to go forward with the development process (Ries, 2011). With this contingent strategy, Dropbox was able to reduce its exposure to market risk and save costly development cycles that would have otherwise been wasted on a product that did not meet the requirements of the market.

10.5 Adaptable Strategies and Agility

One of the skills necessary for managing uncertainty is the ability to pivot, which means altering direction when the current strategy is not producing the desired results. As a result of discovering that its users were primarily interested in the capabilities of photo-sharing, Instagram shifted its focus from being location-based social networking software known as Burbn to focusing only on photo-sharing. By taking this strategic move, Instagram was able to swiftly develop, which ultimately led to Facebook purchasing the company for a price of one billion dollars (McNish and Silcoff, 2015).

The capacity to manage environmental hazards will be more readily available to entrepreneurs who are willing to embrace adaptation, experiment with a variety of tactics, and respond to feedback from the market. With the help of these backup plans, they can minimize risks while simultaneously increasing the likelihood of creative and successful outcomes.

10.6 An Overview of the Way Forward for Entrepreneurship

Changing societal expectations, advancements in the global economy, and advances in technology are all contributing factors that are causing the landscape of entrepreneurship to undergo rapid transformation. Entrepreneurs who are looking to the future must anticipate these changes and be prepared to adjust to them to maintain their competitiveness and sustainability. In the future, the future of entrepreneurship will be defined by new opportunities as well as obstacles, and a mindset characterized by continuous education, inventiveness, and flexibility will be needed.

10.6.1 Technological Disruption and Digital Transformation

The ongoing digital revolution is one of the primary causes driving the shift that has occurred in the realm of entrepreneurship. Artificial intelligence (AI), blockchain technology, the Internet of Things (IoT), and big data analytics are among the technologies that are causing industries to undergo transformations and creating whole new markets. Individuals who are quick enough to adapt to new technologies and make use of them will be able to provide entrepreneurs with a competitive advantage.

10.6.2 Automation and Artificial Intelligence

Artificial intelligence and automation will continue to bring about changes in the way businesses operate, including the simplification of industrial processes and the facilitation of more individualized connections with customers. The use of AI-driven solutions by start-ups enables them to automate mundane tasks such as marketing, customer care, and financial analysis, which in turn enables them to scale their operations more efficiently. A good example would be AI-driven start-ups.

UiPath, a leading robotic process automation (RPA) business, along with other companies that are based on artificial intelligence, have become major disruptors in the automation of repetitive labor in industries such as banking, healthcare, and logistics. These business owners are working on inventing solutions that enable organizations to reduce their costs and improve their operational efficiency, which in turn enables them to expand their operations more quickly and into new markets. There is a connection between the role that artificial intelligence plays in entrepreneurial efforts and the production of products. Companies such as OpenAI, for example, use machine learning to construct generative artificial intelligence tools that can generate new content, visuals, and software code. As a result, these tools have the potential to revolutionize several industries, including the entertainment industry, marketing, and software development.

10.6.3 The Decentralized Finance and Blockchain Technology

The technology known as blockchain is causing a shift in the landscape of entrepreneurship by enabling new forms of trust and security to be used in digital transactions. Blockchain technology is used by business owners to construct decentralized platforms that eliminate the need for intermediaries and provide both security and transparency in several industries, including the banking, supply chain management, and real estate sectors. An example of this would be blockchain firms that provide decentralized financing (DeFi).

Established industries are being disrupted by new businesses that are powered by blockchain technology. Entrepreneurs who are behind websites such as Uniswap and Aave are leading this change in democratizing access to financial services and questioning established banking institutions. Decentralized finance (DeFi) companies provide blockchain-based financial services such as lending, borrowing, and trading. These companies are doing this without the need for traditional banks. Additionally, blockchain technology is used in areas such as intellectual property management. In this context, distributed networks have the potential to provide more secure methods of monitoring ownership and preventing piracy, which may be of assistance to enterprises operating in creative industries.

10.6.4 Implementation of the Internet of Things (Iot) and Intelligent Infrastructure

The adoption of the Internet of Things in a variety of businesses provides company owners with new opportunities for innovation. Through the Internet of Things (IoT), physical items can collect and transmit data in real time, which enables the creation of intelligent ecosystems that optimize the use of resources and improve the service supply. A growing number of entrepreneurs are establishing businesses centered on connected healthcare, smart cities, and smart homes to capitalize on the massive amounts of data generated by Internet of Things devices.

Companies such as Nest, which Google recently acquired, have been at the forefront of developing smart home equipment such as thermostats. These devices can learn the preferences of their users and automatically adjust the temperature settings to maximize energy efficiency. These types of business owners continue to innovate by creating solutions that connect several aspects of day-to-day life and provide clients experiences that are faultless.

10.7 A Purpose-Driven Approach to Entrepreneurship and Its Development

Because an increasing number of enterprises are now focusing not only on being profitable but also on having a positive impact on society and the environment, the future of entrepreneurship will be increasingly driven by a sense of purpose. This shift is driven by consumers, investors, and workers, who are increasingly demanding that firms prioritize sustainability, ethics, and inclusivity the highest priority in their operations.

10.7.1 Sustainability Social Enterprise

One kind of entrepreneurship that is gaining popularity is known as social entrepreneurship, which aims to solve social concerns while maintaining a profitable business model. Creative solutions are being implemented by entrepreneurs to address pressing global issues such as poverty, climate change, and access to healthcare globally. One example is Patagonia's business strategy, which is environmentally responsible.

This outdoor apparel company, Patagonia, exemplifies what it means to be a purpose-driven business. Patagonia, which was founded by Yvon Chouinard, has made sustainability a primary emphasis of business operations by using recycled materials, advocating for the preservation of the environment, and committing to donating a portion of its profits to environmental groups (Chouinard, 2016). These types of models serve as sources of inspiration for entrepreneurs, who are gradually establishing businesses that prioritize the triple bottom line, which includes profit, people, and the environment. In addition, firms that are focused on sustainability are pushing the construction of circular economy models. These models include the production of items that can be reused, repaired, and recycled, hence reducing waste and the effect on the environment.

10.7.2 Globalization and the Shift toward Emerging Markets

Measures that consider environmental, social, and governance (ESG) factors, in addition to impact investment, indicate that a wider society is moving toward more responsible economic activity. What investors are looking for more than anything else is support for new businesses and enterprises that demonstrate a strong commitment to social and environmental causes. Financial availability and customer loyalty are increasing for those that align their firms with environmental, social, and governance (ESG) goals. As an example, the plant-based revolution that Beyond Meat launched.

Businesses such as Beyond Meat have successfully capitalized on the widespread demand among consumers for alternatives to traditional meat that are less harmful to the environment and derived from plants. In addition, Meat has undergone rapid expansion because of its efforts to combat the negative impacts of animal husbandry on the environment and to promote healthier food. The company's products are presently offered in large supermarkets and restaurants worldwide (Creswell, 2023). It is clear that businesses that are focused on the future might benefit from the intersection of innovation, sustainability, and wellbeing.

Third, we have globalization and a shift against rising markets. The worldwide environment for entrepreneurs is undergoing a significant transformation because of the growing significance of emerging markets. Rapid growth in entrepreneurial activity is driven by factors such as increasing internet penetration, the rise of the middle class, and the availability of additional financing in regions such as Africa, Southeast Asia, and Latin America.

10.7.3 Technology Hubs in Emerging Markets

Business owners in developing areas often vent into well-established industries and adopt cutting-edge technologies such as mobile payments, e-commerce, and fintech. These entrepreneurs produce innovative solutions that are tailored to meet the needs of the local community. Mobile payment systems such as M-Pesa in Kenya have revolutionized the concept of financial inclusion (Jack and Suri, 2014). These systems provide individuals who do not have bank accounts with the ability to access financial services via their mobile phones. In addition, the proliferation of global venture capital and incubators that are centered on emerging markets is beneficial to entrepreneurs in these regions. Increasingly, investors are focusing their attention on information technology (IT) hubs such as Lagos (Nigeria), Bangalore (India), and São Paulo (Brazil), which are poised to fuel the subsequent wave of innovation around the globe.

10.7.4 The Future of Work and Gig Economy

In addition, the trajectory of entrepreneurship is intricately intertwined with the changing nature of employment. There is a shift in the way entrepreneurs start and expand their businesses because of the gig economy and the trend toward remote work. Currently, business owners may utilize digital platforms to operate organizations that are more compact and flexible, to delegate tasks to independent contractors, and to have access to talent from all over the globe.

10.7.5 Digital Nomad and Gig economy

It is now much easier for companies to communicate with freelancers from all over the world because of the proliferation of platforms such as Upwork and Fiverr. These platforms have reduced the necessity for traditional full-time employees. A consequence of this is the emergence of the gig economy, which is characterized by businesses expanding more efficiently by employing independent workers for specific tasks (Sundarajan, 2016). At the same time, the concept of the digital nomad is becoming more widespread, as company owners who run entirely remote companies can live and work from any location on the planet. Startups are now able to operate without being constrained by local regulations, which is a move that is opening new opportunities for entrepreneurs across the globe.

10.7.6 Entrepreneurship in the Age of Resilience

Entrepreneurship will increasingly concentrate on resilience, which is the ability to withstand and adapt to shocks, as the world confronts crises that have never been seen before. Emergencies such as pandemics and climate change are examples of such crises. To thrive in uncertain circumstances and survive disruptions, entrepreneurs need to develop robust and adaptable business models that can survive disruptive events.

10.7.7 Innovation Driven by the Crisis

The COVID-19 outbreak demonstrated how quickly and adaptable company owners may be to ensure that their customers' requirements are met. Numerous start-ups in the health technology industry, for example, hastened the development of telemedicine systems to offer solutions for healthcare that may be delivered remotely. Similarly, firms in the e-commerce and logistics industries adapted their operations to accommodate disruptions in the supply chain by implementing new delivery techniques and increasing their use of automation. For entrepreneurs to be able to establish businesses that not only survive but also gain opportunities for growth and innovation as a result of catastrophes, they should prioritize resilience in their plans for the business world.

10.8 Conclusion

Risk management is an essential aspect of entrepreneurship, and it necessitates the implementation of a proactive and dynamic plan to successfully navigate the unpredictability of the entrepreneurial route When it comes to risks, entrepreneurs face a wide range of challenges, including but not limited to market volatility, operational inefficiencies, regulatory obstacles, and technological advancements. The capacity of entrepreneurs to adapt to their environments is ensured by their awareness of these risks and the formulation of strategies to mitigate them via the use of both analytical and intuitive decision-making processes. At the same time as technological advancements and shifting societal expectations are driving the development of entrepreneurship, the entrepreneurial mindset must also evolve to accommodate the new reality. The dual-process model of decision-making, which combines intuition with logic, enables entrepreneurs to make rapid yet sensible conclusions. This contrasts with contingency approaches, which include effectuation, which provides the necessary flexibility to pivot and respond to environmental uncertainty.

In the future, we can see that the ever-present globalization of markets, social impact concerns, and technological innovation will continue to have an increasing influence on entrepreneurship. The creation of purpose-driven businesses reflects the growing attention being given to ethical and environmental concerns. Moreover, emerging technologies such as artificial intelligence, blockchain, the Internet of Things, and the gig economy are causing industries to change and creating new opportunities for entrepreneurs. The entrepreneurs who are most likely to be successful in the ever-evolving landscape of entrepreneurship are those who are resilient, adaptable, and focused on the future. These entrepreneurs will be able to convert challenges into opportunities for innovation and growth. It is thus more important to embrace uncertainty with a combination of foresight, agility, and strategic thinking to effectively manage risk than to avoid ambiguity because of this. The capacity to continuously innovate, adapt to disruptive forces, and establish sustainable firms that not only achieve profitability but also address more general needs of society will be the defining characteristic of entrepreneurship in the years to come.

Bibliography

Carreyrou, J. *Bad Blood: Secrets and Lies in a Silicon Valley Startup*. New York: Knopf, 2018.

Chouinard, Y. *Let My People Go Surfing: The Education of a Reluctant Businessman*. New York: Penguin Books, 2016.

Creswell, J. (2023). Plant-Based Food Companies Face Critics: Environmental Advocates. *New York Times*. Available at: www.nytimes.com/2021/10/15/business/beyond-meat-impossible-emissions.html (Last accessed: August 04, 2024)

Isaacson, W. *Steve Jobs*. New York: Simon & Schuster, 2011.

Jack, W., and T. Suri. "Risk Sharing and Transactions Costs: Evidence from Kenya's Mobile Money Revolution." *American Economic Review* 104, no. 1 (2014): 183–223. https://doi.org/10.1257/aer.104.1.183.

Kahneman, D. *Thinking, Fast and Slow*. New York: Farrar, Straus and Giroux, 2011.

Lucas, H. C., Jr., and J. M. Goh. "Disruptive Technology: How Kodak Missed the Digital Photography Revolution." *Journal of Strategic Information Systems* 18, no. 1 (2009): 46–55. https://doi.org/10.1016/j.jsis.2009.01.002.

McNish, J., and S. Silcoff. *Losing the Signal: The Untold Story Behind the Extraordinary Rise and Spectacular Fall of BlackBerry*. New York: Flatiron Books, 2015.

Ries, E. *The Lean Startup: How Today's Entrepreneurs Use Continuous Innovation to Create Radically Successful Businesses*. New York: Crown Currency, 2011.

Sarasvathy, S. D. "Causation and Effectuation: Toward a Theoretical Shift from Economic Inevitability to Entrepreneurial Contingency." *Academy of Management Review* 26, no. 2 (2001): 243–263.

Stone, B. *The Everything Store: Jeff Bezos and the Age of Amazon*. New York: Little, Brown and Company, 2013.

Stone, B. *The Upstarts: How Uber, Airbnb, and the Killer Companies of the New Silicon Valley Are Changing the World*. New York: Little, Brown and Company, 2017.

Sundararajan, A. *The Sharing Economy: The End of Employment and the Rise of Crowd-Based Capitalism*. Cambridge, MA: MIT Press, 2016.

Tidd, J., and J. Bessant. *Managing Innovation: Integrating Technological, Market and Organizational Change*. 5th ed. Hoboken, NJ: Wiley, 2013.

Vance, A. *Elon Musk: Tesla, SpaceX, and the Quest for a Fantastic Future*. New York: ECCO, 2015.

Vuori, T. O., and Q. N. Huy. "Distributed Attention and Shared Emotions in the Innovation Process: How Nokia Lost the Smartphone Battle." *Administrative Science Quarterly* 61, no. 1 (2016): 9–51. https://doi.org/10.1177/0001839215606951.

Zuboff, S. *The Age of Surveillance Capitalism: The Fight for a Human Future at the New Frontier of Power*. New York: PublicAffairs, 2019.

Case Study: Melanie's AI Healthcare Start-Up

Siyath Thamuditha Gallage and Adnan ul Haque

In a successful Information Technology firm, working at the middle level management Melanie is considering resigning from her stable corporate to start her own tech entrepreneurial venture. She is primarily focusing on improving telehealth services through developing an AI-powered healthcare solution. Driven by her axiological stance, she aims to operate in rural areas, reflecting her early childhood experiences of growing up in rural areas, where access to healthcare facilities was limited. Before pursuing her plan, Melanie must assess the risks inherent to her entrepreneurial journey. The key risks she identified are as follows:

Strategic Risk

Melanie critically assesses her strategy to enter in the market, contemplating whether she should invest her resources entirely in the U.S. market or explore international opportunities as well. To manage this strategic risk, she prototypes a pilot program in one county. This allows her to assess and check her business model prior to expanding the business scope to serve a larger market.

Financial Risk

Quitting a stable job for an entrepreneurial venture is both overwhelming and extremely risky, especially given the higher chance of a new startup failure. Instead of remaining reliant primarily on her personal savings, she opts for a hybrid financing strategy. Rather than solely relying on her personal savings, she adopts a hybrid financing strategy, combining capital venture with her savings. This move creates a 'safety net' and allows her to secure funding for quick development of products and marketing.

Legal and Regulatory Risk

After recognizing the complex legal framework of the healthcare sector, she consults professionals and legal experts in the field during the early stages of her business. This strategically pre- emptive approach enables her to remain compliant with industrial laws and regulations. Moreover, enabling Melanie to acquire patents for her innovative AI algorithms, thereby safeguarding her intellectual property.

Market Risk

Melanie recognizes immediately that navigating the healthcare sector is difficult because of its rigid regulatory environment. Additionally, the unique needs of the target audience further increase challenges. She conducts extensive market research to deal with these risks and assess an acceptable level of demand for her potential product. During her research, Melanie not only identifies a gap in telehealth services but also explores the potential of how awareness could be enhanced, especially in the underserved rural communities. This insight reinforces and solidifies her market position.

Decision-Making Process

Melanie pursues a twin-track method as data-driven analysis with intuitive insights combined together in her decision-making. The several years of relevant industry experience she possesses and strongly develops an attitude to maintain faith in her own instincts. Nonetheless, she also values the meticulous and robust information gathered from market research studies and consulting experts. By maintaining this balanced approach, she enables herself to be flexible and adaptive in a highly dynamic, challenging and competitive environment so she can meet the market and consumers' needs in an effective and efficient manner.

Future Considerations

Moving forward, Melanie must identify, anticipate, manage, and address emerging risks, such as changing consumer preferences, buying behaviour, and technological disruptions. She proceeds by deciding to implement a lean start-up framework, emphasizing the creation of a minimum viable product (MVP). This approach helps her to quickly gather the feedback from the consumers and modify her product through iterative improvements.

Reflection Questions

- According to you, what are some of the most critical risks Melanie encountered while launching her own entrepreneurial venture? Justify your statements?
- Critically evaluate Melanie's strategic approach to address strategic, financial, legal, and market risks. What additional measures should she consider?
- Explain why it is essential for entrepreneurs to balance between intuitive and logical analysis when making decisions. How can a twin-track approach impact the entrepreneurial venture's outcome?
- What other challenges might Melanie encounter in a volatile, uncertain, complex, and ambiguous (VUCA) environment? Suggest strategies to overcome these challenges.
- As an inspiring entrepreneur, what lessons can you learn from Melanie's approach to decision-making and risk management?

Chapter 11

From Margins to Markets

Exploring Barriers and Pathways for Transgender Entrepreneurs

Harmandeep Kaur, Riffat Faizan and Adnan ul Haque

11.0 Introduction

Entrepreneurship has often been a source of innovation, social mobility, and economic development (Crenshaw, 1989; Balachandra et al., 2019; Faizan et al., 2019). On the other hand, it is not guaranteed that all types of entrepreneurs will have equal access to resources in the entrepreneurial landscape. Distinct and unique challenges are faced by marginalized groups, including transgender entrepreneurs, who, because of their gender identity, encounter difficulties not only in starting but also in maintaining their ventures. Although scholars have shown more interest in entrepreneurial marginalized groups, gender intersection, and societal exclusion, the study of transgender entrepreneurship is still understudied (Hughto et al., 2015). Unique barriers are faced by transgender individuals, and the exploration of potential opportunities for them remains largely unexplored in the mainstream entrepreneurship literature (Galloway et al., 2015). Thus, this chapter fills the gap in the literature by critically evaluating the constraints and opportunities encountered by transgender entrepreneurs.

Owing to discrimination and social exclusion, transgender entrepreneurs experience difficulties in securing funding and accessing financial resources, often resulting from cultural and societal stereotypes. Additionally, their participation in business activities is further hindered by institutional barriers, such as complex and rigid bureaucratic processes and recognition of legal gender (Darden et al., 2022; S et al., 2024). Furthermore, the struggles for transgender entrepreneurs are often further intensified by the dominance of the cisgender and heteronormative norms within the entrepreneurial ecosystem, resulting in bias and invisibility (Martinez Dy et al., 2014). Conversely, transgender individuals benefit from digital economies and platforms, as they offer potential opportunities by reducing reliance on traditional business practices and conventional capital structures (Murad and Rambley, 2024). A solid foundation for transgender entrepreneurship is provided in the shape of the digital economy, as it plays a vital role in bypassing gender discrimination while developing niche markets and nurturing support within the trans community.

11.1 Literature Review

11.1.1 Broadening the Scope of Transgender Entrepreneurship

A systematic review of transgender entrepreneurship broadens the scope of the entrepreneurship literature, especially focusing on marginalized groups' opportunities and

DOI: 10.4324/9781003504351-11

challenges. Intersectional factors of identity, such as race, sexual orientation, and class, are explored through transgender entrepreneurs' real-life experiences. This chapter reflects on potential opportunities (especially emerging trends in the digital economy) prevailing within the existing entrepreneurial ecosystem while addressing the specific challenges faced by transgender individuals. Professional networks and personal connections play vital roles in the formation of social capital, which is important for the success of entrepreneurship. Nonetheless, a unique challenge for transgender entrepreneurs is exclusion from networks that could help them build social capital.

11.1.2 The Limited Focus on Transgender Entrepreneurship in Existing Literature

The literature on the intersection of gender and entrepreneurship is limited, with an extensive focus remaining on women entrepreneurs and minority groups (Crenshaw, 1989; Faizan and Haque, 2016; Kaur and Haque, 2024). Nonetheless, transgender entrepreneurship still remains understudied to a greater extent. Distinct economic and social constraints impact transgender individuals in the entrepreneurial space because of transgenders' non-conforming gender identity. According to Rietveld and Patel (2022), a higher level of discrimination is faced by transgender individuals than by other marginalized groups, which significantly affects their access to essential resources in entrepreneurial ecosystems. Moreover, transgender entrepreneurs face a double challenge that includes (i) the typical challenges that all types of entrepreneurs face: setting up a business and additional (ii) societal and social bias that hinders their access to funding, participation in mentorship programs, and developing social networks (Murad and Rambley, 2024). However, access to funding remains the most notable barrier for transgender entrepreneurship (Darden et al., 2022). In other words, among these challenges, access to capital remains the most prominent barrier.

11.1.3 Subconscious Biases and Limited Access to Funding

A study by Galloway et al. (2015) revealed that entrepreneurial ventures owned by transgender individuals often receive underfunding because of subconscious biases and negative perceptions. Hughto et al. (2015) argued that while male entrepreneurs benefit from biased structures and that female entrepreneurs receive a lesser portion of financial assistance, transgender individuals face even greater financial limitations due to heightened prejudice and societal norms. Interestingly, Galloway et al. (2015) reported that transgender women face greater difficulties than transgender men do because of exclusions from financial institutions amid societal norms and pressures.

11.1.4 The Role of Social Capital and Network Exclusion

The latest work of Thoroughgood et al. (2020) also confirmed that social capital is relatively low for transgender entrepreneurs, which is due to limited social network support, resulting in slower progress in comparison to that of general entrepreneurial ventures. Studies have shown that personal and professional networks play a critical role in the success of the entrepreneurial venture, as they form the social capital crucial for businesses (Faizan and Haque, 2016; Rietveld and Patel, 2022). Nonetheless, the study of Thoroughgood et al.

(2020) revealed that exclusion from social networks is the result of very little understanding of transgender identities and prejudice in social circuits. Heteronormative and cisnormative standards are dominant in the entrepreneurial ecosystem, which marginalizes transgender individuals because they struggle to form legitimacy and access mentorship support (Galloway et al., 2015). Interestingly, transgender individuals are also excluded from LGBTQ+ business networks (Moser et al., 2022).

11.1.5 Opportunities in the Digital Economy for Transgender Entrepreneurs

Despite these challenges, the digital economy has opened new opportunities for transgender entrepreneurs, even though barriers remain significantly high (Murad and Rambley, 2024). E-commerce and social media platforms allow transgender entrepreneurs to bypass traditional channels such as banks and venture capitalists, increasing their independence (Murad and Rambley, 2024). These digital platforms help transgender entrepreneurs target niche markets and foster inclusive business environments within the LGBTQ+ community (Thoroughgood et al., 2020). Digital entrepreneurship also allows transgender individuals to build personal brands linked to their gender identity, helping them reach broader audiences in a safe space. Social and geographic barriers are minimized in digital markets, enabling transgender entrepreneurs to operate in a secure environment (Moser et al., 2022).

11.1.6 Intersectionality: Understanding Compounded Barriers and Resilience

A lack of an intersectional approach to exploring transgender entrepreneurship has been identified as a significant gap in the academic literature. Crenshaw's (1989) concept of intersectionality provides insights into how distinct identity markers—such as gender, race, sexual orientation, and class—intersect to shape experiences of privilege and discrimination. The barriers faced in entrepreneurship by transgender individuals are further intensified for those with multiple marginalized identities (Jefferson et al., 2013). For example, greater discrimination is experienced by transgender entrepreneurs than by their white counterparts because of the compounded effects of transphobia and racial bias. These compounded effects restrict business networks and access to financial resources (Jefferson et al., 2013). Additionally, transgender women are rendered particularly vulnerable to social exclusion and violence, significantly hindering their entrepreneurial ventures and aspirations (Hughto et al., 2015).

However, intersectionality also presents potential opportunities. Resilient strategies are often developed by transgender entrepreneurs through the adoption of adaptive approaches and by targeting niche markets (Darden et al., 2022). An intersectional framework is essential for providing a comprehensive view of the various challenges faced by transgender entrepreneurs and how intersecting identity factors shape their business experiences (Moser et al., 2022).

11.2 Distinct Barriers for Transgender Entrepreneurs

This section discusses different barriers and challenges faced by transgender entrepreneurs.

11.2.1 Institutional and Legal Barriers in Transgender Entrepreneurship

A focus on institutional and legal barriers faced by transgender entrepreneurs has been highlighted by recent studies, such as those conducted by Moser et al. (2022). One of the critical hurdles identified is the legal recognition of gender identity. In many countries, the process of changing the gender marker on legal documents is considered lengthy and complex, making it difficult for transgender entrepreneurs to apply for loans or business registration (Hughto et al., 2015; Galloway et al., 2015). Legal discrimination is also faced by transgender entrepreneurs, including exemptions from employment protections, which deter them from pursuing or starting entrepreneurial ventures (Darden et al., 2022). Studies suggest that better performance is exhibited by transgender entrepreneurs in regions with more progressive recognition laws, where stronger support networks and greater access to entrepreneurial resources are available (Moser et al., 2022). Nonetheless, legal protection and recognition are insufficient if structural inequalities and biased cultural attitudes persist (Martinez Dy et al., 2014).

11.2.2 Social Norms, Biases, and Exclusion in Entrepreneurial Activities

Societal norms, biases, discrimination, and social exclusion negatively affect the participation of transgender individuals in entrepreneurial activities. In addition, transgender entrepreneurs struggle to build strong supportive and meaningful networks, as they are often viewed as outsiders, even within LGBTQ+ communities. As a result, they experience limited access to financial assistance and restricted opportunities for mentoring programs, which hinders their ability to develop social capital. The literature reveals that these barriers are outweighed by opportunities (Köllen, 2016; Galloway et al., 2015; Moser et al., 2022; Jefferson et al., 2013; Darden et al., 2022; Murad and Rambley, 2024). Interestingly, the work of Murad and Rambley (2024) also revealed that in emerging economies, transgender entrepreneurs face additional challenges such as bullying and harassment.

11.2.3 Financial Barriers and Institutional Discrimination

Compared with other entrepreneurial groups, transgender entrepreneurs access financial resources at significantly lower levels. Institutional discrimination and investor biases further reduce their access to essential funding for businesses starting and running businesses (Köllen, 2016; Martinez Dy et al., 2014; Rietveld and Patel, 2018; Balachandra et al., 2019; Gamarel et al., 2020). A thorough review identified one of the most significant barriers for transgender entrepreneurs as access to financial resources. Negative perceptions and subconscious biases contribute further to a belief among investors that transgender individuals represent greater risk, making them reluctant to fund transgender-led entrepreneurial ventures. Additionally, trans women of color are further excluded from financial support because of compounded discrimination.

11.2.4 Legal and Structural Barriers to Transgender Entrepreneurship

The literature also identifies systematic discrimination against transgender entrepreneurs stemming from institutional barriers that negatively impact their businesses. Furthermore, reports of harassment and bullying experienced by transgender entrepreneurs are common (Murad and Rambley, 2024). Despite reforms and evolving legal frameworks aimed at supporting LGBTQ+ communities, the legal system has remained rigid, hierarchical, and time-consuming, making it difficult for loans to be applied for or for commercial business activities to be commenced by transgender individuals (Moser et al., 2022; Jefferson et al., 2013. The absence of legal recognition for transgender identities further contributes to these challenges through in-depth analysis (Martinez Dy et al., 2014; Moser et al., 2022). In regions lacking legal recognition of transgender identities, weak structural support and exclusion from employment protections are common experiences for these individuals (Martinez Dy et al., 2014; Moser et al., 2022; Murad and Rambley, 2024).

11.3 Digital Platforms: New Opportunities and Shifting Trends

An in-depth review of the literature has revealed many challenges faced by transgender individuals, with compounded effects impacting their entrepreneurial ventures. However, potential opportunities are also presented by the emergence of e-commerce, social media, and other digital platforms. These platforms enable the bypass of traditional channels, providing greater independence and opportunities to reach a wider audience. The shift from traditional entrepreneurship to digital entrepreneurship has facilitated the creation of personal brands and entry into niche markets that were previously overlooked by mainstream channels and businesses (Martinez Dy et al., 2014 Galloway et al., 2015; Moser et al., 2022, Jefferson et al., 2013).

The literature also emphasizes that the barriers faced by transgender entrepreneurs extend beyond economic constraints to include institutional and social patterns, such as social exclusion and stigma. The compounded effects on transgender entrepreneurship are influenced by race, sexual orientation, gender, and class. Additionally, support from LGBTQ+ communities is often not extended to transgender entrepreneurs within their networks, further reducing social support. Despite these challenges, trends are changing that are creating safe spaces for transgender entrepreneurs on digital platforms.

Recent studies related to artificial intelligence (AI) have shown that psychological responses to AI can vary by gender (Velinov et al., 2024). It has been suggested that different psychological responses might be experienced by transgender entrepreneurs, although whether these responses are positive is still unknown. Furthermore, the development of strategies related to customer loyalty on digital platforms must be prioritized, as customer loyalty and recommendations are considered vital to business success (Hughto et al., 2015). Health and safety considerations must also be emphasized (Dylan, 2024), as it is known that entrepreneurial activities affect the personal well-being of individuals. Psychological well-being is linked to adaptability and performance (Velinov et al., 2024), so ensuring that the psychological well-being of transgender individuals remains intact is essential.

11.4 Conclusion

In-depth analysis of entrepreneurial ecosystems reveals both challenges and opportunities for transgender entrepreneurs. However, the challenges and difficulties are relatively greater than the opportunities. The most prevalent difficulties include institutional investor biases, lack of access to funding, inadequate social capital, discrimination and social exclusion, even within the trans community itself, where trans women face more hurdles than other trans women do.

Although increasing awareness and a culture of inclusivity are being developed in many countries, the social support network and access to financial resources for transgender individuals to start and manage businesses remain restricted. Moreover, inclusion and support for transgender individuals within LGBTQ+ communities are largely absent. Nonetheless, the emergence of the digital economy and the growth of digital platforms provide safer spaces for transgender entrepreneurs, offering opportunities to reach wider audiences, establish themselves in niche markets, bypass traditional barriers, and develop personal brands. This suggests that the way forward for transgender entrepreneurs is to utilize digital platforms effectively.

Bibliography

Balachandra, L., T. Briggs, K. Eddleston, and C. Brush. "Don't Pitch Like a Girl!: How Gender Stereotypes Influence Investor Decisions." *Entrepreneurship Theory and Practice* 43, no. 1 (2019): 116–137.

Crenshaw, K. "Demarginalizing the Intersection of Race and Sex: A Black Feminist Critique of Antidiscrimination Doctrine, Feminist Theory, and Antiracist Politics." *University of Chicago Legal Forum* 1989, no. 1 (1989): 139–167.

Darden, B. B., F. W. Kellermanns, and E. L. Best. "Entrepreneurial Fear of Failure: Transgender versus Cis-Gender Entrepreneurs." *Journal of Business Venturing Insights* 18 (2022): e00332.

Dylan, S. "Building Your Personal Brand as an LGBTQ+ Entrepreneur." 2024. Accessed November 10, 2024. https://scottdylan.com/blog/pride-month/building-your-personal-brand-as-an-lgbtq-entrepreneur/.

Faizan, R., and A. U. Haque. "The Relationship between Societal Attributes, Feminine Leadership & Management Style: Responses from Pakistan's Urban Region Female-Owned Businesses." *European Journal of Business and Management* 8, no. 23 (2016): 171–191.

Faizan, R., A. U. Haque, A. Cockrill, and J. Aston. "Females at Strategic Level Affecting Logistics Firms' Competitiveness: Qualitative Comparative Analysis." *Forum Scientiae Oeconomia* 7, no. 1 (2019): 57–71.

Galloway, L., I. Kapasi, and K. J. C. Sang. "Entrepreneurship, Leadership, and the Value of Feminist Approaches to Understanding Them." *International Small Business Journal* 33, no. 5 (2015): 477–489.

Gamarel, K. E., L. Jadwin-Cakmak, W. M. King, A. Lacombe-Duncan, R. Trammell, L. A. Reyes, C. Burks, B. Rivera, E. Arnold, and G. W. Harper. "Stigma Experienced by Transgender Women of Color in Their Dating and Romantic Relationships: Implications for Gender-Based Violence Prevention Programs." *Journal of Interpersonal Violence* 37, nos. 9–10 (2022): NP8161–NP8189.

Hughto, J. M. W., S. L. Reisner, and J. E. Pachanks. "Transgender Stigma and Health: A Critical Review of Stigma Determinants, Mechanisms, and Interventions." *Social Science & Medicine* 147 (2015): 222–231.

Jefferson, K., T. B. Neilands, and J. Sevelius. "Transgender Women of Color: Discrimination and Depression Symptoms." *Ethnic Inequality in Health and Social Care* 6, no. 4 (2013): 121–136.

Kaur, H., and A. U. Haque. "The Impact of Occupational Stress on the Performance of Employees in Competitive Sectors: Systematic Review." *International Journal of Applied Business and Management Studies* 9, no. 1 (2024): 1–7.

Köllen, T., ed. *Sexual Orientation and Transgender Issues in Organizations: Global Perspectives on LGBT Workforce Diversity*. Springer, 2016.

Martinez Dy, A., L. Martin, and S. Marlow. "Developing a Critical Realist Positional Approach to Intersectionality." *Journal of Critical Realism* 13, no. 5 (2014): 447–466.

Moser, J., J. E. Booth, and A. Beauregard. "Challenges and Opportunities for LGBTQI+ Inclusion at Work." In *Handbook on Management and Employment Practices*, 481–501. Springer, 2022.

Murad, M., and N. A. S. B. Rambley. "Factors Leading Marginalized Transgenders towards Digital Entrepreneurship in Pakistan." *Journal of Entrepreneurship and Business Venturing* 4, no. 1 (2024): 257–281.

Rietveld, C. A., and P. C. Patel. "Gender Inequality and the Entrepreneurial Gender Gap: Evidence from 97 Countries (2006–2017)." *Journal of Evolutionary Economics* 32 (2022): 1205–1229.

S, G. S. M., R. A. B., G. B., S. S., R. S., and E. E. "Transgender Entrepreneurs: An Alternative Path to Social Integration." In *Corporate Practices: Policies, Methodologies, and Insights in Organizational Management*, edited by S. Kot, B. Khalid, and A. U. Haque, 1–20. Springer, 2024. https://link.springer.com/chapter/10.1007/978-981-97-0996-0_10#citeas

Thoroughgood, C. N., K. Sawyer, and J. R. Webster. "Creating a Trans-Inclusive Workplace." *Harvard Business Review*, 2020. Accessed November 10, 2024. https://hbr.org/2020/03/creating-a-trans-inclusive-workplace.

Velinov, E., P. Strach, V. Vassilev, N. Gergova, and N. Konovalova. "Psychological Well-Being and Readiness of Employees for Organizational Changes from Tertiary Education Institutions." *Forum Scientiae Oeconomia* 12, no. 1 (2024): 39–52.

Case Study: Navigating the Entrepreneurial Landscape: A Case Study of Transgender Entrepreneur

Harmandeep Kaur

The awareness and recognition by the entrepreneurial landscape regarding the unique difficulties transgender entrepreneurs faced over the course of the last several decades have significantly increased. The focus of this case is on a transgender entrepreneur, Alver, a pioneer of gender-inclusive fashion who set up an online boutique. Alver's entrepreneurial journey demonstrates the institutional difficulties, social and societal stigmas, and structural obstacles and barriers that transgender entrepreneurs face while pursuing their own businesses and small-scale ventures.

At the start, the biggest obstacle for Alver was to secure funding. A trend of prejudice, discrimination and bias among investors was evident and reflected in traditional banks' usual reluctance to lend funds to transgender people running and managing businesses. Due to limited access to funds, Alver was compelled to start his own venture through crowdfunding initiatives and bootstrapping (personal saving and resources). Although these obstacles existed, Alver nevertheless successfully managed and marketed his venture by using digital platforms for specialized audiences, establishing a significant online presence that conveys the message of the brand's inclusivity.

In Alver's entrepreneurial journey, another important factor that played a pivotal role was social barriers. The sense and feeling of isolation mounted for Alver when many LGBTQ+ support groups initially ignored his entrepreneurial venture. Nonetheless, Alver found enormous support once the awareness and recognition grew widely about the significance of

intersectionality in the business world. The establishment of relationships and strategic partnership with other LGBTQ+ businesses started to thrive, resulting in the formation of a supportive network that not only promoted collaboration but also enhanced the transgender business owners' visibility worldwide.

The concept of inclusivity grew and was more openly embraced by the corporate world as Alver's venture continued to grow. Opportunities for Alver further expanded as he participated in training programs and pitch events that were customized by major corporations with the intention of helping marginalized groups. This helped in attaining essential and invaluable resources as well as initiated the process of removing the prejudices and biases that were hindering for long transgender individuals' participation in the entrepreneurial world for so long. Alver did not give up the hope and continued to make the most of the available opportunities, irrespective of how small the margin was. Although there are still many difficulties and obstacles to tackle, the growth and expansion of digital platforms and increasing acceptance regarding intersectional identities have offered transgender entrepreneurs' opportunities to thrive. The story of Alver's entrepreneurial journey is a testament to hope, adaptability, and resilience against all odds.

Reflection Questions

- What different systemic difficulties Alver have encountered when attempting to secure capital for their business?
- Briefly explain how digital platforms played a role in the success of Alver's entrepreneurial journey.
- How has the changing business environment affected the resources accessible to transgender entrepreneurs, as reflected in the case of Alver?
- Why is it essential for LGBTQ+ support networks to include transgender entrepreneurs in their initiatives?

Chapter 12

Entrepreneurial Stress and Structural Support

Irfan ul Haq and Riffat Faizan

12.0 Behind the Curtain: Stress and Entrepreneurs

Stress can be defined as the imbalance between environmental demands (Lazarus, 1966; Haque and Aston, 2016; Haque, 2023; Kaur and Haque, 2024) and an individual's ability to cope with the consequential demands (Contrada and Baum, 2011). However, eustress, also known as good stress or little stress, is useful for focus and performance, as it triggers the release of adrenaline in the body (Sapolsky, 2004; Faizan and Haque, 2019; Haque, 2020). The brain region that processes emotions is called the amygdala; it sends distress signals to the hypothalamus, which functions as a command center for the body. The hypothalamus communicates through the nervous system, which triggers a response to either escape the threat or confront the perceived stress (Sapolsky, 2004; McEwen, 2007). This phenomenon is described as the "fight-or-flight" reaction (Selye, 1936; Haque, 2023). While eustress is good for entrepreneurs, as it helps individuals perform in the demanding field, distress or bad stress must be identified and managed to ensure the mental well-being of entrepreneurs (Haque and Yamoah, 2021; Haq et al., 2024a).

Entrepreneurial stress refers to the physical, emotional, and psychological strain that is inherent in the uncertainties, demands, and challenges of starting a new venture (Rauch et al., 2018). In other words, we can argue that entrepreneurial stress can be referred to as entrepreneurial distress. Contributing factors that worsen stress include vulnerability to socioeconomic conditions and resource scarcity (Clough et al., 2019). Thus, the potential impact of entrepreneurial stress affects individuals' health as well as the success of entrepreneurial ventures. Furthermore, this stress encompasses a range of pressures, such as financial instability, extended work hours, market competition, decision-making dilemmas and the constant need to adapt to changes. By recognizing these stressors, effective strategies can be developed and implemented to manage entrepreneurial stress (Lerman et al., 2020).

Prolonged and unmanaged stress can lead to health issues such as insomnia, anxiety, depression, and an increased risk of burnout (Hobfoll et al., 2018; Haque, 2022). A plethora of research confirms that personal relationships may become strained due to financial pressure and time constraints, which can lead to decreased productivity and hinder innovation (Freeman, 2015; Thompson, 2019). In other words, professional and personal well-being are at stake. In the absence of proper coping mechanisms, sustaining long-term resilience in facing these challenges could be difficult (Freeman, 2015; Bregman, 2019). Thus, developing a sustainable long-term coping mechanism is imperative to ensure the long-term physical and mental well-being of entrepreneurs.

DOI: 10.4324/9781003504351-12

12.1 Dissect and Dismantle: Understanding the Causes of Entrepreneurial Stress

Several factors contribute to entrepreneurial stress, each stemming from the unique demands and challenges of starting and running a business. Financial pressure is one of the primary sources of entrepreneurial stress, as it directly impacts the viability and success of the business. Research shows a significant relationship between financial hardship and impaired well-being among entrepreneurs (Annink, 2016; Haq et al., 2024a). Securing initial funding is a constant constraint; for entrepreneurs, managing loans, investor expectations, and potential financial losses can be particularly intimidating.

Although entrepreneurial stress is often perceived as challenging, recognizing its positive aspects can transform it into a catalyst for growth and success. For example, entrepreneurs can use financial stress as motivation to develop effective financial management strategies. Seeking professional advice, diversifying funding sources, and maintaining a buffer for unexpected expenses are essential strategies for mitigating financial stress in entrepreneurship. However, since entrepreneurs differ in their personalities, their perceptions of stress and resilience may vary (Haque, 2024).

High levels of economic uncertainty and significant time and deadline pressure are also prominent stressors in entrepreneurial ventures (White and Gupta, 2020). Hence, the viability of a business is often closely linked to financial pressure. As a business grows, the need for additional support in the form of staff and funding increases to expand market shares. Furthermore, achieving and maintaining profitability is a constant concern for entrepreneurs, compounded by uncertainties in market demand, economic fluctuations, and financial instability. Eustress, or "good stress," encourages entrepreneurs to seek cost-effective solutions and explore alternative approaches to operational challenges (Haque et al., 2020). Thus, striking a fine balance is essential to ensure that stress remains manageable and controlled.

Entrepreneurs often put their personal finances on the line (Haq et al., 2024a). The risk of losing personal savings, mortgaging homes, or draining retirement funds adds significant stress, particularly if the business faces difficulties. However, this situation also encourages the optimization of resources, reduces unnecessary expenses, and promotes efficiency and sustainability. Managing these financial burdens while ensuring continued growth adds another layer of pressure. Effectively managing stress enhances leadership capabilities, as entrepreneurs learn to make tough decisions under pressure (Haque, 2024).

In many cases, entrepreneurs use their personal assets and finances—such as savings, remortgaging, or even retirement funds—to support their ventures. They operate under the pressure of being responsible for the well-being of their entrepreneurial ventures (Grant and Ferris, 2012). Therefore, effective and efficient decision-making, organizational leadership, and precise control over various processes are crucial.

Compared with employees, entrepreneurs experience higher levels of stress (Cardon and Patel, 2015). When an entrepreneur experiences work-related stress, it can negatively impact their subordinates. As stress levels rise, work quality tends to decline, leading to decreased overall productivity and effectiveness, especially as the demand to stay competitive increases. In addition, business growth may present entrepreneurs with challenges in managing internal team dynamics. Conflicts within the team can also be a source of entrepreneurial stress (Bentlage, 2017). Role conflicts and unclear job responsibilities within a team can increase stress and lead to internal tensions.

Because entrepreneurs serve as role models for their employees, they can harness stress as fuel ambition and drive them to achieve ambitious goals. The pressure to succeed may inspire creative problem solving and innovation within the business (Haq et al., 2024b). In the early business stages, the success of a business relies heavily on the founder's individual performance and contribution (Rauch and Frese, 2007; Bentlage, 2017). This heavy reliance on the founder's input also increases stressors due to ambiguity and undefined roles and responsibilities, as entrepreneurs often juggle multiple roles, such as being manager, marketer and accountant. This multitasking can overwhelm entrepreneurs as they balance conflicting demands.

The ability to self-regulate and cope with stress in the entrepreneurial process can be hindered by negative emotions (Przepiorka & Blachino, 2016). Additionally, the relationship between stress levels and concerns about business failure can impair an entrepreneur's decision-making ability, potentially leading to poor strategic choices and accelerating the timeline for business failure.

12.2 The Equation: Unravelling the Impact of Entrepreneurial Stress

The stress experienced by entrepreneurs is a complex issue arising from the distinct demands and uncertainties associated with entrepreneurship endeavors. The constant pressure for innovation and growth, market competition, financial uncertainties, and venture setbacks greatly impact the well-being of entrepreneurs.

Financial uncertainty, often in the form of bootstrapping – relying on limited resources or self-funding – can be a significant contributor to stress. The stress level can intensify due to challenges in cash flow management, inconsistent revenue streams, and financial forecasting difficulties. Entrepreneurs perform diverse roles across the organization, including operations, finance, marketing, and, at times, even customer service. Balancing workload and time management becomes challenging, leading to burn out and reduced productivity. The pressure to stay competitive in the market adds further stress, as entrepreneurs strive to remain ahead in the competitive landscape. Additionally, persistent fatigue and fear of failure can lead to the development and worsening of mental health issues. Over time, these stressors may contribute to chronic stress, which can deteriorate physical and emotional well-being, leading to depression, isolation and reluctance to seek help due to perceived stigma.

While stress is an inevitable aspect of the entrepreneurial journey, its impact can be mitigated through proactive strategies and support systems. The first step is to identify and recognize the sources of stress, prioritize mental health, and foster resilience so that entrepreneurs can sustain their mental well-being while navigating the complexities of business ownership.

12.3 Building Stability: Structural Support for Entrepreneurs

The intrinsic uncertainties and challenges of entrepreneurial endeavors are inherent key aspects of entrepreneurship, which vary significantly depending on environmental factors and the operating environment. Therefore, there is an evident need for effective support systems within the private sector. Allocating time properly, defining work boundaries, and maintaining a work–life balance can foster healthy habits and help minimize stress, paving the way for developing resilience.

In addition, embracing change and learning from setbacks can strengthen resilience in the face of challenges. Entrepreneurial stress is a significant issue that requires proactive management and support. By acknowledging its sources, understanding its impact, and implementing effective coping strategies, entrepreneurs can enhance their resilience and well-being. Ultimately, addressing entrepreneurial stress not only benefits individual entrepreneurs but also contributes to a more sustainable and innovative entrepreneurial ecosystem.

12.3.1 Mentorship System

The mentorship system plays a crucial role in supporting entrepreneurial well-being by pairing less experienced entrepreneurs with seasoned mentors who can provide guidance, share experiences, and offer emotional support as coping mechanisms for stressors. One-on-one mentoring, peer-group mentoring, and reverse mentoring programs enable goal alignment through matching programs, where mentors are paired with their mentees based on shared goals, personalities, and expertise. However, finding the right mentor–mentee match can be a crucial element in entrepreneurial success. Mentors offer strategic advice on business planning, market strategies, and operational efficiencies, providing entrepreneurs with invaluable insights and lessons learned. Moreover, mentorship programs offer emotional support to help entrepreneurs overcome setbacks and challenges, fostering resilience through encouragement and knowledge transfer. However, sustaining a long-term mentoring relationship can be challenging because of the time commitment required from both mentees and mentors. Mentors assist mentees in making informed decisions by sharing industry-specific knowledge, trends, and best practices. Additionally, with access to a broader network of mentors, entrepreneurs can learn to develop critical skills such as leadership, negotiation, and problem solving. The mentorship system helps entrepreneurs focus on goals and minimizes stress levels.

12.3.2 Wellness Programs

Wellness programs support business leaders and entrepreneurs by enhancing their mental, physical, and emotional well-being. The high-stress nature of entrepreneurship can reduce productivity and lead to burnout. However, the introduction of wellness programs that focus on mental and physical health can empower entrepreneurs, enabling them to achieve a clear work–life balance and a proactive approach to managing stress. Good mental and physical health contributes to improved decision-making through clearer thinking and better judgment. A well-rounded wellness routine enhances creativity and innovation, fostering healthier entrepreneurs who are more focused, energized, and productive when addressing challenges. Entrepreneurs can benefit from flexible work hours and environments that support work–life balance. Tailoring wellness initiatives to meet the specific needs of entrepreneurs helps address stressors in a proactive manner. Moreover, wellness programs can help overcome the stigma associated with seeking emotional wellness support. Trained mental health professionals specializing in stress management, depression, and anxiety are essential for these programs, and continuous evaluation and feedback are necessary to match the programs to entrepreneurs' evolving needs. Wellness programs are essential for fostering a thriving and sustainable entrepreneurial ecosystem.

12.3.3 Financial Planning Services

Financial planning services are a powerful tool for entrepreneurs, significantly reducing stress by providing clarity, stability, and strategic guidance. Access to financial advisors who assist entrepreneurs in managing financial stress and planning for long-term stability can be highly effective. Financial education empowers entrepreneurs to manage cash flow effectively and optimize expenses, allowing them to focus confidently on growing their businesses. Entrepreneurs often face unique financial challenges due to fluctuating business environments, which contributes to stress and anxiety; proactive financial planning addresses these challenges. Knowledge of financial planning provides entrepreneurs with tools to mitigate financial risk and develop strategies for sustainable growth and effective decision-making. Financial stability reduces the fear of uncertainty, offering a clear understanding of cash flow, expenses, and revenue projections. Skills in cash flow management, debt consolidation, expense management, and investment planning reduce financial anxiety, providing clarity and control over financial situations and helping entrepreneurs navigate uncertainties. With a solid financial foundation, entrepreneurs can concentrate on strategic growth initiatives without being hindered by financial worries.

12.3.4 Mental Support App – 24/7

A 24/7 mental support app for entrepreneurs would provide easy access to licensed therapists and counsellors, helping entrepreneurs cope with various stressors (Haq et al., 2024b). This app offers a reliable, accessible support system that accommodates entrepreneurs' hectic and often inconsistent schedules (Haque et al., 2024), ensuring privacy, anonymity, and quick access. The affordability of mental health support is a significant factor, as SMEs may struggle to justify higher costs for such services. In the digital age, features such as reminders and goal-setting options on the app help entrepreneurs remain engaged and on track with self-care routines.

12.3.5 Awareness Balance Control (ABC) Model

Awareness, balance, and control models (Haque et al., 2018; Haque, 2020) are imperative in ensuring self-understanding for entrepreneurs by developing awareness of their behavior, emotions and thoughts. This model aids in identifying various stressors and allows for early intervention (Haq et al., 2024b). In other words, entrepreneurs become aware of their mental state, seek balance, and gain control over their actions, enhancing self-efficacy. Through the ABC model, entrepreneurs can achieve mental clarity, cope with anxiety, and reduce the impact of stress, improving their resilience in this demanding field.

12.3.6 Educational Workshops

Educational workshops are a critical component of entrepreneurial development, providing invaluable knowledge, skills, and networking opportunities. These workshops empower entrepreneurs to navigate challenges and seize opportunities for sustainable growth. Investing in learning through workshops enhances entrepreneurs' competitiveness in constantly evolving business landscaping. Workshops focused on business planning and strategy help entrepreneurs outline their mission, vision, objectives, and strategies. Sessions on goal setting, aligning business activities, and long-term planning introduce strategic thinking. Education on operational efficiency and technology adoption enables entrepreneurs to extend their reach, integrate innovative ideas, and implement lean methodologies. In addition, workshops help develop leadership capabilities and effective team management and foster a positive organizational culture, equipping entrepreneurs to manage conflicts, negotiate solutions, and maintain a harmonious workplace. Engaging industry experts as facilitators encourages innovation through practical exercises, simulations, and case studies. Sessions led by successful entrepreneurs and professional industry trainers as invaluable insights into these workshops

12.4 Navigating Turbulence: Effective Coping Strategies

Entrepreneurial stress is a common challenge; however, with targeted coping strategies and effective techniques, its impact can be managed and minimized. Entrepreneurs can significantly improve their resilience and well-being by establishing work–life balance and a reliable support system as an initial coping mechanism. Time management, physical and mental health practices, and organizational strategies all assist in managing stress, which not only contributes to the success of entrepreneurial ventures but also provides personal fulfillment. By identifying, prioritizing, and focusing on high-impact responsibilities, entrepreneurs can distinguish between urgent and important tasks. Creating structured schedules is an effective tool for managing tasks efficiently and for allocating appropriate time for both work and personal activities. In addition, effective task delegation frees up time for essential activities, especially strategic decision-making.

In addition, fostering a positive mindset and organizational culture enables entrepreneurs to focus on overcoming setbacks and planning for future growth. Viewing setbacks as opportunities for learning can be a vital part of an entrepreneurial journey, promoting a better understanding of the evolving business landscape and revealing growth opportunities. Adaptability in response to unexpected challenges enhances operational efficiency and supports effective organizational strategies. Automated tools, management software, and communication technologies reduce workload, whereas realistic goal setting and breaking large goals into manageable tasks help to avoid overload and burnout. Moreover, keeping up with industry trends through continuous learning not only enhances knowledge and skills but also increases confidence and reduces stress by preparing entrepreneurs for the challenges ahead.

12.5 Embracing the Journey: Empowering Entrepreneurs for Success

Entrepreneurship is often viewed as a path to freedom, innovation, and financial success (Haq et al., 2024b); however, this journey is not without significant challenges, with stress being a primary obstacle (He et al., 2018). One such example of resilience is Adolf Dassler, Adidas' founder, who faced intense competition from other shoemakers in Bavaria, Germany. Dassler gathered direct feedback from the athletes to understand their specific needs. This process was highly draining, stressful, and energy consuming; however, it helped Dassler to improve designs by focusing on athletes' requirements and pain points, leading to the establishment of Adidas as a renowned brand. Entrepreneurs can navigate similar challenges actively observing areas of improvement and through effective listening.

By developing resilience in the face of challenges and effectively managing various adversities, entrepreneurs can navigate the challenges of their journey more effectively, ensuring both personal well-being and business growth. Entrepreneurial resilience is defined as the process by which an individual builds and uses his/her capability endowments to interact with the environment in a way that positively adjusts and maintains functioning prior to, during, and following adversity (Sheppard et al., 2020). Therefore, for entrepreneurs, it is critical to be adaptive and proactive in dealing with adversity, facilitating both personal and organizational success. Entrepreneurs can overcome adversity to promote entrepreneurial health and success (Newman et al., 2018). Entrepreneurs can rely on their psychological resources, such as psychological resilience, for positive adoption. Psychological resources, such as psychological resilience, are needed for positive adaptation despite adversity (Sutcliffe and Vogus, 2003). Since entrepreneurial stress can have a profound psychological impact, an entrepreneur's psychological resilience can be an effective tool to interact with the environment in a way that leads to a positive outcome.

The term adversity is defined as "an unfortunate event or circumstance or the state of serious and continued difficulty" (Fan et al., 2014, p. 252). In the context of entrepreneurship, the term can translate into losing an important investor (i.e., an acute event) or facing a high likelihood of venture failure over extended periods (that is, chronic circumstances). The experience of adversity and significant challenges, along with positive adaptation despite these obstacles, highlights the resilience and strength of individuals. It underscores the ability to navigate and overcome obstacles, transforming difficult experiences into opportunities for growth and development.

Moreover, entrepreneurs draw on their individual capability endowments to cope with adversity. The capability endowments include affective or emotional capabilities, such as positive emotions such as optimism or hope, and emotional regulation (Hayward et al., 2010); cognitive endowments, such as knowledge or creativity; and behavioral endowments, such as seeking social support (Sheppard et al., 2020). These capabilities enable entrepreneurs to overcome various adversities through positive adaptation. Furthermore, this adaptation stems from an entrepreneur's ability to recover through resilience.

Entrepreneurs may retain a sense of happiness, optimism, and vitality even during tough times, which helps them remain motivated and focused on their goals (Sheppard et al., 2020; Hartmann et al., 2022). Positive attitudes toward entrepreneurship give individuals the necessary persistence in uncertain environments (Pérez-López et al., 2016; González-López et al., 2019). This resilience can be seen, for example, in their ability to deliver a compelling pitch that attracts investors or partners, despite earlier setbacks. Moreover, resilience allows entrepreneurs to bounce back, adapt strategies, and ultimately achieve success. In other words, resilience also manifests in the new skills and capabilities that entrepreneurs develop as they navigate challenges. This includes their ability to learn from failures and apply those lessons to future ventures. For instance, they might gain insights into market strategies, customer relations, or operational efficiencies that enhance their ability to successfully launch new ventures in the future.

12.6 Conclusion

In conclusion, entrepreneurial stress is an unavoidable aspect of the entrepreneurial journey. It can significantly impact personal well-being as well as business success. Nonetheless, through the adoption of proactive coping strategies, including effective time management, support systems, mentorship, and resilience-building practices, entrepreneurs can efficiently and effectively deal with different types of stressors. Additionally, these adversities and challenges provide crucial growth opportunities.

Bibliography

Annink, A. "Using the Research Journal During Qualitative Data Collection in a Cross-Cultural Context." *Entrepreneurship Research Journal* 7 (2016): Article ID: 20150063. https://doi.org/10.1515/erj-2015-0063.

Bentlage, J. "The Entrepreneurial Stress Circle – a Grounded Theory Approach." University of Twente Student Theses, 2017. https://essay.utwente.nl/72889/.

Bregman, M. "The Relationship Between Entrepreneurship, Business and Mental Health." *Pop Culture Intersections* 36 (2019). https://scholarcommons.scu.edu/engl_176/36.

Clough, B. A., M. Zarean, I. Ruane, N. J. Mateo, T. A. Aliyeva, and L. M. Casey. "Going Global: Do Consumer Preferences, Attitudes, and Barriers to Using E-Mental Health Services Differ Across Countries?" *Journal of Mental Health* 28, no. 1 (2019): 17–25. https://doi.org/10.1080/09638237.2017.1370639.

Contrada, R. J., and A. Baum (Eds.). *The handbook of stress science: Biology, psychology, and health.* Springer Publishing Company, 2011.

Cardon, M. S., and P. C. Patel. "Is Stress Worth it? Stress-related Health and Wealth Trade-offs for Entrepreneurs." *Applied Psychology: An International Review*, 64, no. 2 (2015): 379–420. https://doi.org/10.1111/apps.12021

Faizan, R., and A. U. Haque. "Working Efficiency of Contrasting Genders Under Eustress, Distress, Hyper-Stress, and Hypo-Stress." *Prabandhan: Indian Journal of Management* 12, no. 11 (2019): 32–46.

Fan, S., Z. L. Tian, J. Lin, and B. L. Wang. "Review and Prospect of Companies Hypocrisy Based on Social Responsibility Perspective." *Foreign Economics & Management* 36 (2014): 2–12.

Freeman, D., R. Emsley, G. Dunn, D. Fowler, P. Bebbington, E. Kuipers, S. Jolley, H. Waller, A. Hardy, and P. Garety. "The Stress of the Street for Patients with Persecutory Delusions: A Test of the Symptomatic and Psychological Effects of Going Outside into a Busy Urban Area." *Schizophrenia Bulletin* 41, no. 4 (2015): 971–979. https://doi.org/10.1093/schbul/sbu173.

González-López, M. J., M. C. Pérez-López, and L. Rodríguez-Ariza. "Clearing the Hurdles in the Entrepreneurial Race: The Role of Resilience in Entrepreneurship Education." *Academy of Management Learning & Education* 18, no. 3 (2019): 457–483. https://doi.org/10.5465/amle.2016.0377.

Haq, I., Haque, A. U., and N. A. A. Rahim. "Entrepreneurial Stress and Mental Well-Being: Pre- and Post-COVID-19 Comparative Analysis of SMEs in Canada." *Forum Scientiae Oeconomia* 12, no. 1 (2024a): 53–71.

Haq, I. U., Haque, A. U., A. Kaur, and N. A. A. Rahim. "Occupational Stress Affecting Innovative Capabilities and Innovative Work Behavior of Migrant Entrepreneurs." *Polish Journal of Management Studies* 9, no. 2 (2024b): 238–253. https://doi.org/10.17512/pjms.2024.29.2.12.

Haque, A. U. "Varying Occupational Stress and Organisational Commitment Within the University Staff of Contrasting Economies (Cross-Sectional Comparative Study of Middle Range Public

Universities in Pakistan and the UK)." *Research Repository* (2020). https://repository.uwtsd.ac.uk/id/eprint/1570/.

Haque, A. U. *Handbook of Research on the Complexities and Strategies of Occupational Stress.* IGI Global, 2022. https://doi.org/10.4018/978-1-6684-3937-1.

Haque, A. U. Handbook of Research on Dissecting and Dismantling Occupational Stress in Modern Organizations. IGI Global, 2023. https://doi.org/10.4018/978-1-6684-6543-1.

Haque, A. U. *How Occupational Stress Impact the Innovative Work Behaviour and Innovative Entrepreneurial Capabilities of Migrant Entrepreneurs in Contrasting Economies?* In: Hyams-Ssekasi, D., Daskalaki, E. (eds) Migration and Entrepreneurship in the Global Context. Palgrave Studies in Entrepreneurship and Society. Palgrave Macmillan, Cham, 2024. DOI: 10.1007/978-3-031-34067-3_2

Haque, A. U., and J. Aston. "A Relationship Between Occupational Stress and Organizational Commitment of I.T Sector's Employees in Contrasting Economies." *Polish Journal of Management Studies* 14, no. 1 (2016): 95–105.

Haque, A. U., Aston, J., Kozlovski, E., and Caha, Z. "Role of External CSR and Social Support Programme for Sustaining Human Capital in Contrasting Economies." *Polish Journal of Management Studies* 22, no. 1 (2020): 147–168.

Haque, A. U., and F. A. Yamoah. "The Role of Ethical Leadership in Managing Occupational Stress to Promote Innovative Work Behaviour: A Cross-Cultural Management Perspective." *Sustainability* 13, no. 17 (2021): 9608. https://doi.org/10.3390/su13179608.

Hartmann, S., J. Backmann, A. Newman, K. M. Brykman, and R. J. Pidduck. "Psychological Resilience of Entrepreneurs: A Review and Agenda for Future Research." *Journal of Small Business Management* 60, no. 5 (2022): 1041–1079. https://doi.org/10.1080/00472778.2021.2024216.

Hayward, M. M., W. R. Forster, S. D. Sarasvathy, and B. L. Fredrickson. "Beyond hubris: How highly Confident Entrelireneurs Rebound to Venture Again." *Journal of Business Venturing* 25 no. 6 (2010): 569–578.

He, V. F., C. Sirén, S. Singh, G. Solomon, and G. Von Krogh. "Keep Calm and Carry On: Emotion Regulation in Entrepreneurs' Learning from Failure." *Entrepreneurship Theory and Practice* 42, no. 4 (2018): 605–630. https://doi.org/10.1177/1042258718783428.

Hobfoll, S. E., J. Halbesleben, J.-P. Neveu, and M. Westman. "Conservation of Resources in the Organizational Context: The Reality of Resources and Their Consequences." *Annual Review of Organizational Psychology and Organizational Behavior* 5 (2018): 103–128. https://doi.org/10.1146/annurev-orgpsych-032117-104640

Kaur, H., and A. U. Haque. "The Impact of Occupational Stress on the Performance of Employees in Competitive Sectors: Systematic Review." *International Journal of Applied Business and Management Studies* 9, no. 1 (2024): 1–7.

Lazarus, R.S. "Cognition and Motivation in Emotion." *American Psychologist* 46 (1996): 352. http://dx.doi.org/10.1037/0003-066X.46.4.352

Lerman, D. C., M. J. O'Brien, L. Neely, N. A. Call, L. Tsami, K. M. Schieltz, W. K. Berg, J. Graber, P. Huang, T. Kopelman, and L. J. Cooper-Brown. "Remote Coaching of Caregivers via Telehealth: Challenges and Potential Solutions." *Journal of Behavioral Education* 29, no. 2 (2020): 195–221. https://doi.org/10.1007/s10864-020-09378-2

McEwen, B. S. "Physiology and Neurobiology of Stress and Adaptation: Central Role of the Brain." *Physiological Reviews* 87, no. 3 (2007): 873–904.

Newman, E. L., M. Z. Leonard, D. T. Arena, R. M. M. de Almeida, and K. A. Miczek. "Social Defeat Stress and Escalation of Cocaine and Alcohol Consumption: Focus on CRF." *Neurobiology of Stress* 9 (2018): 151–165. https://doi.org/10.1016/j.ynstr.2018.09.007

Przepiorka, A., and A. Blachnio. "Time Perspective in Internet and Facebook Addiction." *Computers in Human Behavior* 60 (2016): 13–18. https://doi.org/10.1016/j.chb.2016.02.045

Rauch, A., and M. Frese. "Let's Put the Person Back into Entrepreneurship Research: A Meta-Analysis on the Relationship Between Business Owners' Personality Traits, Business Creation, and Success." *European Journal of Work and Organizational Psychology* 16, no. 4 (2007): 353–385. https://doi.org/10.1080/13594320701595438

Rauch, S., E. Jasny, K. E. Schmidt, and B. Petsch. "New Vaccine Technologies to Combat Outbreak Situations." *Frontiers in Immunology* 9 (2018): 1963. https://doi.org/10.3389/fimmu.2018.01963

Sapolsky, R. M. "Stress and Cognition." In *The Cognitive Neurosciences*, 3rd ed., edited by M. S. Gazzaniga, 1031–1042. Boston Review, 2004.

Selye, H. "A Syndrome Produced by Diverse Nocuous Agents." *Nature* 138 (1936): 32. https://doi.org/10.1038/138032a0

Sheppard, J. P., J. Burt, M. Lown, E. Temple, R. Lowe, R. Fraser, J. Allen, G. A. Ford, C. Heneghan, F. D. R. Hobbs, S. Jowett, S. Kodabuckus, P. Little, J. Mant, J. Mollison, R. A. Payne, M. Williams, L. M. Yu, R. J. McManus, and OPTIMISE Investigators. "Effect of Antihypertensive Medication Reduction vs Usual Care on Short-Term Blood Pressure Control in Patients with Hypertension Aged 80 Years and Older: The OPTIMISE Randomized Clinical Trial." *JAMA* 323, no. 20 (2020): 2039–2051. https://doi.org/10.1001/jama.2020.4871

Sutcliffe, K. M., and T. J. Vogus. "Organizing for Resilience." In *Positive Organizational Scholarship: Foundations of a New Discipline*, edited by K. S. Cameron, J. E. Dutton, and R. E. Quinn, 94–110. Berrett-Koehler, 2003.

Thompson, R. R., N. M. Jones, E. A. Holman, and R. C. Silver. "Media Exposure to Mass Violence Events Can Fuel a Cycle of Distress." *Science Advances* 5, no. 4 (2019): eaav3502. https://doi.org/10.1126/sciadv.aav3502

White, J. V., and V. K. Gupta. "Stress and Well-Being in Entrepreneurship: A Critical Review and Future Research Agenda." In *Entrepreneurial and Small Business Stressors, Experienced Stress, and Well-Being*, edited by P. L. Perrewé, P. D. Harms, and C.-H. Chang, 65–93. Emerald Publishing, 2020. https://doi.org/10.1108/S1479-355520200000018004

Case Study: The Journey of Mariyah Joseph – Overcoming Entrepreneurial Stress

Adnan ul Haque and Harmandeep Kaur

Background

EcoAuraCandles is an entrepreneurial venture founded by Mariyah Joseph in her mid-30s. The company manufactures eco-friendly (sustainable) candles. She started this venture two years ago, driven by her love for a green earth – her passion for environmental sustainability. The aim was to promote her philosophy of saving the earth by creating a positive impact. However, soon she faced the harsh realities of the entrepreneurial journey, which is not smooth. She was excited, yet overwhelmed, by several stressors such as finding a balance between professional commitments and personal responsibilities, financial burdens, and a looming fear of failure.

Identifying and comprehending the Stressors

Mariyah found herself facing increasing demands as EcoAuraCandles gained popularity. Orders began to flood in, exceeding the earlier capacity limit. Being swamped with orders, she worked late into the night and woke up early in the morning. She found herself struggling to complete orders and manage inventory in efficient and effective manner while also trying to balance adequate customer service and execute marketing initiatives. She was burning out, with visible sign of anxiety due to the ever-growing pressure.

Establishing Support Systems to Encourage Stability

Mariyah approached a local entrepreneurship network for support, and she received invaluable mentorship assistance as her business and health suffered from uncontrollable stress. Her mentor was a very seasoned business professional who provided invaluable advice on how to effectively delegate business activities and manage time efficiently. The mentor's guidance proved vital in helping her overcome these challenges and avoid common pitfalls. Furthermore, besides mentorship Mariyah joined a customized health and wellness program specifically designed for business professionals. She benefited from stress reduction and mindfulness, which were emphasized in the program as techniques for stress management. Additionally, she sought financial planning services to manage her cash effectively, preparing her for future growth and development.

Using Technology to Aid

Mariyah opted to use an application specifically designed for entrepreneurs' mental health, ensuring her mental health needs were addressed. The application granted access to guided meditations at any time, day or night – essentially 24/7. In addition to that, its community forum allowed her to share her stories and receive support from other entrepreneurs. In other words, it served as both a form of ventilation therapy and a source of community support.

Educational Workshops and Continuing Education

She actively participated in training and educational seminars, especially on effective business practices and stress management. These training sessions provided her with a deeper understanding of the business environment as well as practical and relevant coping strategies.

Results

Mariyah combined financial planning, health and wellness initiatives, mentorship, and continuous education to develop a more viable and comprehensive business model. With the passage of time, she mastered organizational skills, learned to set priorities, balanced work and life by managing her workload, and built a strong support network. Now EcoAuraCandles has moved out of survival mode and is gearing up for growth and further success. She credits her proactive approach and never-giving-up attitude in effectively managing stress.

Reflection Questions

- What were the stressors affecting Mariyah, and how were her personal and professional life impacted?
- Reflect on how Mariyah benefited from wellness programs and mentorship? What other techniques could be employed to assist other entrepreneurs?
- How did financial planning enable Mariyah? How could entrepreneurs manage their stress through financial management?
- Examine how the adoption of technology – such as mental health apps – impacts the mental health of the entrepreneurs?

Chapter 13

The Impact of Artificial Intelligence on Modern Entrepreneurship

Adnan ul Haque, Diya Nitinbhai Patel and Pavlos Gkasis

13.0 Introduction

Context, connectedness, and complexity in the rapidly changing global business environment have significantly increased the competitiveness of various stakeholders in multiple economic sectors (Haque et al., 2017). Modern-day entrepreneurship is no exception to dynamic changes in the environment, and several transformations, especially in redefining and refining business strategies, operational efficiencies, stakeholder engagement, and customer interactions in diverse industries, can be attributed to the emergence of artificial intelligence (AI). This chapter explores the impact of AI on entrepreneurship through assessing its applications and the advantages, challenges, and future implications that stem from its use.

13.1 Understanding AI in Entrepreneurship

AI is "a system's ability to correctly interpret external data, to learn from such data, and to use those learnings to achieve specific goals and tasks through flexible adaptation" (Kaplan and Haenlein, 2019). Poole and Mackworth (2010) considered AI as an agent that studies and acts as an intelligent agent to analyze and synthesize computed information. Essentially, it can be described as programming human intelligence in machines to think, learn, and respond like humans do.

For entrepreneurs, AI offers various solutions, including task customization and automation, quick synthesis and analysis of large amounts of data, and accurate prediction of trends and capabilities, all of which were previously limited. Russell and Norvig (2021) stated that AI has the ability to perform a wide range of activities that require human intelligence, such as translation, speech recognition, visual perception and presentation, and decision-making. Through the lens of entrepreneurship, these activities could be pivotal in improving service automation, optimizing resources, enhancing operational efficiency, customized marketing, and predictive analytics.

13.2 AI for Innovation and Competitiveness

Entrepreneurs benefit from AI to further improve their capabilities by enhancing competitiveness and iterative innovation (Horn et al., 2022). According to the work of Davenport and Ronanki (2018), businesses can gain invaluable insights from datasets in real time by using AI-powered and supported analytics, which could then help them

DOI: 10.4324/9781003504351-13

in their strategic business planning and decision-making processes. In other words, entrepreneurs could benefit from AI-powered and supported analytics to make more informed decisions, manage risk, and develop plans with rational strategic directions by extracting valuable insights from large datasets in real time. AI is an intelligent agent that takes information from the environment and functions to respond via perceived actions (i.e., perceived response) (Russell and Norvig, 2021). Thus, entrepreneurs could focus on more creative endeavors because more routine tasks could be facilitated by AI. It offers a rapid approach, calculated measures, and appropriate actions for routine tasks. Brynjolfsson and McAfee (2017) argued that to gain a competitive edge in a saturated market, the introduction of AI could help emerging businesses and startups by offering quick responses to market demands while ensuring that products and services are novel and useful.

13.3 Key AI Technologies and Entrepreneurship

13.3.1 Machine Learning (ML)

One of the subfields of AI is machine learning (ML); it creates algorithms to support systems to learn and use this knowledge to create experiences without being explicitly programmed. In other words, algorithms use enriched experiences of tasks and feedback to improve the functionality of the assigned tasks. Interestingly, patterns are easily identified, and predictions are made effectively by ML algorithms through the analysis of large datasets, which indicates that these algorithms are not only able to forecast consumer behavior but also able to detect operational irregularities (Russell and Norvig, 2021). Hence, entrepreneurs could benefit from ML by using large datasets to understand consumer behavior, buying patterns, and preferences. Moreover, the supply chain process could be improved by earlier detection of operational inaccuracies and irregularities.

13.3.2 Natural Language Processing (NLP)

Natural Language Processing (NLP) focuses on the interactions that take place between human language and computers. Language translation tools for global communication, sentiment analysis for social media monitoring, and chatbots for customer satisfaction are powered by NLP (Jurafsky and Martin, 2019). These tools could help entrepreneurs and new startups improve their presence on social media platforms and enhance their engagement and interaction with potential target audiences.

13.3.3 Computer Vision

The visual information from the real world that is extracted and interpreted by machines is described as computer vision (Szeliski, 2010). The wide range of applications, from autonomous vehicles, which are specifically equipped with vision-based navigation systems, to facial recognition software, are prominent examples of computer vision (Szeliski, 2010). Entrepreneurs could benefit from different types of computer vision to make their products more appealing and attractive to customers.

13.4 The Impact of AI on Traditional Sectors

13.4.1 Disruption Across Economic Sectors

Traditional sectors are disrupted by AI through increased productivity, cost reduction, and process optimization. Kumar (2018) stated that AI-driven innovations are significantly transforming the retail, manufacturing, healthcare, and finance sectors. Startups in traditional sectors could benefit from AI-driven innovations; to support this argument, the following cases are extracted from more traditional sectors:

13.4.2 Healthcare

Personalized treatment plans, predictive diagnostics, and analyses of medical images can be generated from AI applications. Jiang et al. (2017) reported that AI is utilized by IBM's Watson Health for medical literature analysis as well as for examining patient data, which helps clinicians make informed and data-driven treatment decisions.

13.4.3 Retail

To a greater extent, the retail sector has been reshaped by AI-driven tools and techniques to ensure that organizations have personalized marketing campaigns, optimization of enterprise resources and inventory management, and improved customer experiences. For example, the browsing history of customers and their preferences, which are the result of AI usage, have been effectively incorporated by Amazon to drive sales and better target its audience (Marr, 2024).

13.4.4 Finance

Early detection and prevention of fraudulent activities, personalized investment advice, and improved trading strategies are supported by AI-powered algorithms in the financial sector. Davenport and Bean (2021) discussed the case of Wealthfront using AI to offer automated investment services that are customized according to the profiles of individual

Table 13.1 AI Technologies in Entrepreneurial Ventures

AI Technology	*Description*	*Example Applications*
Machine Learning (ML)	Algorithms that learn from data and improve over time without explicit programming.	Predictive analytics, fraud detection
Natural Language Processing (NLP)	Enables machines to understand, interpret, and generate human language.	Chatbots, sentiment analysis, language translation
Computer Vision	Real-world visual information interpreted by AI such as detection of objects and recognition of images	Facial recognition, autonomous vehicles

Source: *Own illustration based on the literature*

investors. Similarly, AI algorithms could be constructively used by entrepreneurs not only to develop and tailor products and/or services according to everyone's profile but also to ensure that fraudulent activities are detected and prevented in a timely manner.

13.5 Opportunities and Challenges

An extensive review of the literature confirms that many different opportunities are presented by AI, specifically for innovation and growth, but it also creates challenges, which entrepreneurs must navigate to fully capitalize on its potential. Some of these challenges are as follows:

13.5.1 Ethical Considerations

While there are many advantages to AI, its application also presents moral dilemmas that business owners must resolve to guarantee sustainable and ethical growth. The need for careful consideration of ethical implications further escalates due to the inherent biases of AI algorithms. The use of AI has raised significant concerns regarding data privacy and the adverse social impact that it might trigger. Thus, entrepreneurs need to consider the adoption of ethical AI frameworks to increase stakeholders' trust and confidence while mitigating ethics-related risks (Mittelstadt et al., 2016). The ethical concern regarding AI algorithms is that there is a tendency for biases in training data that could lead to discriminatory outcomes in decision-making processes. More specifically, the training data may contain biases that AI algorithms can reinforce or even make worse. Racial or gender biases, for example, could be inherited by a hiring algorithm that was trained on historical employee data, resulting in discriminatory hiring practices. To ensure that their AI models are trained on a variety of representative datasets, entrepreneurs need to be aware of the quality of their data.

According to the work of Floridi et al. (2018), algorithm transparency, diversified representation in the dataset, and unbiased (fair) assessments are essential for dealing with biases. Therefore, algorithmic auditing and continuous monitoring are necessary to address this problem.

In addition to implementing AI, entrepreneurs should consider how their actions affect society as a whole and investigate ways to train their employees to enhance their respective skill sets (Bessen, 2019). These issues must be considered by entrepreneurs while using AI-powered tools and applications. The ethical application of AI necessitates striking a balance between social responsibility and innovation, ensuring that technology is utilized to advance society overall.

13.5.2 Regulatory Compliance

AI applications often involve sensitive data handling and algorithmic transparency requirements, necessitating compliance with data protection regulations such as the GDPR in Europe or the CCPA in California (Floridi et al., 2018). Thus, entrepreneurs are likely to face the challenge of how to handle sensitive information and transparency requirements in different geographical locations.

For AI systems to function well, enormous volumes of data are frequently needed, which raises questions regarding data security and privacy. Laws such as the California

Consumer Privacy Act (CCPA) and the General Data Protection Regulation (GDPR) must be followed by entrepreneurs utilizing AI in customer-facing applications. According to Mittelstadt et al. (2016), compliance not only safeguards user data but also increases consumer trust.

13.5.3 Skills Gap

Job displacement is another worrisome aspect. There is increasing concern about job displacement as AI automates tasks that have historically been done by humans, particularly in low-skilled positions. While AI can increase productivity, it can also result in serious unemployment-related societal problems.

Specialized skills are highly required in fields such as data sciences, ML, and software engineering (Ng, 2021). Hence, AI technology integration would further increase the demand for training and developing the required skills. Ng (2021) hinted that startups may face challenges in recruiting and retaining AI talent amidst high demand and competition from tech giants (Ng, 2021). For startups and small-scale businesses, AI proposes numerous applications that are not only impactful but also easily accessible. For example, AI offers personalized marketing by implementing customer-focused marketing strategies for small-scale businesses.

According to Davenport and Ronanki (2018), through the effective use of AI algorithms, businesses such as HubSpot or Mailchimp can personalize their email marketing campaigns based on their customers' preferences and behavior. The rates of conversion and customer engagement increase because of these tools, so they help effectively target potential customers.

Another benefit of AI is that it provides timely support to customers through AI chatbots, which are vital for small-scale businesses and startups. Such solutions could help entrepreneurs, through customer queries in real time, in tracking customer behavior and enhancing customer engagement (Ng, 2021). In addition, these solutions are affordable; thus, small-scale businesses, such as Intercom and Tawk, use them aggressively (Ng, 2021). This allows small businesses to offer better customer service and boost efficiency with even smaller teams.

Effective inventory management is also a key feature of using AI in businesses. According to Brynjolfsson and McAfee (2017), small businesses manage inventories more efficiently by automating orders, predicting demand accurately, and identifying and tracking slow-moving products through Stitch Labs, an AI tool. For startups that are usually working on tight budgets with limited resources, such levels of automation can effectively reduce operational inefficiencies to a greater extent (Brynjolfsson and McAfee, 2017). Lastly, AI tools enable businesses to compete effectively in the market, reduce costs, and increase the overall customer experience (Brynjolfsson and McAfee, 2017).

13.6 Innovating Business Models with AI

Entrepreneurs can now rethink conventional methods of creating value and providing services via AI, which has emerged as a major force behind business model innovation. New opportunities for product customization, increased operational effectiveness, and improved customer experience have been made possible with the use of AI. To offer tailored recommendations on the basis of user preferences and behavior, AI-powered platforms such as Netflix and Spotify, for example, have transformed the way that content is delivered (Kaplan and Haenlein, 2019). AI is used by e-commerce platforms such as Shopify to assist business owners in managing customer information, optimizing inventory, and customizing marketing campaigns.

Automation tools powered by AI eliminate manual labor, enabling companies to grow rapidly and concentrate on innovation (Ng, 2021). A great example of the above is AI as a Service (AIaaS): There is no need to create AI infrastructure from the ground up since entrepreneurs can integrate scalable AI tools into their business models using AIaaS platforms such as Microsoft Azure and Amazon Web Services (AWS) (Russell and Norvig, 2021). In addition, on-demand services are another important element. Real-time supply and demand matching has been made possible by AI, allowing companies such as Uber and Lyft to optimize their services by using AI-driven algorithms that forecast user demand while they can also dynamically modify prices (Brynjolfsson and McAfee, 2017).

13.7 Strategies for Responsible AI Use

Transparent AI development and inclusive data practices are two strategies for the responsible use of AI. To enable users and stakeholders to comprehend AI's decision-making process, entrepreneurs should embrace AI frameworks that incorporate transparency as a fundamental tenet (Mittelstadt et al., 2016). However, to reduce bias, AI systems are trained on a variety of datasets. Diversity should be a top priority for entrepreneurs, both in the teams that develop AI and in the data they gather (Floridi et al., 2018).

13.8 Overcoming Challenges in AI Entrepreneurship

The adoption of AI involves a number of difficulties, ranging from workforce concerns to technical obstacles. However, entrepreneurs can overcome these obstacles by employing strategic approaches:

13.8.1 Addressing AI Skills Gap

It is imperative for entrepreneurs to invest in their teams' training in AI-related competencies such as ML and data science. Affordable learning opportunities can be made available to startups through partnerships with educational institutions or online learning platforms such as Coursera and Udemy (Ng, 2021).

13.8.2 Navigating Regulations

The laws pertaining to AI should be kept up to date by authorities and regulatory bodies. On the other hand, by proactively implementing best practices for algorithmic transparency and data privacy, companies can steer clear legal pitfalls (Floridi et al., 2018).

13.8.3 Building Consumer Trust

By being open to how AI is used and ensuring that ethical practices are followed, entrepreneurs can increase the level of trust that people have in AI solutions. Customers' concerns about bias and privacy can be alleviated with a clear communication strategy that highlights the advantages and safeguards of AI (Mittelstadt et al., 2016).

13.8.4 Managing Costs of AI Implementation

In regard to implementing cutting-edge AI technologies, startups and small businesses frequently face financial constraints. By using open-source tools such as Hugging Face or TensorFlow or scalable AI services such as AIaaS platforms (AWS, Google Cloud AI, etc.), entrepreneurs can reduce expenses (Russell and Norvig, 2021). These platforms offer pay-per-use models for AI that are easily accessible and do not require significant investments in proprietary infrastructure.

13.8.5 Addressing Ethical Dilemmas

The ethical implications of the AI tools that entrepreneurs use must be openly discussed with all relevant parties, including investors, customers, employees, and regulators. Public trust can be increased, and accountability can be established by working with AI ethics boards or outside audits (Floridi et al., 2018).

13.9 Recommendations

AI adoption needs to take place gradually and in a scaffolded manner. AI applications that are simple to deploy and offer quantifiable, obvious advantages, such as chatbots powered by AI that automate marketing or customer support, should be incorporated through a stepwise process. This will make it possible for companies to scale up gradually and experiment with little risk. Additionally, investments should be made in promoting AI literacy. By taking courses and earning certifications in AI, data science, and ML, entrepreneurs and their teams can improve their AI literacy and skills. Online learning environments such as edX, Udemy, and Coursera provide flexible and reasonably priced learning options. Moreover, it is important to foster and endorse ethical practices related to AI usage. By creating moral AI guidelines, conducting algorithms audits, and protecting data privacy in accordance with local laws such as the CCPA or GDPR, you can guarantee equity and openness in AI models. There is also a need for frequent and close collaboration between AI experts. To create AI systems that are reliable, moral, and in line with corporate objectives, entrepreneurs should not be afraid to consult with AI specialists or work with organizations and technology partners. Being constantly updated about regulatory changes is also essential. Given how quickly AI regulations are changing, it is essential for business owners to remain up to date on legal requirements, such as data protection laws, to prevent future legal risks and possible compliance problems.

13.10 Conclusion

By enabling companies to innovate, automate, and scale in previously unexplored ways, AI is revolutionizing modern entrepreneurship. AI gives startups and small businesses the ability to compete more successfully in the global market through individualized customer experiences and optimized operations. The adoption of AI is not without its difficulties, however, particularly in regard to ethics, skill shortages, and regulatory compliance. When creating business models, entrepreneurs must consider the ethical, social, and regulatory aspects of AI. Through responsible AI integration that prioritizes openness, equity, and customer confidence, companies can maximize AI benefits while reducing risk. AI in entrepreneurship has a promising future, with ongoing developments providing chances for expansion and creativity. Leaders in the developing digital economy are likely entrepreneurs who apply AI in a thoughtful and balanced way.

Acknowledgment

We would like to express our gratitude to Dr. Angela Antohi-Kominek for suggesting the topic of this chapter.

Bibliography

Bessen, J. E. *Automation and Jobs: When Technology Boosts Employment. Boston University*. School of Law, Law and Economics Research Paper No. 17-09, 2019. http://dx.doi.org/10.2139/ssrn.2935003

Brynjolfsson, E., and A. McAfee. *Machine, Platform, Crowd: Harnessing Our Digital Future*. W.W. Norton & Company, 2017.

Davenport, T. H., and R. Bean. "The Pursuit of AI-Driven Wealth Management." *MIT Sloan Management Review*, 2021. Accessed November 1, 2024. https://sloanreview.mit.edu/article/the-pursuit-of-ai-driven-wealth-management/

Davenport, T. H., and R. Ronanki. *Artificial Intelligence for the Real World*. Harvard Business Review Press, 2018. Accessed November 1, 2024. https://www.bizjournals.com/boston/news/2018/01/09/hbr-artificial-intelligence-for-the-real-world.html

Floridi, L., J. Cowls, M. Beltrametti, R. Chatila, P. Chazerand, V. Dignum, C. Luetge, R. Madelin, U. Pagallo, F. Rossi, B. Schafer, P. Valcke, and E. Vayena. "AI4People—An Ethical Framework for a Good AI Society: Opportunities, Risks, Principles, and Recommendations." *Minds & Machines* 28 (2018): 689–707. https://doi.org/10.1007/s11023-018-9482-5

Haque, A. U., E. Aydin, and E. Uysal. "A Comparison of Effectiveness of Global Leaders and Domestic Leaders in the Electronic Retail Industry." *Global Journal of Management and Business Research (G)* 17, no. 3 (2017): 11–20.

Horn, C., O. Ivarsson, C. Lindhé, *et al.* "Artificial Intelligence, 3D Documentation, and Rock Art—Approaching and Reflecting on the Automation of Identification and Classification of Rock Art Images." *Journal of Archaeological Method and Theory* 29 (2022): 188–213. https://doi.org/10.1007/s10816-021-09518-6

Jiang, F., Y. Jiang, H. Zhi, Y. Dong, H. Li, S. Ma, Y. Wang, Q. Dong, H. Shen, and Y. Wang. "Artificial Intelligence in Healthcare: Past, Present, and Future." *Stroke and Vascular Neurology* 2 (2017): 230–243. https://doi.org/10.1136/svn-2017-000101

Jurafsky, D., and J. H. Martin. *Speech and Language Processing*. 3rd ed. Pearson, 2019.

Kaplan, A., and M. Haenlein. "Siri, Siri, in My Hand: Who's the Fairest in the Land? On the Interpretations, Illustrations, and Implications of Artificial Intelligence." *Business Horizons* 62, no. 1 (2019): 15–25. https://doi.org/10.1016/j.bushor.2018.08.004

Kumar, V. *Transforming Traditional Industries with AI: A Roadmap to Modernization*. Tech Innovations Press, 2018.

Marr, B. *The Amazing Ways Amazon Is Using AI Robots*, 2024. Available on: www.forbes.com/sites/bernardmarr/2024/09/20/the-amazing-ways-amazon-is-using-ai-robots/ (Last accessed: 30 September, 2024).

Mittelstadt, B. D., P. Allo, M. Taddeo, S. Wachter, and L. Floridi. "The Ethics of Algorithms: Mapping the Debate." *Big Data & Society* 3, no. 2 (2016): 1–21. https://doi.org/10.1177/2053951716679679

Ng, A. *AI Transformation Playbook: How to Lead Your Company into the AI Era.* 2021. Accessed November 1, 2024. https://landing.ai/case-studies/ai-transformation-playbook

Poole, D., and A. Mackworth. *Artificial Intelligence: Foundations of Computational Agents.* Cambridge University Press, 2010. https://doi.org/10.1017/CBO9780511819346

Russell, S. J., and P. Norvig. *Artificial Intelligence: A Modern Approach.* 4th ed. Pearson, 2021.

Szeliski, R. *Computer Vision: Algorithms and Applications.* Springer, 2010. Accessed November 1, 2024. https://link.springer.com/chapter/10.1007/978-3-030-51110-4_2#Sec6

Case Study: Sandra's AI-Driven Startup

Harmandeep Kaur

Sandra founded EcoTecSol, a startup that specializes in sustainable consumer goods. In a quest to transform the world through eco-friendly products, Sandra has incorporated several AI technologies into her company operations and customer interaction. With a small budget but big vision, Sandra faces both opportunities and challenges as she works to integrate AI into her business.

AI Technologies Adopted

Machine Learning (ML)

She uses ML algorithms to study customer purchase trends and preferences. With data as the driver, she customizes her product offerings accordingly, optimizes her inventory management, and is therefore able to stock up on items that are in demand.

Natural Language Processing (NLP)

In addition to this, Sandra has integrated an AI-powered chatbot into her website to enhance customer service experience. It uses NLP to handle customer queries, recommend products, and gather feedback by learning from every conversation to provide even better answers.

Computer Vision

EcoTecSol utilizes computer vision to streamline its supply chain. Image recognition monitors product quality at every level of production, allowing Sandra to swiftly identify defects and waste, ensuring that only the best products reach her clients.

Challenges Faced

The promising application of AI comes with a lot of challenges for Sandra:

Ethical Considerations

She is worried that her AI algorithms could be biased, affecting their fairness toward customers and undermining their level of satisfaction. To address this, she opts to embed ethics into her design of AI systems, so it is fair and transparent to customers.

Regulatory Compliance

Operating a business in a global marketplace requires Sandra to address several regulations for data protection, such as GDPR and CCPA, which help protect customer information and maintain compliance.

Skills Gap

EcoTecSol, being a small startup, faces challenges in finding and retaining skilled AI talent. Sandra is looking to build collaborative relationships with local universities to create internships that would attract fresh talent.

Future Directions

Sandra wants EcoTecSol to spread its wings by developing new AI-powered business models. These models should incorporate customer feedback more effectively and enhance personalized marketing efforts. According to Sandra, addressing ethical concerns and investing in talent development are of paramount importance for any organization aspiring to become a frontrunner in sustainable entrepreneurship.

Reflection Questions

- How do the AI technologies implemented by Sandra contribute to her startup's operational efficiency and customer satisfaction?
- What specific ethical considerations does Sandra need to consider when deploying AI technologies in her business?
- Discuss the implications of data protection regulations on Sandra's operations. How can she be able to use AI while ensuring compliance?
- What are some strategies Sandra could use to overcome the skills gap regarding AI in her startup?
- Given the opportunities provided by AI, what new business models could Sandra consider to further increase EcoTecSol's growth and sustainability?

Chapter 14

Entrepreneurial Leadership and Decision-making

Adnan ul Haque

14.0 Characteristics of Entrepreneurial Leadership

Traditional leadership and entrepreneurial actions and traits have been combined to form a distinct form of leadership, which is regarded as 'entrepreneurial leadership'. Broadly defined, entrepreneurial leadership is focused on identifying and seizing new opportunities that would enable innovation and drive others toward a common goal (Renko et al., 2015). Interestingly, Renko et al. (2015) argued that the shared vision is often evident in volatile, uncertain, and resource-constrained environments. Additionally, Kuratko (2016) argued that entrepreneurial leaders, unlike traditional managers, frequently operate in high-risk situations that demand tenacity and the ability to quickly readjust to changing circumstances.

14.1 Visionary Thinking

In the context of entrepreneurial leadership, visionary thinking can be defined as a processing act reflecting innovation and motivation toward a vision, which offers not only an organizational purpose but also a direction (Gupta et al., 2004; Haque et al., 2017). According to Gupta et al. (2004), the ambition of a leader to transform the industry or develop unique value propositions is often demonstrated through this vision. One of the most distinctive features of entrepreneurial thinking is visionary thinking because it allows entrepreneurial leaders to surpass the status quo and develop creative solutions (Renko et al., 2015). Interestingly, Renko et al. (2015) argued that a clear vision helps the team maintain a steady focus on collective goals but also provides a clear roadmap in difficult circumstances. In contrast, it is evident that at times, excessive risk-taking is the result of overly visionary leaders (Kuratko, 2016). This is because such individuals often become excited and heavily focus on countless possibilities in the future while ignoring current realities (Kuratko, 2016). One example of a visionary-thinking leader could be Elon Musk, who has transformed his vision into reality. For instance, Tesla and SpaceX reflect the perfect embodiment of the visionary thinking of an entrepreneurial leader. Space travel and renewable energy reflect the vision of Musk, which not only distinguished his entrepreneurial venture from those of other competitors but also redefined industries with many possibilities, attracting his workforce and customers (Vance, 2015; Sudjiman, 2024).

DOI: 10.4324/9781003504351-14

14.2 Resilience and Adaptation

The tendency to bounce back from setbacks while ensuring adaptability—refining and setting responsive strategies according to the situation—reflects resilience (Luthans and Youssef, 2007). In other words, resilience is the ability to adjust strategies when circumstances change and to quickly return to one's feet after experiencing adversity. The challenges in an uncertain environment are frequently unpredictable; therefore, entrepreneurial leadership heavily relies on adaptability and resilience to sustain operations in such a competitive environment. The flux in the environment applies further pressure on leaders to operate effectively and address complexities, connectedness, and context within the global paradigm (Haque et al., 2017). Thus, resilience and adaptability become more essential.

In other words, the ability to adapt easily, as well as being resilient, is highly significant within entrepreneurial leadership because unique challenges continually emerge in the environment. Hayward et al. (2010) explained that resilient leaders are those who ensure that morale remains high in their teams even in tough times and that consistency is maintained in pursuit of accomplishing long-term goals. Nonetheless, Shepherd et al. (2015) argued that leaders need to be cautious because overemphasizing resilience can have a drastic negative impact on both entrepreneurs and their ventures. At times, adaptation requires calculated change, yet some leaders overcome their reluctance in the name of resilience. As a result, they continue with outdated methods that can ultimately lead to self-destruction. In other words, continuing certain procedures to demonstrate resilience might lead entrepreneurs down paths that are not viable and may result in severe negative consequences (Shepherd et al., 2015).

Nonetheless, there is no doubt that entrepreneurial leaders frequently demonstrate greater resilience. For example, Spanx's founder, Sara Blakely, demonstrated a higher level of exceptional resilience when faced with doubts and initial reluctance from manufacturers and investors (Kaufman, 2014). However, it did not deter her from pursuing her passion. Through her persistence, focus, and flexibility ultimately helped her create a billion-dollar company, disrupting trends and transforming the shapewear market (Kaufman, 2014).

14.3 A Creative Attitude—aka Innovative Mindset

Drucker (1985) defined a creative way of thinking (aka creative mindset) that includes openness to change, and exploring new approaches and solutions to preexisting problems demonstrates an innovative mindset. Within entrepreneurial leadership, a creative attitude is one of the significant traits (Drucker, 1985). Entrepreneurial leaders are bound to exhibit innovativeness that enables them to maintain relevance and a competitive advantage. One of the earlier concepts of "creative destruction" was introduced by Schumpeter in 1942 (Haq et al., 2024), who highlighted that only innovation could lead firms to disrupt the market and seize new opportunities (Shane and Venkataraman, 2000). In other words, to seize new opportunities and change the dynamics of the market with the product and services offering unique propositions, entrepreneurs must continuously innovate.

One example is the founder of Netflix – Reed Hastings. With a highly imaginative and creative mindset, he decided to disrupt the entertainment industry by transitioning from renting DVDs to streaming services and, lately, producing original content. This illustrates that to stay ahead of industry trends and other competitors, new technologies must be embraced with an open mindset (McCord, 2019). Nonetheless, Shane and Venkataraman

(2000) argued that burnout could result from excessive focus on innovation because the relentless efforts to focus on innovation may cause stress. Additionally, recent studies confirm that innovative work behavior and entrepreneurial capabilities are significantly impacted by distinct types of stressors (Haq, Haque and Rahim, 2024; Haq et al., 2024; Haque, 2024). Thus, innovation frequently contributes to stress among team members because of experimentation and demand for ideation.

14.4 Risk Management and Risk-Taking

Urbański et al. (2019) defined risk management as a rational and strategic practice aimed at reducing potential losses. In the context of entrepreneurial leadership, however, the concept of risk-taking involves the attempt to seize opportunities when outcomes are uncertain. Kuratko et al. (2015) indicated that risk-taking is frequently considered the most important trait of entrepreneurial leadership, capturing the essence of leading operations in all types of situations. Risk-taking is seen as a hallmark trait because it reveals a leader's relentless drive to expand the horizon and operate in underserved markets (Kuratko et al., 2015; Kuratko, 2016). In other words, the risk-taking ability of entrepreneurial leaders enables them to explore territories that have not yet been thoroughly explored, as they stretch and push boundaries to a new level.

However, critics argue that some entrepreneurs may take uncalculated risks without proper risk assessment and risk analysis, which could lead to a collapse of the business enterprise (Timmons et al., 2010). Thus, reckless risk-taking is neither an appropriate nor wise move in business. The ability to take calculated risks, along with the successful management of those risks, constitutes a defining feature of effective entrepreneurial leadership. The founder of one of the largest online businesses, Amazon, Jeff Bezos, is a master of calculated risk. He is known for assessing options and employing a balanced approach to taking risks (Stone, 2013). Bezos took calculated risks when he decided to expand his e-commerce platform by launching Amazon Web Services (AWS), strategically assessing the advantages and disadvantages (Stone, 2013). Undoubtedly, his calculated moves contributed to the growth of the company, eventually transforming it into a global market leader.

14.5 Team Building and Formation

According to Ireland et al. (2003), entrepreneurial leaders place high emphasis on the importance of forming diverse yet strong teams, encouraging collaboration, and allowing team members autonomy so that they take responsibility for their performed tasks. This approach aims to create an atmosphere of cooperation that inspires innovation as well as growth (Ireland et al., 2003). It is also essential for business expansion that an organization functions openly without any restrictions. In other words, the organization is free from direct involvement of the founder while functioning in an environment (Chen and Lai, 2010). It is important for the growth of an organization to empower teams so that they adapt to dynamic environments. A study by Chen and Lai (2010) revealed that empowered teams not only enjoy high morale but are also highly productive, which helps achieve the objectives of enterprises.

Nonetheless, other schools of thought argue that empowerment is not sufficient to ensure that it will reap rewards and make enterprises successful (Manz and Sims, 2001). They suggest that the direction, accountability and structure of the organization are more important for the growth and success of the organization (Manz and Sims, 2001). The reason is that empowerment does not have its own true framework or personal accountability, which could result in a lack of proper direction (Manz and Sims, 2001). For example, in the case of Zappos, Tony Hsieh was a company CEO who did not just exemplify participatory leadership by empowering his team through creating an environment that nurtured autonomy and innovation. His move to implement "Holacracy" – an organizational system that operates without conventional managerial hierarchies – reflects his commitment to employee empowerment and entrepreneurial leadership. In other words, his practice speaks volumes about his entrepreneurial leadership commitment to fostering a culture of employee empowerment.

Nonetheless, in highly autonomous settings, operating without structure presents unique challenges (Hsieh, 2010). Entrepreneurial leaders often make decisions in volatile, uncertain, complex, and ambiguous (VUCA) environments, with imperfect knowledge and uncertain consequences. Entrepreneurial leaders must make decisions on the basis of calculated risks. According to Haque et al. (2017), uncertainty refers to situations where possible outcomes are not fully known, making conventional risk assessment tricky and difficult. According to Sarasvathy (2001), the ability of entrepreneurial leaders to make efficient and effective decisions under time pressure results from knowledge that integrates intuition backed by analytical methodologies.

14.6 Making Intuitive vs. Analytical Decisions

Intuitive decision-making relies on instinct or experience to guide choices, whereas analytical (logical) decision-making is based on facts, seeking rationality, and systematic analysis in making choices (Dane and Pratt, 2007). Often, the availability of reliable data is limited due to uncertainty; hence, entrepreneurs find themselves in a situation to rely on intuition despite evidence-based decisions being always preferred because of their rigor and objectivity (Dane and Pratt, 2007). Experienced entrepreneurs usually make decisions on the basis of intuition, supported by following recognized patterns, which enables them to respond promptly to new opportunities (Dane and Pratt, 2007). For example, Howard Schultz used both an analytical and intuitive approach when deciding to transform Starbucks from a coffee bean retailer into a coffee chain. Without Shultz's rational approach and intuition, Starbucks might never have emerged as a global brand, despite early trends showing that moving away from the original business model was risky (Schultz and Yang, 1997). Nonetheless, subjective errors and distinct biases can result from heavy reliance on intuition, especially under conditions of pressure or discomfort (Kahneman, 2011).

14.7 Adaptability and Scenario Planning

Scenario planning promotes adaptability and agility in responding to shifting circumstances because it helps in the preparation for several probable potential future events (Schoemaker, 1995). In times of uncertainty, scenario planning is highly useful, as it encourages leaders to consider various scenarios and ensure that employees have all relevant information and are adequately prepared. Schoemaker (1995) argued that by creating different scenarios, leaders can remain flexible and adjust according to the situation's demands. In other words, leaders keep their options open and redefine their approach as situations unfold.

For example, Airbnb used scenario planning to accommodate various types of recovery periods on the basis of public health events during the COVID-19 pandemic. This practice enabled the company to stay agile when international tourism was negatively impacted and dropped to new lows across the globe. Airbnb promptly adjusted its policies according to the situation and shifted its focus to domestic audiences, particularly to travel options that supported the recovery of business during this period (Yohn, 2020).

Nonetheless, Mintzberg (1994) argued that too much scenario planning can lead to the development of a situation of "analysis paralysis"—a situation where excessive consideration of options hinders decision-making. In other words, the risk of delayed decision-making can result from extensive scenario planning.

14.8 Prompt Decisions

Eisenhardt (1989) explained that at times, entrepreneurs do not have sufficient information, but they must make immediate decisions, requiring prompt actions so that they can act quickly to seize opportunities and/or minimize potential risks. Entrepreneurial leaders must grasp opportunities before they slip away in dynamic environments by making fast decisions. The ability to "decide and act" immediately and adapt action plans as required by the situation are key attributes of effective leaders (Eisenhardt, 1989). Nonetheless, hurried decisions are likely to yield poor results, especially when risks are not properly assessed (Kahneman, 2011). This can lead to severe mistakes that may prove very costly for the entrepreneur (Kahneman, 2011). For example, the former CEO of Uber, Travis Kalanick, was known for his fast decisions, which led to large expansion and rapid growth of the company (Isaac, 2017). However, reputational risks and regulatory issues emerged that might have been avoided with a more considered approach.

14.9 Biases in Decision Making

Kahneman (2011) stated that systematic errors in judgment, which are based on either emotional or cognitive shortcuts, are referred to as biases in decision-making. Anchoring, confirmation, and overconfidence are a few of the biases to which entrepreneurs, like all other decision-makers, are vulnerable. Research has shown that entrepreneurs often exhibit overconfidence bias, as they strongly believe in the success of their entrepreneurial venture despite having limited data at hand (Busenitz and Barney, 1997). The ability to make balanced (neither overly logical nor highly emotional) decisions depends on awareness of all types of biases. In this context, it is important to note that not all biases are harmful, such as optimism bias (super confidence), which can spark hope and give entrepreneurs the courage to pursue ambitious goals (Simon et al., 2000). In other words, at times, entrepreneurs need optimism bias so that they have the confidence to fulfill their ambitions. For instance, Theranos' founder, Elizabeth Holmes exhibited confirmation bias and maintained overconfidence, believing her innovation would succeed, whereas extensive evidence pointed in the opposite direction. Her bias played a significant role in decision-making, which lacked objective scrutiny. Eventually, it was one of the primary reasons for the collapse of Theranos Company (Carreyrou, 2018).

14.10 Team Formation and Management

Hackman and Hackman (2002) argued that team building and leadership are crucial in entrepreneurship because effective teams are essential for responding quickly and efficiently to the pressures and challenges of innovation. Effective teams are characterized by good leadership, clear roles, open communication, trust, and shared goals. Beyond gathering talented people, the entrepreneurial leader should foster a culture of cooperation where the collective talent of all team members is maximized.

14.10.1 Define Responsibilities and Rules

Well-defined roles and responsibilities ensure that each member of the team knows their specific role and how it fits within the larger context of the overall goal. This structure enhances responsibility, explicitly defines expectations, and decreases misunderstandings (Katzenbach and Smith, 1993; Kaur et al., 2024). With the frequent overlap of roles and changes prevalent in entrepreneurial teams, there is a strong need to clarify assigned roles. According to Hackman and Hackman (2002), greater role clarity helps reduce duplication of effort and increases the efficient division of labor among members. For instance, in the early days of Microsoft, there was a clear division of labor between Paul Allen and Bill Gates, allowing each to perform to their strengths: Allen oversaw product development, whereas Gates handled the actual writing of software. Because the roles were clear, the team was more efficient and presented foundational attributes that paved the way for Microsoft's success years later (Wallace and Erickson, 1993).

On the other hand, excessively rigid role demarcations can also make team members both unable and unwilling to contribute beyond their narrow sphere, hence discouraging creativity altogether.

14.10.2 Encouraging Open Communication

Open communication within teams forms trust, fosters the free exchange of ideas, and ensures that problems are caught at the earliest possible phase. It enables team members to voice their concerns, share constructive criticism, and collaborate on solutions. Because open communication allows creative ideas to be shared without fear of backlash, it is crucial for fostering creativity. According to Edmondson (1999), teams characterized by "psychological safety" are more willing to take risks and employ innovative problem-solving methods. For example, Google's "20% Time" policy allows employees to work on their side projects for up to 20% of their time, thus fostering open communication and encouraging knowledge sharing among teams (Bock, 2015). Innovative products such as Gmail and AdSense resulted from this concept and demonstrated that open communication can positively impact innovation. Critics argue that open communication needs to be balanced with discretion to avoid information overload, which leads to ineffectiveness in decision making (Daft and Lengel, 1986; Kaur, 2023; Kaur et al., 2024).

14.10.3 Fostering Unity and Trust

Effective collaboration relies on trust and cohesion, which creates a positive atmosphere, making members feel committed to their common goals and confident in one another's competencies. Team cohesion and trust are significant elements of any team; their absence can lead to ineffectiveness, especially when teams are working in challenging environments. Cohesion provides a sense of direction among team members, whereas trust reinforces cooperation and decreases events of conflict (Costa et al., 2001). For example, Pixar Animation Studios has been renowned for its small teams, built through a "braintrust" model, which encourages open and frank feedback sessions among team members. In such a setting, teams were able to work in harmony with movies such as Finding Nemo and Toy Story, which became instant blockbusters all the time (Catmull and Wallace, 2023). Critics, however, argue that high cohesion can foster the "groupthink" phenomenon, where the desire for harmony overrides the expression of minority opinions, potentially leading to lower-quality decisions.

14.10.4 Embracing Diversity and Inclusion

Shore et al. (2011) explained that while diversity in teams refers to actively seeking out different viewpoints and experiences, inclusion involves the assurance of being valued and included within the dynamics of the team. Diversity and inclusiveness are essential to creativity because various perspectives introduce a level of complexity that encourages challenging problem-solving and novel insights. Research has shown that diverse teams are better able to generate fresh ideas and adapt to changing situations (Van Knippenberg et al., 2004). For example, the success of Johnson & Johnson in different global markets can be attributed to a company's commitment to diverse and inclusive policies. This commitment is evident in their efforts toward diverse recruitment and team-building practices. At Johnson & Johnson, diverse teams collaborate to produce healthcare and wellness products customized to different consumer groups (Barton and Hirsch, 2016).

However, effectively harnessing diversity requires knowledge and skills, as different points of view may lead to miscommunication and conflict (Jehn et al., 1999; Haq and Faizan, 2023).

14.10.5 Lead by Example

As suggested by Gandz (2002), leaders who lead by example provide a model for responsibility and dedication. They demonstrate the values, behaviors, and work habits expected from others on their team. Leaders who exemplify honesty, hard work, and flexibility motivate their team to do the same (Haque and Yamoah, 2021). Kouzes and Posner (2017) explained that leaders who act as models inspire loyalty and commitment among team members because they are seen as actively involved rather than simply overseeing it. For example, Indra Nooyi, the former chief executive officer (CEO) of PepsiCo, has been widely recognized for her interactive leadership style and commitment to social responsibility (Sorkin et al., 2014). She embraced diversity and transparency by staying close to her staff and embodying the values of PepsiCo—a quality that helped the brand adapt to changing consumer preferences (Sorkin et al., 2014). Critics, however, point out that leaders who try to take on every role risk becoming micromanagers, which can limit trust and independence among team members (Pearce and Conger, 2003).

14.11 Strategic Decision-making in Entrepreneurship

Strategic entrepreneurial decision-making involves determining long-term objectives, performing informational analysis, and making informed decisions that guide and direct the company toward long-term success. In industries, the entrepreneur usually operates in dynamic and high-pressure environments. Strategic entrepreneurial decisions made by entrepreneurial firms can significantly impact their profitability and positioning in their competitive environments (Eisenhardt, 1989).

14.11.1 Characteristics of Entrepreneurial Strategic Decision-Making

Entrepreneurs depend on strategic decision-making to set goals that align with the purpose and vision of their companies, allocate resources effectively, and respond to market fluctuations. The key difference from ordinary routine decision-making is that strategic decision-making involves choices that have a significant influence on the organization and its further direction.

For example, Elon Musk took a well-calculated risk that enabled Tesla to enter the mass market by opting to focus on affordable electric vehicles instead of luxury models. Although this strategy involved a considerable number of risks, it cemented Tesla as one of the influential players in the automobile industry (Vance, 2017).

Complex and sometimes unpredictable strategic decisions can drive innovation but also carry substantial risks. For time-constrained firms, rapid information processing and fluid thinking are pivotal dimensions of effective strategic decision-making (Haque and Yamoah, 2021). However, if too much information is evaluated without careful prioritization, this speed in decision-making can lead to "analysis paralysis" (Langley, 1995).

14.11.2 Strategic Decision-making Techniques

Entrepreneurs frequently use intuition or heuristics in making strategic decisions by drawing on prior experiences and industry knowledge (Gigerenzer, 2007). For example, at Apple, Steve Jobs was renowned for his innovative stance on product development. Since there were no market precedents, his bold decision to introduce the iPhone represented strategic management guided by a vision rather than due to any existing demand (Isaacson, 2011). In other words, a decision is based on intuition rather than data. Critics argue that intuitive decisions can carry the risk of judgment or decisions being compromised by cognitive biases, although such decisions can also be faster and more adaptive (Faizan and Zehra, 2016).

14.12 Integrity and Ethics in Entrepreneurial Management

Ethics and integrity in entrepreneurship involve the steadfast application of morality and honesty in all business practices, which inspires confidence among stakeholders and fosters a healthy corporate culture (Ciulla, 2004). In practice, entrepreneurial leaders often play a vital role in setting moral standards, as they directly influence how an organization thinks and acts.

14.12.1 Integrity and Ethics in Entrepreneurship

Integrity is an unwavering commitment to moral principles, especially under challenging circumstances, whereas ethics are a set of moral values that help guide behaviors (Ciulla, 2004). Ethics and integrity within entrepreneurship contexts involve transparency, respect for stakeholders, and accountability. For instance, Patagonia's founder, Yvon Chouinard, built his company on values such as fair wages and respect for natural resources. Owing to these values, Patagonia has a stronger reputation than many other companies operating in the same industry. Its commitment to ethical practice further reinforces employee commitment and customer loyalty (Chouinard, 2005).

Additionally, integrity and ethical behavior build trust among customers, employees, and investors, fostering long-term profitability (Trevino et al., 2003). The evidence suggests that businesses that are perceived as ethical and lead to integrity attract more engaged employees and loyal customers. Trevino et al. (2003) argues that organizations practicing ethical behavior have more employee commitment and loyal customers. However, companies may sometimes feel pressure to compromise moral principles to meet earnings (Faizan and Zehra, 2016).

14.12.2 Challenges in Maintaining Integrity and Ethics

Startups frequently find it difficult to balance moral obligations with financial demands, especially in their initial phase when there are financial constraints. Labor standards or product quality may be sacrificed to save costs and expenditures, creating a moral dilemma for entrepreneurs (Dees, 1998). Compromised ethics displayed by health tech firms – Theranos, exaggerating the capabilities and features of their products, leading to legal issues and long-term damage to their reputation. This example shows the risks of prioritizing financial goals over moral principles (Carreyrou, 2018). Startups are characterized by uncertainties, quick changes, and resource limitations, which pose serious challenges for entrepreneurial leaders. For entrepreneurs, maintaining a balance requires motivating the team and earning investor trust while navigating these obstacles (Kuratko, 2016).

14.12.2.1 Balancing Pragmatism and Vision

Balancing pragmatism and vision involve managing routine details while maintaining a forward-thinking approach. This balance requires the ability to adapt flexibly while remaining on track with long-term enterprise goals (Baum et al., 1998). For instance, the aim of Jeff Bezos to expand Amazon beyond books initially received skepticism. However, his adaptive, step-by-step expansion strategy allowed Amazon to thrive and demonstrated how vision and practicality can work in tandem (Stone, 2013).

While setting a direction requires vision, an excessive focus on long-term goals may lead management to neglect immediate needs. In support of this, the study by Baron and Markman (2003) revealed that the executives who practice practical flexibility can accommodate necessary modifications without risking the firm's failure. However, visionary management may sometimes block pragmatic adjustments, which can hinder operational improvement and reduce teamwork enthusiasm (Katz and Gartner, 1988).

14.12.2.2 Scaling and Resource Scarcity Management

One of the most common challenges startups face is the scarcity of resources, which negatively affects the organization's operational efficiency (Brush et al., 2001). Strategic decisions on the scalability and allocation of resources are often guided by cash flow considerations and investment in leadership roles. For example, Sara Blakely, the founder of Spanx, relied on cost-effective strategies and reinvested revenues for nearly two decades. By managing resources prudently, Spanx accomplished sustainable growth without needing external investment (Bankoff, 2016).

The scarcity of resources often forces entrepreneurial leaders to innovate and seek new partnerships or solutions. While resource scarcity may trigger innovation, it can overburden leaders to deliver rapid results, sometimes leading to burnout or overextension (Greve and Salaff, 2003; Faizan et al., 2022).

14.12.2.3 Managing Uncertainty and Building Resilience

From fluctuating consumer demand to market swings, uncertainty is a constant companion for the entrepreneur. For entrepreneurial leaders to pivot and survive, they must be resilient, possessing the ability to "stand after being bent"—a quality that enables them to bounce back quickly from adversity (Shepherd et al., 2015). For example, the founders of Airbnb showed persistence during the financial crisis in 2008. They managed to stay afloat in such tough lending conditions by using several creative ways of keeping the business running. Their flexibility and tenacity eventually helped Airbnb become one of the leading players in the hospitality industry (Gallagher, 2017).

While resilience is essential, some argue that without the ability to realize when a course correction is needed, resilience can lead to stubbornness (Sarasvathy, 2001). For example, highly resilient leaders (aka overly resilient leaders) may hold onto unprofitable ideas or fail to recognize that the environment calls for a change (Hayward et al., 2010).

14.13 Conclusion

It is concluded that entrepreneurial leaders must adopt a balanced approach to ensure that adaptability remains intact when making decisions in complex business environments. Ethical decision-making and effective team management enable them to perform better. The success of entrepreneurial leaders is characterized by prompt yet calculated decision-making, flexibility in uncertain situations, and adaptation of inclusive approaches to build teams. Ethical standards help them mitigate biases, strengthen their reputation, and foster trust. Strategic visions and pragmatic actions enable entrepreneurial leaders to address complex challenges, capitalize on opportunities, and achieve sustainable growth.

Bibliography

Bankoff, C. "How Selling Fax Machines Helped Make Spanx Inventor Sara Blakely a Billionaire." *The Vindicated*, 2016. Accessed November 2, 2024. https://nymag.com/vindicated/2016/10/how-selling-fax-machines-helped-sara-blakely-invent-spanx.html.

Barton, A. L., and J. K. Hirsch. "Permissive Parenting and Mental Health in College Students: Mediating Effects of Academic Entitlement." *Journal of American College Health: J of ACH* 64, no. 1 (2016): 1–8. https://doi.org/10.1080/07448481.2015.1060597.

Baum, J. R., E. A. Locke, & S. A. Kirkpatrick. "A Longitudinal Study of the Relation of Vision and Vision Communication to Venture Growth in Entrepreneurial Firms." *Journal of Applied Psychology* 83 (1998): 43. https://doi.org/10.1037/0021-9010.83.1.43.

Bock, M. A. "Beyond the First Story: Technology and the Emerging Practices of Alternative Journalism." In *The Routledge Companion to Alternative and Community Media*, edited by Chris Atton, 30. London: Routledge, 2015.

Brush, C. G., P. G. Greene, M. M. Hart, and H. S. Haller. "From Initial Idea to Unique Advantage: The Entrepreneurial Challenge of Constructing a Resource Base." *Academy of Management Executive* 15 (2001): 64–78. https://doi.org/10.5465/AME.2001.4251394.

Busenitz, L. W., and J. B. Barney. "Differences between Entrepreneurs and Managers in Large Organizations: Biases and Heuristics in Strategic Decision-Making." *Journal of Business Venturing* 12 (1997): 9–30. https://doi.org/10.1016/S0883-9026(96)00003-1.

Carreyrou, J. *Bad Blood: Secrets and Lies in a Silicon Valley Startup*. Toronto, Canada: Penguin Random House, 2018. ISBN 9781524731656.

Catmull, E., and A. Wallace. *Creativity, Inc. (The Expanded Edition)*. New York: Penguin Random House, 2023.

Chen, Y., and M. Lai. "Factors Influencing the Entrepreneurial Attitude of Taiwanese Tertiary-Level Business Students." *Social Behavior and Personality* 38 (2010): 1–12.

Chouinard, Y. Let My People Go Surfing: The Education of a Reluctant Businessman. 2005. Amazon.

Ciulla, J. B. "Ethics and Leadership Effectiveness." In: *The Nature of Leadership*, edited by J. Antonakis, A. T. Cianciolo, & R. J. Sternberg, 302–327. London: Sage Publications, Inc., 2004.

Costa, P. T. Jr., A. Terracciano, and R. R. McCrae. "Gender Differences in Personality Traits Across Cultures: Robust and Surprising Findings." *Journal of Personality and Social Psychology* 81, no. 2 (2001): 322–331.

Daft, R. L., and R. H. Lengel. "Organizational Information Requirements, Media Richness, and Structural Design." *Management Science* 32, no. 5 (1986): 554–571. https://doi.org/10.1287/mnsc.32.5.554.

Dane, E., & M. G. Pratt. "Exploring Intuition and its Role in Managerial Decision Making." *The Academy of Management Review* 32, no. 1 (2007): 33–54. https://doi.org/10.2307/20159279.

Dees, J. G. "The Meaning of Social Entrepreneurship." *Stanford Social Innovation Review*, 1998.

Drucker, P. F. *Innovation and Entrepreneurship*. New York: Harper & Row, 1985.

Edmondson, A. "Psychological Safety and Learning Behavior in Work Teams." *Administrative Science Quarterly* 44, no. 2 (1999): 350–383. https://doi.org/10.2307/2666999.

Eisenhardt, K. M. "Building Theories from Case Study Research." *The Academy of Management Review* 14, no. 4 (1989): 532–550. https://doi.org/10.2307/258557.

Faizan, R., I. U. Haq, A. Faridi, and A. Baloch. "Occupational Stress and Workplace Creativity (WPC): Understanding the Relationship." *International Journal of Applied Business and Management Studies* 7, no. 2 (2022): 1–10.

Faizan, R., & N. Zehra. "Quality Work–Life as Predictor to Organisational Commitment Under Contrasting Leadership Styles: I.T Responses from Pakistan's Private Software Houses." *Global Journal of Management and Administration* 16, no. 6 (2016): 9–23. https://mpra.ub.uni-muenchen.de/73973/.

Gallagher, M. S. "The Influence of Social Media on Teens' Self-Esteem." MA thesis, Department of Psychology, College of Science and Mathematics, Rowan University, 2017. Accessed November 1, 2024. https://rdw.rowan.edu/cgi/viewcontent.cgi?article=3440&context=etd; https://rdw.rowan.edu/etd/2438/

Gandz, J. "Train Dogs, Develop Leaders." *Ivey Business Journal* 66, no. 5 (2002): 8–9.

Gigerenzer, G. *Gut Feelings: The Intelligence of the Unconscious.* New York: Penguin Books, 2007.
Greve, A., and J. W. Salaff. "Social Networks and Entrepreneurship." *Entrepreneurship Theory and Practice* 28, no. 1 (2003): 1–22. https://doi.org/10.1111/1540-8520.00029.
Gupta, V., I. C. MacMillan, and G. Surie. "Entrepreneurial Leadership: Developing and Measuring a Cross-Cultural Construct." *Journal of Business Venturing* 19 (2004): 241–260. https://doi.org/10.1016/S0883-9026(03)00040-5.
Hackman, J. R., and R. J. Hackman. *Leading Teams: Setting the Stage for Great Performances.* Brighton, MA: Harvard Business Press, 2002.
Haq, I. U., and R. Faizan. "Communication Within the Workplace: Systematic Review of Essentials of Communication." *International Journal of Applied Business and Management Studies* 8, no. 2 (2023): 1–18.
Haq, I., A. U. Haque, and N. A. A. Rahim. "Entrepreneurial Stress and Mental Well-Being: Pre- and Post-COVID-19 Comparative Analysis of SMEs in Canada." *Forum Scientiae Oeconomia* 12, no. 1 (2024): 53–71.
Haq, I. U., A. U. Haque, H. Kaur, and N. A. A. A. Rahim. "Occupational Stress Affecting Innovative Capabilities and Innovative Work Behavior of Migrant Entrepreneurs." *Polish Journal of Management Studies* 9, no. 2 (2024): 238–253. https://doi.org/10.17512/pjms.2024.29.2.12.
Haque, A. U. "How Occupational Stress Impacts the Innovative Work Behaviour and Innovative Entrepreneurial Capabilities of Migrant Entrepreneurs in Contrasting Economies?" In *Migration and Entrepreneurship in the Global Context*, edited by D. Hyams-Ssekasi and E. Daskalaki, 15–30. Cham: Palgrave Macmillan, 2024. https://doi.org/10.1007/978-3-031-34067-3_2.
Haque, A. U., E. Aydin, and E. Uysal. "A Comparison of Effectiveness of Global Leaders and Domestic Leaders in Electronic Retail Industry." *Global Journal of Management and Business Research (G)* 17, no. 3 (2017): 11–20.
Haque, A. U., and F. A. Yamoah. "The Role of Ethical Leadership in Managing Occupational Stress to Promote Innovative Work Behaviour: A Cross-Cultural Management Perspective." *Sustainability* 13, no. 17 (2021): 9608. https://doi.org/10.3390/su13179608.
Hayward, M. L. A., W. R. Forster, S. Sarasvathy, and B. Fredrickson. "Beyond Hubris: How Highly Confident Entrepreneurs Rebound to Venture Again." *Journal of Business Venturing* 25, no. 6 (2010): 569–578. https://doi.org/10.1016/j.jbusvent.2009.03.002.
Hsieh, T. "How I Did It: Zappos's CEO on Going to Extremes for Customers." *Harvard Business Review*, July 2010. Accessed November 2, 2024. https://hbr.org/2010/07/how-i-did-it-zappos-ceo-on-going-to-extremes-for-customers.
Ireland, R. D., M. A. Hitt, and D. G. Sirmon. "A Model of Strategic Entrepreneurship: The Construct and its Dimensions." *Journal of Management* 29, no. 6 (2003): 963–989. https://doi.org/10.1016/S0149-2063_03_00086-2.
Isaac, M. "How Uber Deceives the Authorities Worldwide." *The New York Times*, March 3, 2017. Accessed November 2, 2024. /www.nytimes.com/2017/03/03/technology/uber-greyball-program-evade-authorities.html.
Isaacson, W. *Steve Jobs.* New York: Simon & Schuster, 2011.
Jehn, K. A., G. B. Northcraft, and M. A. Neale. "Why Differences Make a Difference: A Field Study of Diversity, Conflict and Performance in Workgroups." *Administrative Science Quarterly* 44, no. 4 (1999): 741–763. https://doi.org/10.2307/2667054.
Kahneman, D. *Thinking, Fast and Slow.* New York: Farrar, Straus and Giroux, 2011.
Katz, J., & W. B. Gartner. "Properties of Emerging Organizations." *The Academy of Management Review* 13, no. 3 (1988): 429–441. https://doi.org/10.2307/258090.
Katzenbach, J. R., and D. K. Smith. "The Discipline of Teams." *Harvard Business Review* 71, no. 2 (1993): 111–120.
Kaufman, J. C., ed. Creativity and Mental Illness. Cambridge, United Kingdom: Cambridge University Press, 2014. https://doi.org/10.1017/CBO9781139128902.

Kaur, H. "The Impact of Occupational Stress on the Performance of Employees: Systematic Review." *International Journal of Applied Business and Management Studies* 8, no. 2 (2023): 19–34.

Kaur, H., A. U. Haque, and P. Gkasis. "The Impact of Varying Styles of Leadership on Team Dynamics and Project Success." *Forum Scientiae Oeconomia* 12, no. 3 (2024): 51–69. https://doi.org/10.23762/FSO_VOL12_NO3_3.

Kouzes, J. M., & Z. B. Posner. *The Leadership Challenge.* 7th ed. New Jersey, USA: Jossey-Bass, 2017.

Kuratko, D. F. *Entrepreneurship: Theory, Process, Practice.* 10th ed. Boston: Cengage Learning, 2016.

Kuratko, D. F., M. H. Morris, and M. Schindehutte. "Understanding the Dynamics of Entrepreneurship Through Framework Approaches." *Small Business Economics* 45, no. 1 (2015): 1–13. https://doi.org/10.1007/s11187-015-9627-3.

Langley, A. "Between 'Paralysis by Analysis' and 'Extinction by Instinct'." *Sloan Management Review* 36 (1995): 63–76.

Luthans, F., and C. M. Youssef. "Emerging Positive Organizational Behavior." *Journal of Management* 33 (2007): 321–349.

Manz, C. C., and H. P. Sims Jr. *The New Super Leadership: Leading Others to Lead Themselves.* Oakland, CA: Berrett-Koehler Publishers, 2001.

Markman, G. D., & R. A. Baron. "Person-Entrepreneurship Fit: Why Some People Are More Successful as Entrepreneurs Than Others." *Human Resource Management Review* 13, no. 2 (2003): 281–301. https://doi.org/10.1016/S1053-4822(03)00018-4.

McCord, B. "Taking Up the Revolutionary Call: Principles to Guide a Purpose-Driven AI Future." *Harvard Data Science Review* 1, no. 1 (2019).

Mintzberg, H. *The Rise and Fall of Strategic Planning.* New York: Free Press, 1994.

Pearce, C. L., & J. A. Conger, eds. *Shared Leadership: Reframing the Hows and Whys of Leadership.* London, United Kingdom: SAGE Publications, Inc., 2003. https://doi.org/10.4135/9781452229539.

Renko, M., A. E. El Tarabishy, A. Carsrud, and M. Brännback. "Understanding and Measuring Entrepreneurial Leadership Style." *Journal of Small Business Management* 53, no. 1 (2015): 54–74. https://doi.org/10.1111/jsbm.12086.

Sarasvathy, S. D. "Causation and Effectuation: Toward a Theoretical Shift from Economic Inevitability to Entrepreneurial Contingency." *The Academy of Management Review* 26, no. 2 (2001): 243–263.

Schoemaker, P. J. H. "Scenario Planning: A Tool for Strategic Thinking." *Sloan Management Review* 36 (1995): 25–40.

Schultz, H., and D. J. Yang. *Pour Your Heart Into It: How Starbucks Built a Company One Cup at a Time.* 1st ed. New York: Hyperion, 1997.

Shane, S., and S. Venkataraman. "The Promise of Entrepreneurship as a Field of Research." *Academy of Management Review* 25, no. 1 (2000): 217–226.

Shepherd, D. A., T. A. Williams, and H. Patzelt. "Thinking About Entrepreneurial Decision Making: Review and Research Agenda." *Journal of Management* 41, no. 1 (2015): 11–46. https://doi.org/10.1177/0149206314541153.

Shore, L. M., A. E. Randel, B. G. Chung, M. A. Dean, K. Holcombe Ehrhart, and G. Singh. "Inclusion and Diversity in Work Groups: A Review and Model for Future Research." *Journal of Management* 37, no. 4 (2011): 1262–1289. https://doi.org/10.1177/0149206310385943.

Simon, M., S. M. Houghton, and K. Aquino. "Cognitive Biases, Risk Perception, and Venture Formation: How Individuals Decide to Start Companies." *Journal of Business Venturing* 15, no. 2 (2000): 113–134.

Sorkin, D. H., S. Mavandadi, K. S. Rook, K. A. Biegler, D. Kilgore, E. Dow, & Q. Ngo-Metzger. "Dyadic Collaboration in Shared Health Behavior Change: The Effects of a Randomized Trial to Test a Lifestyle Intervention for High-Risk Latinas." *Health Psychology: Official Journal of the Division of Health Psychology, American Psychological Association* 33, no. 6 (2014): 566–575.

Stone, B. *The Everything Store: Jeff Bezos and the Age of Amazon.* New York: Little, Brown, 2013.

Sudjiman, D. "Elon Musk: Decoding Leadership Style of a Visionary." *LinkedIn Pulse*, 2024. Accessed November 2, 2024. www.linkedin.com/pulse/elon-musk-decoding-leadership-style-visionary-david-sudjiman-ockuc/.

Timmons, J. A., S. Spinelli, and P. C. Ensign. *New Venture Creation*. 1st ed. New York: McGraw-Hill, 2010.

Trevino, L. K., M. Brown, & L. P. Hartman. "A Qualitative Investigation of Perceived Executive Ethical Leadership: Perceptions from Inside and Outside the Executive Suite." *Human Relations* 55 (2003): 5–37. https://doi.org/10.1177/0018726703056001448.

Urbański, M., A. U. Haque, and I. Oino. "The Moderating Role of Risk Management in Project Planning and Project Success: Evidence from Construction Businesses of Pakistan and the UK." *Engineering Management in Production and Services* 11, no. 1 (2019): 23–35.

van Knippenberg, D., C. K. W. De Dreu, and A. C. Homan. "Work Group Diversity and Group Performance: An Integrative Model and Research Agenda." *Journal of Applied Psychology* 89, no. 6 (2004): 1008–1022. https://doi.org/10.1037/0021-9010.89.6.1008.

Vance, A. *Elon Musk: Tesla, SpaceX, and the Quest for a Fantastic Future*. New York: Harper Collins, 2015.

Wallace, J., and J. Erickson. *Hard Drive: Bill Gates and the Making of the Microsoft Empire*. New York: Wiley & Sons, 1993. ISBN 0471568864.

Yohn, D. L. "How Airbnb Survived the Pandemic—And How You Can Too." *Forbes*, 2020. Accessed November 2, 2024. www.forbes.com/sites/deniselyohn/2020/11/10/how-airbnb-survived-the-pandemic--and-how-you-can-too/.

Case Study: G-Inov Technologies – A Journey of Leadership and Decision-Making

Harmandeep Kaur, Adnan ul Haque and Riffat Faizan

Background

In 2021, Margareta Hopkins founded "G-Inov Technologies," a company with the objective of providing renewable energy solutions. The company specialized in the installation of solar panels for residential customers. Margareta, who earned her master's in environmental engineering and proposed an eco-friendly mindset, formed the startup to transform her dream into reality. Through this venture, she sought to provide each household with the opportunity to attain clean energy at an affordable price.

The Initial Challenges

Several challenges were faced by G-Inov Technologies in the very first year. These challenges included scarcity of financial resources and fierce competition from already established players in the electricity business. Margareta then decided to adopt value-based pricing, where customers would pay based on the amount of energy saved. Furthermore, she offered free consultations for first-time customers to build momentum. This strategic move enabled her to attract consumers while also building trust within the community.

Strategic Decision-Making

Due to increased demand, Margareta immediately understood the need to change the company strategy. In other words, the need to evolve the business model was promptly realized. This was a tough decision because in English there is a common saying that "If it ain't broke, don't fix it.". The decision before her was whether she should focus on further growing her installation services and operations or invest resources into developing a proprietary technique that would yield more efficient solar panels. However, this choice meant diverting resources away from her installation business.

Based on a study of current trends in the sector and discussions with her team members, she decided to invest in technological development. She aimed to position G-Inov Technologies as a distinct brand among competitors while also adding value in the long run.

Ethics and Community Engagement

During her success, Margareta equated ethical behavior with community involvement. Through a carefully designed program, she was able to prove her commitment to social responsibility by providing installation services at low costs for low-income families. She not only fulfilled her duties as a morally obligated person but also contributed significantly to the image of G-Inov Technologies by gaining loyalty from customers. Exemplary leadership attributes were demonstrated.

Current Situation

By 2024, G-Inov Technologies had proven itself as one of the leading companies in renewable energy. Nonetheless, Margareta now faces two sensitive issues: on the one hand, the fast pace of technical change in the sector is a common trend, and on the other hand, she must balance the firm's growth with its core values. She is challenged to decide how to maintain a strong business culture while achieving a balance between fresh ideas and her continued commitment to environmental responsibility.

Reflection Questions

- How did Margareta manage to overcome the early challenges faced by G-Inov Technologies?
- What impact did the decision of Margareta to invest money in technical advancement have on the company, in terms of competitive advantage?
- Explain some of the ways in which the brand reputation and customer loyalty were shaped by G-Inov Technologies' ethical practices.
- What are the major considerations that Margareta should consider ensuring that core values are not compromised while facing upscaling?

Chapter 15

Factors Contributing to Failures in Intrapreneurship

Adnan ul Haque, Harmandeep Kaur and Irfan ul Haq

15.0 Introduction

According to Hernández-Perlines et al. (2022), intrapreneurship is entrepreneurship within organizational settings. A plethora of studies have defined the concept of intrapreneurship in various ways. For instance, it is considered as the demonstration of entrepreneurial behavior within the existing organization rather than starting a new venture (Antoncic and Hisrich, 2001). It can also refer to lower-level employees introducing ideas and techniques to bring innovation within the company (Alt and Craig, 2016) or the corporate renewal process within the well-established organization. The work of Antoncic and Hisrich (2003) reflects that, instead of taking a new venture within the competitive market, the individual innovates and contributes to the improvement of structure. Thus, one could argue that intrapreneurship is a form of entrepreneurship where a competent individual introduces their innovation within the existing organization.

During the last few decades, entrepreneurship has changed from an emergent area to an established area of research, with a remarkable number of publications. Several studies indicate that the origins of entrepreneurship can be traced back to the beginning, which underlines the growing interest of academia in this field (Valencia et al., 2016). One of the dimensions is that researchers attempt to analyze how entrepreneurship positively contributes to the development of the economy through job creation (Barber, 2007), either in new firms or in the renewal of existing firms (Burgelman, 1983; Honig, 2001; Yang et al., 2009; Parker, 2011; Gawke et al., 2019). Conversely, the innovation that firms must achieve has also been a point of interest for academics as a source of competitiveness in an increasingly globalized economy. In this respect, several studies have been conducted by experts (Kuratko and Audretsch, 2013; Bierwerth et al., 2015). Organizational efficiency and innovation have become central to the agenda (Naveed et al., 2022). Entrepreneurship involves both new venture creation and intrapreneurship (Antoncic and Hisrich, 2003). According to Douglas and Fitzsimmons (2013), entrepreneurship is discussed together with intrapreneurship. The former refers to taking risks involved in the creation and management of an independent company. In contrast, intrapreneurship means the identification and exploitation of an idea by employees for their company (Bosma et al., 2013).

According to the researchers, intrapreneurship is entrepreneurship within an already existing organization, which describes emergent behavioral intentions and behaviors of an organization related to departures from the customary and conventional approach (Antoncic and Hisrich, 2003). Intrapreneurs are not venturing into a new business in a

DOI: 10.4324/9781003504351-15

competitive market but are internal entrepreneurs who work within the structures of an already established company.

Intrapreneurship is the process of generating entrepreneurial behavior within an already existing organization. This method aims to harness innovative capacity and agility from entrepreneurship by leveraging the resources and capabilities of the parent company. Despite the potential benefits associated with intrapreneurship, many efforts often lead to critical failure for various reasons (Antoncic and Hisrich, 2001). Hence, this chapter systematically explores the available literature in identifying and analyzing these influential factors leading to such failures.

15.1 Overview of Intrapreneurship

This concept was popularized by Gifford Pinchot in the 1980s, when intrapreneurship was utilized to describe the methods entrepreneurs use internally within large organizations to ensure that innovation and growth occur. Accordingly, intrapreneurs can behave like entrepreneurs while having access to all the internal resources and capabilities of their parent companies. In this way, it is an apparent attempt to combine the best of both worlds: the dynamism of a start-up combined with the stability of a large corporation.

15.2 Importance of Intrapreneurship

Intrapreneurship is an essential ingredient that allows organizations to maintain the competitive advantages enjoyed by them for a considerable period of time, since markets evolve very quickly. It fosters creativity, encourages innovation, and institutionalizes a mindset of continuous improvement (Kuratko, Montagno, and Hornsby, 1990). Organizations such as 3M and Google have already gained advantages from intrapreneurial initiatives in their efforts to develop breakthrough products and services (Carrier, 1994). However, there are traces in the literature indicating that intrapreneurship could fail (Huang, 2021; Onetti, 2021; Hussain, 2023). Thus, it is essential to examine those factors contributing to intrapreneurship failure.

15.3 Factors Contributing to Intrapreneurship Failures

The following are various factors that lead to the failure of intrapreneurship within organizations. These challenges are explained below in two broad areas: managerial and technological challenges.

15.3.1 Managerial Challenges

15.3.1.1 Inadequate Supportive Culture

A company is usually devoid of an intrapreneurial culture within the workplace, which is a vital component for encouraging innovation. Companies might not build the right climate for intrapreneurs, even when all resources are available (Lukes and Stephan, 2017; Duncan et al., 1988).

15.3.1.2 Poor Work Relationships

Poorly designed compensation systems promote problems of justice/fairness in individual-based approaches and free riding in team-based approaches. These problems ultimately affect team performance through intrapreneurial efforts.

15.3.1.3 Low Motivation Among Employees

As paid workers and not entrepreneurs, employees may be unwilling to take the risks associated with intrapreneurship. Since initiatives often fail to attract participation, many employees do not engage themselves in generating innovative ideas (Gibbs et al., 2017; Perry-Smith and Coff, 2011).

15.3.1.4 Poor Incentives

The inability to align rewards properly with intrapreneurial activities introduces motivational hurdles. Research has shown that relying solely on intrinsic motivation for employee commitment is not enough (Rigtering et al., 2019).

15.3.1.5 Conflicts Between Employees and Managers

Conflicts between employees and management can lead intrapreneurs to leave and establish their venture outside the organization since their ideas are not supported by management (Klepper, 2001).

15.3.2 Technological Challenges

The following are some of the technological challenges:

15.3.2.1 Inadequate IT Infrastructure

Most organizations lack the technological means and processes to harness and manage intrapreneurial ideas properly. Thus, proper IT infrastructure is an important foundation for supporting intrapreneurship (Alsalim, 2020; Huang et al., 2021; Hussain & Afzal, 2023).

15.3.2.2 Systems Isolation

Most firms create isolated IT systems that fail to facilitate the required collaboration and innovation processes. There is a lack of sophisticated digital platforms connecting resources (Kissimoto et al., 2023).

15.3.2.3 Inaccessibility to Open Platforms

An inability to engage externally with open intrapreneurial platforms makes the firm tend to lose collaboration and innovation opportunities. These could be due to deficits or deficiencies in the commercialization and new product development capabilities of firms

(Hsieh and Wu, 2019). Despite its potential, intrapreneurship often encounters significant hurdles. A review of the literature reveals several factors contributing to the failure of intrapreneurial initiatives.

15.4 Disadvantages Faced by Managers

15.4.1 Lack of Support Culture

A corrective approach involves the establishment of principles that trigger creativity and risk-taking in addition to commitment from leadership, which is a critical factor for creating an innovative culture. The argument by Martins and Terblanche (2003) suggests that it is crucial for leaders to accept the fact that failure is part of the process of innovation and encourages experimentation with eagerness. Such a culture would also be supported by consistent feedback systems (Schein, 1992).

15.4.2 Destructive Relations at Work

One of the ways companies can try to improve work relationships is through designing pay systems that encourage cooperation rather than competition. For example, free riding could be reduced with the help of team-based awards for group performance (Gibbs et al., 2017). Additionally, training in conflict resolution and interpersonal skills are other efficient techniques for improving relations inside the office.

15.4.3 Low Motivation Level of Staff

Businesses must create a sense of ownership within the workforce regarding the work that is being pursued. In the opinion of Kuratko (2016), involving employees in the goal-setting process and providing autonomy in decision-making functions will increase employee involvement. With respect to the enhancement of intrinsic motivation, Kisimoto et al. (2023) add that opportunities for job development could help.

15.4.4 Lack of Rewards

Reward systems should be targeted at activities carried out by the intrapreneurial team. As suggested by O'Reilly and Tushman (2011), for businesses to truly recognize innovative work, they must develop a holistic approach to pay, including extrinsic and intrinsic rewards. Incentive systems need to be continuously monitored and adjusted based on employee response to ensure long-term motivation.

15.4.5 Conflict Between Employees and Managers

It is very important to establish open lines of communication between management and workers. As indicated by Klepper (2001), feedback sessions and check-ins held regularly may be useful in resolving issues before they escalate. Training managers in conflict management techniques may provide them with the necessary skills to handle disputes non-violently.

15.5 Challenges About Technology

15.5.1 Inability to Build Sufficient Information Technology Infrastructures

The way for organizations to break through this barrier is by investing in a strong information technology infrastructure that supports the use of collaboration tools and software used in project management. Their efficiency may be further enhanced by the incorporation of training (Alsalim, 2020; Huang et al., 2021; Hussain, 2023). The weaknesses in information technology are identified.

15.5.2 System Isolation

The solution to the problem of systems separation is for organizations to integrate their information technology systems with platforms that facilitate information sharing across departments. According to Kissimoto et al. (2023), the implementation of enterprise-wide platforms that encourage collaboration and communication may be an effective way to support innovative projects.

15.5.3 Inability to Access Open Platforms

While innovative platforms are operated by third parties, there is potential to increase the level of collaboration opportunities. By leveraging external expertise and sources, business corporations should be active in seeking partnership opportunities with start-up, academic, and industrial consortia (Hsieh and Wu, 2019). Additionally, investing in open projects of innovation is yet another added advantage that enhances the capacity to create new products.

15.6 Organizational Culture of the Company

Therefore, leaders must model the behaviors they wish to see in their employees and create a psychologically safe space at work where employees can express views freely without anxieties about reprisal (Schein, 1992). All this may be encouraged by frequent training to highlight the need to be flexible and innovative (Martins and Terblanche, 2003).

15.6.1 Lack of Management Support

Management, in turn, should actively endorse intrapreneurial initiatives by giving them enough resources and prominence. To give legitimacy to these projects and to ensure that they receive continuous support (Hornsby et al., 2002), a dedicated team or role should be developed to nurture intrapreneurship.

15.6.2 Lack of Sufficient Resources

The solution lies in the fact that organizations must prioritize intrapreneurial activities alongside core operations and set aside specific funds for intrapreneurial endeavors to overcome resource limitations. A flexible mechanism of resource allocation can be put in place to quickly respond to new ideas (Burgelman, 1983).

15.6.3 Negative Responses to Change

The solution should be a change management strategy where employees are engaged in the transformation process. According to Kotter (1996), training and seminars for participants will reduce resistance by addressing their grievances and educating them about new activities.

15.6.4 Poor Communication

There should be open channels of communication and processes among the parties involved. In cases where digital technologies are used to facilitate information dissemination and periodic updates, one can stay in touch with all the stakeholders concerned (Daft and Lengel, 1986).

15.6.5 Lack of Well-Defined Goals and Objectives

It is desirable for business organizations to utilize a goal-setting framework such as the SMART formula (specific, measurable, achievable, relevant and time bound) to clarify expectations. As Locke and Latham (2002) mention, employees can be given the attention and focus required through frequent discussions regarding such goals.

15.6.6 Insufficient Training and Development

The antidote is investing in continuous training programs and seminars that may improve the competency of employees and create a culture of lifetime learning. Nonaka and Takeuchi (1995) also claim that collaboration with educational institutions may provide opportunities for access to advanced technological knowledge and capabilities.

15.6.7 Lack of Patience and Short-term Focus

The solution lies in the fact that businesses need to emphasize the importance of a long-term perspective by making continuous investments in the field of innovation. During this process of innovation, leaders must congratulate themselves on even minor achievements and emphasize the need to be patient (Christensen, 1997).

15.6.8 Limitations Imposed by Bureaucracy

To overcome this, the power of decisions and speed up processes should be delegated to individuals to minimize bureaucratic obstacles. A decentralized structure can easily provide quicker responses to opportunities rather than a centralized structure, where decisions must pass through multiple layers of hierarchy (Mintzberg, 1979).

15.7 Real-Life Examples of Intrapreneurship Failures

15.7.1 Kodak

The failure of Kodak to capitalize on its digital photography technology is among the most well-documented cases of intrapreneurial mismanagement. Although Kodak managed to develop the technology early on, the company focused on protecting its film business and restricted the intrapreneurial drive toward digital development (Tripsas and Gavetti, 2000). This case illustrates how a culture with limited openness to risk can stifle innovation, even when disruptive technology is at hand.

15.7.2 Nokia

One notable example of how organizational inertia can derail innovation is the failure of Nokia to penetrate the smartphone market. According to Vuori and Huy (2016), resistance to change and a lack of vision in adapting to new technological landscapes prevented Nokia from competing effectively with more agile competitors, such as Apple.

15.7.3 Xerox

The Xerox PARC invented new technologies such as GUI. However, Xerox was unable to gain any benefit from these inventions. To be precise, this example demonstrates the general failures of a lack of management support and resources for intrapreneurship (Chesbrough, 2002).

15.7.4 IBM

The failure of IBM's OS/2 operating system to outcompete Microsoft Windows is a good example of internal resistance and a lack of focus on the customer. Unless sufficient attention is given to the demands of the market and internal advocacy, intrapreneurial projects generally end in fiasco (Ferguson and Morris, 1994).

15.8 Cross-case Analysis and Recommendations for Successful Intrapreneurship

These themes stand out most across these cases: supportive management, resource availability, and a good organizational culture. Successful intrapreneurship requires an enabling environment that empowers employees to innovate and provides time and resources to bring new ideas to the market. Intrapreneurship can be encouraged in an organization using the following strategies for success.

15.8.1 Building a Supportive Culture

An innovation-friendly culture embraces risks and values experimentation, notwithstanding the possibility of failure. As Schein (1992) says, this offers a secure environment in which employees can pursue seemingly unorthodox ideas.

15.8.2 Gaining Management Buy-in

Top management participation is essential for intrapreneurial success. According to Kanter (1985), this not only gives legitimacy to intrapreneurship but also helps coordinate resource allocation and prioritization across the organization.

15.8.3 Providing Enough Resources

Financial, technological, and human resources are crucial for intrapreneurial projects. As Burgelman (1983) has shown, without such resources, the ideas of employees cannot be developed or expanded on an appropriate scale.

15.8.4 Stimulating Open Communication

Clearly defined communications ensure that intrapreneurial efforts are in close coordination with organizational goals, therefore reducing misunderstandings (Daft and Lengel, 1986).

15.8.5 Setting Clear and Achievable Goals

Well-defined goals focus on and motivate effort (Locke and Latham, 2002). Well-set objectives may assist in determining guidelines and measuring intrapreneurial efforts.

15.8.6 Providing Ongoing Training and Development

Intrapreneurs need opportunities for learning. As Nonaka and Takeuchi (1995) noted, knowledge acquisition and the enhancement of skills are integral parts of the process of innovation.

15.8.7 Taking the Long-term View

This means being realistic about intrapreneurial projects and allowing appropriate time for their development and maturation. According to Christensen (1997), an expectation of quick results can hamper the potential to innovate.

15.8.8 Limiting Bureaucratic Obstacles

Reducing bureaucratic processes will accelerate decision-making, which is one of the primary requisites of an innovative environment. According to Mintzberg (1979), limiting bureaucracy can facilitate the ability of intrapreneurs to act quickly and bring products to the market.

15.9 Conclusion

This chapter has identified and analyzed the key factors responsible for the failure of intrapreneurial initiatives. Understanding such factors will enable organizations to design strategies more appropriately and effectively to support intrapreneurship. Further research is needed in a variety of contexts, along with the creation of more detailed frameworks that should be realized to address these challenges.

Bibliography

Alsalim, F. I. "The Role of Information Technology Management in Supporting Managerial Innovation." *Management Science Letters* 10, no. 11 (2020): 2483–2490.

Alt, E and J. B. Craig. "Selling issues with solutions: Igniting social intrapreneurship in for-profit organizations." *Journal of Management Studies* 53, no. 5 (2016): 794–820.

Antoncic, B., and R. D. Hisrich. "Intrapreneurship: Construct Refinement and Cross-Cultural Validation." *Journal of Business Venturing* 16 no. 5 (2001): 495–527.

Antoncic, B. and R. D. Hisrich. "Clarifying the Intrapreneurship Concept." *Journal of Small Business and Enterprise Development* 10, no. 1 (2003): 7–24.

Barber, H. D. The Importance of Entrepreneurship to Economic Growth, Job Creation and Wealth Creation, 33 Can.-U.S. L.J. 25 (2007). Available at: https://scholarlycommons.law.case.edu/cuslj/vol33/iss1/8 (Last accessed: 10 June 2024).

Bosma, N., S. Wennekers, M. Guerrero, J. E. Amorós, A. Martiarena, and S. Singer. *The Global Entrepreneurship Monitor. Special report on entrepreneurial employee activity.* London: GERA, 2013.

Burgelman, R. A. "A Process Model of Internal Corporate Venturing in the Diversified Major Firm." *Administrative Science Quarterly*, vol. 28 no. 2 (1983): 223–244.

Carrier, C. "Intrapreneurship in Large Firms and SMEs: A Comparative Study." *International Small Business Journal*, 12. No. 3 (1994): 54–61.

Chesbrough, H. W. "Graceful Exits and Missed Opportunities: Xerox's Management of Its Technology Spin-Off Organizations." *Business History Review*, vol. 76, no. 4 (2002): 803–837.

Christensen, C. M. *The Innovator's Dilemma: When New Technologies Cause Great Firms to Fail.* Harvard Business Review Press, 1997.

Daft, R. L., and R. H. Lengel. "Organizational Information Requirements: A Situational Approach." *Management Science*, vol. 32, no. 5 (1986): 554–571, 1986.

Ferguson, C. H., and C. R. Morris. *Computer Wars: The Fall of IBM and the Future of Global Technology.* New York, NY: Times Books, 1994.

Hernández-Perlines, F., A. Ariza-Montes, and C. Blanco-Gonzalez-Tejero. "Intrapreneurship Research: A Comprehensive Literature Review." *Journal of Business Research*, 153 (2022): 428–444.

Hornsby, J. S., D. F. Kuratko, and S. A. Zahra. "Middle Managers' Perceptions of the Internal Environment for Corporate Entrepreneurship: Assessing a Measurement Scale." *Journal of Business Venturing*, vol. 17, no. 3 (2002): 253–273.

Hsieh, Y. C., and Y. J. Wu. "The Role of Open Innovation in Enhancing Organizational Performance." *Journal of Business Research*, vol. 101 (2019): 99–112.

Huang, L.-Y., S.-M. Yang, and Y.-J Hsieh. "Cultivation of Intrapreneurship: A Framework and Challenges." *Frontiers in Psychology*, Sec. Organizational Psychology, Volume 12 (2021). https://doi.org/10.3389/fpsyg.2021.731990.

Husain, M. "Why Intrapreneurs Are Rare: Examining the Challenges and Obstacles Within Organizations." *LinkedIn*, February 2023. Accessed November 1, 2024. www.linkedin.com/pulse/why-intrapreneurs-rare-examining-challenges-obstacles-mudassar-husain/.

Hussain, A., and S. Afzal. "Lack of Infrastructure and Educational Facilities in Public Schools and its Effects on Quality Education of Students." *Journal of Excellence in Social Sciences*, vol. 2, no. 1 (2023): 37–50. Retrieved from https://journals.smarcons.com/index.php/jess/article/view/160

Kanter, R. M. "Supporting Innovation and Venture Development in Established Companies." *Journal of Business Venturing*, vol. 1, no. 1 (1985): 47–60.

Kissimoto, K. O., C. A. Mattos, and F. J. Laurindo. "The Role of the Organizational and Operational Dimensions in the Open Collaboration Performance: A Strategic Alignment Perspective." *RAUSP Management Journal* 58, no. 1 (2023): 22–38. https://doi.org/10.1108/RAUSP-12-2021-0244.

Klepper, S. "The Evolution of Firms in the Presence of a Dynamic Environment." *Industrial and Corporate Change*, vol. 10, no. 1 (2001): 113–143.

Kotter, J. P. *Leading Change.* Harvard Business Review Press, 1996.

Locke, E. A., and G. P. Latham. "Building a Practically Useful Theory of Goal Setting and Task Motivation: A 35-Year Odyssey." *American Psychologist*, vol. 57, no. 9 (2002): 705–717.

Lukes, M., and U. Stephan. "Measuring Employee Innovation: A Review of Existing Scales and the Development of the Innovative Behavior and Innovation Support Inventories across Cultures." *International Journal of Entrepreneurial Behavior & Research* vol. 23 (2017): 136–158. https://doi.org/10.1108/IJEBR-11-2015-0262

Martins, E. C., and F. Terblanche. "Building Organisational Culture that Stimulates Creativity and Innovation." *European Journal of Innovation Management*, vol. 6, no. 1 (2003): 64–74.

Mintzberg, H. *The Structuring of Organizations: A Synthesis of the Research*. Prentice-Hall, 1979.

Naveed, R. T., H. Alhaidan, H. Al Halbusi, and A. K. Al-Swidi. "Do Organizations Really Evolve? The Critical Link Between Organizational Culture and Organizational Innovation Toward Organizational Effectiveness: Pivotal Role of Organizational Resistance." *Journal of Innovation & Knowledge* 7, no. 2 (2022): 100178.

Nonaka, I., and H. Takeuchi. *The Knowledge-Creating Company: How Japanese Companies Create the Dynamics of Innovation*. Oxford University Press, 1995.

Onetti, A. "Why Most Intrapreneurship Programmes Fail." *Sifted*, March 2021. Accessed November 1, 2024. https://sifted.eu/articles/why-intrapreneurship-programmes-fail.

O'Reilly, C. A., and M. L. Tushman. "Organizational Ambidexterity in Action: How Managers Explore and Exploit." *California Management Review*, vol. 53, no. 4 (2011): 5–22.

Rigtering, J. P. C., G. U. Weitzel, and K. Muehlfeld. "Increasing Quantity Without Compromising Quality: How Managerial Framing Affects Intrapreneurship." *Journal of Business Venturing* 34, no. 2 (March 2019): 224–241.

Schein, E. H. *Organizational Culture and Leadership*. Jossey-Bass, 1992.

Valencia, A., I. Montoya, and A. Montoya. "Intención Emprendedora en Estudiantes Universitarios: Un Estudio Bibliométrico." *Intangible Capital* 12, no. 4 (2016): 881–922. https://doi.org/10.3926/ic.730.

Vuori, T., and Q. N. Huy. "Distributed Attention and Shared Emotions in the Innovation Process: How Nokia Lost the Smartphone Battle." *Administrative Science Quarterly*. Vol. 61, no. 1 (2016): 9–47.

Case Study: The Intrapreneurial Journey of Tech Innovations Inc.

Harmandeep Kaur

An ambitious group of employees at Tech Innovations Inc., a medium-sized technology company including Emily, a software developer with a strong work ethic, decided to undertake a new project with the goal of improving the options available for working remotely. Emily thought they could improve the user experience and speed up operations by integrating artificial intelligence (AI) into the current platform. But very quickly, the process highlighted the difficulties of intrapreneurship within the organization. Despite this, Emily reacted with enthusiasm.

She put together a crew of like-minded colleagues and shared the ideas with her superiors, highlighting that the constraints of remote work represented an unsolved market need and people would benefit from addressing it. However, the executives were not equally receptive, as they had a greater interest in continuing their product mixes without investing in a new venture. Weeks of opposition from her colleagues, who did not want to break their habitual processes, followed for Emily. Many workers were resistant to the new technology because they preferred the established processes already in place.

Owing to this resistance, the crew became much more risk-averse, especially when rumors of layoffs emerged. Emily realized that the culture of the business was dampening her advancement toward her goals. Despite the setbacks, Emily did not give up. She started unofficial sessions for brainstorming to encourage open discussions and creative stance among her team members.

They brainstormed ideas, listened to each other, and even celebrated minor achievements they managed to accomplish. However, the absence of formal administrative support remained a significant concern. This frustration and disengagement were the result of not having the resources needed to further develop their prototype.

One fine day, Emily learned about an invention contest being held across the entire firm, with the purpose of encouraging intrapreneurship. For Emily, that was a golden opportunity, as the reward for the best project was full financing. She managed to motivate her team and ensured they covered all the key dimensions of their proposal with utmost care. In addition to having clearly defined aims and objectives, they also presented their vision with tremendous amounts of enthusiasm and self-confidence.

They were utterly surprised when their proposal was approved and won in the competition. After the management recognized the team's persistence and ingenuity, it finally provided the required resources and support. Soon, the employees immersed themselves in the development process with fresh eagerness, working collaboratively, and overcoming challenges collectively.

Emily trained her workers in state-of-the-art AI technologies, and seminars on lifelong learning played an important role as well. The agile approaches allowed the team to make quick changes driven by feedback and changes in market needs.

The one-of-a-kind, AI-powered remote work solution developed by Tech Innovations Inc. finally launched several months later received widespread positive reviews from customers as well as industry professionals. In addition to revolutionizing the product mix of the company, this effort also revived the culture of the company. Ultimately, Emily's case demonstrated that intrapreneurship succeeds only when management support, a healthy work climate, and effective communication are present.

Reflection Questions

- What were some of the most critical issues that Emily faced and had to overcome during her intrapreneurial days at Tech Innovations Inc.?
- What were the consequences of the lack of support from management toward Emily's project in its formative stages, and how did these results become apparent?
- In what ways did Emily create an environment that encouraged collaboration and creativity among her team members?
- Based on the case, what are some ways businesses can provide more support to their intrapreneurs and the projects that they work on?

Chapter 16

Modern Era Challenges and Business Models for Entrepreneurs

Harmandeep Kaur, Anuraj Sangha and Adnan ul Haque

16.0 Introduction

The entrepreneurial landscape has been reshaped by the rapid evolution of sociocultural shifts, technology, and globalization (Faizan and Haque, 2016). These emerging trends must be addressed not only by entrepreneurs but also by conventional business models, which need to be reorganized and refined to remain competitive. In other words, entrepreneurs need to be proactive and responsive to changes by considering the emerging and latest trends while ensuring that the traditional model is fine-tuned to meet the needs and demands of the competitive dynamic environment. To respond to the shift in dynamics, various business models are increasingly being experimented with by entrepreneurs to fit the modern environment and respond to shifting consumer preferences. In this chapter, business models are explained from the lens of entrepreneurship to highlight the modern challenges and approaches of entrepreneurs to not only survive but also thrive in the dynamic environment. Furthermore, the challenges faced by entrepreneurs in today's marketplace are explored. Additionally, the chapter discusses alternative business models that can be adopted by entrepreneurs in general to survive and thrive in the modern era. The challenges are navigated more effectively with the assistance of key frameworks, such as the customer development model and the product development model. Lastly, the chapter compares the customer development model and the product development model.

16.1 Understanding Business Models

A strategic blueprint that defines how value is delivered, captured and created by an organization is regarded as a business model (Osterwalder and Pigneur, 2010). In other words, a business model is a framework that enables entrepreneurs to focus on three important areas, namely, (a) creating the value of products and/or services, (b) delivering products and/or services to the target audience to satisfy their needs, and (c) ensuring that value is adequately captured. A wide range of business models can be chosen by entrepreneurs today, with each catering to different market needs and resource constraints (Osterwalder and Pigneur, 2010). Thus, a comprehensive understanding of these different models is essential because it helps in the development of sustainable businesses that are not only responsive and adaptable to external pressures but also relevant to the needs of the target audience (Osterwalder and Pigneur, 2010).

DOI: 10.4324/9781003504351-16

16.2 Popular Business Models

A diverse set of business models is available for entrepreneurs today to choose from, depending on their target market, revenue generation strategy, and product and/or service type (Mintzberg, 2015). In other words, depending on the context, entrepreneurs are able to choose their business model from the wide range of available models; however, the essential considerations include relevance and responsiveness to the target market, revenue-generating streams, and types of products and/or services. Some of the most common models are listed below:

16.2.1 Wholesale Model

Products are sold in bulk to retailers or distributors by businesses in this conventional model. In other words, businesses often sell wares in large quantities to wholesalers and retailers under this model. Companies such as Costco are examples of those using the wholesale model as part of their entrepreneurial operations, primarily selling large quantities that are bought, with savings passed on to members (Mintzberg, 2015).

16.2.2 Retail Model

Direct sales to the end consumer are carried out in this retail model. This model is used by traditional brick-and-mortar stores with an online presence, such as Amazon and Walmart, which reach mass markets through a wide range of goods offered at competitive prices (Johnson, 2010).

16.2.3 Franchise Model

In this model, entrepreneurs purchase the right to use a company's business model and brand. Franchisees pay fees to run their businesses under a well-known brand and system, such as McDonald's and Subway (Rubin, 1978).

16.2.4 Marketplace Model

Buyers and sellers are connected through platforms in the marketplace model, without inventory being held. Peer-to-peer transactions are facilitated by websites such as Airbnb and Etsy (Parker et al., 2016).

16.2.5 Pay-as-you-go Model

Customers are charged based on the actual usage of a service in this model. Billing for cloud computing services, such as storage or data transfer, is handled by Amazon Web Services (AWS) based on usage (Teece, 2010).

16.2.6 Free-to-Service Model

In the free-to-service model, revenue is generated through advertisements or other partnerships, while services are offered for free. Revenue is generated through targeted ads, whereas Google's free-to-service model offers free cloud services, email, and search (Evans, 2003).

16.2.7 Subscription Model

Customers are charged a recurring fee by subscription-based businesses for ongoing access to a product or service. One well-known example is Netflix, which offers subscribers unlimited streaming of shows and movies in exchange for a monthly subscription fee (Teece, 2010).

16.2.8 Freemium Model

This model charges for premium features but offers basic services for free. The freemium model is used by companies such as Spotify and LinkedIn, where a restricted version of the platform is accessed by users for free, and additional features such as ad-free content or advanced analytics can be unlocked for a fee (Parker et al., 2016).

16.2.9 Affiliate Model

In this model, revenue is earned by promoting third-party products or services. Influencers and websites can earn commissions through Amazon's Affiliate Program by referring customers to the company's marketplace (Laudon and Traver, 2018).

16.2.10 Razor and Blade Model

In this model, a primary product is sold at a low price (or even at a loss) to generate revenue from complementary goods. Profits are generated from razor blades, while razors are sold at a discount, as demonstrated by Gillette (Cusumano, 2010).

16.2.11 Reverse Razor and Blade Model

Unlike the razor and blade model, this method involves pricing the base product at a premium while providing complementary services or consumables at a reduced cost. Apple employs this strategy by marketing premium-priced iPhones while providing relatively affordable applications via its App Store (Cusumano, 2010).

16.2.12 Brokerage Model

In this model, companies act as intermediaries in transactions between two parties. Companies such as eBay and Uber connect buyers and sellers or drivers and riders and charge a fee for the transaction (Rappa, 2004).

16.3 Analyzing Business Models in Current and Proposed Ventures

Analyzing existing businesses reveals the importance of identifying business models and evaluating their competitiveness in a rapidly evolving landscape. For example, Netflix's subscription model has been effectively tailored for digital streaming; however, pricing strategies and content partnerships are continuously assessed to sustain a competitive advantage (Teece, 2010).

When starting a new business, entrepreneurs need to carefully consider which business model best fits their product and marketing strategy. A startup offering software solutions may determine that the freemium or subscription models are the most suitable, as these models facilitate easy scalability and recurring revenue. In contrast, brokerage or marketplace models may be deemed suitable for a marketplace that targets artisans.

16.4 Alternative Business Models for New Ventures

Entrepreneurs in the modern era can experiment with alternative business models that cater to niche markets and adapt to external forces. Some innovative models include the following:

16.4.1 Platform Business Model

According to Moazed (2024), a platform that develops value by assisting various types of exchanges between several independent groups often involves producers and consumers. In other words, this business model facilitates the connection between users and providers without directly offering the service or product that can be utilized by entrepreneurs. These changes take place with the notion of creating and promoting scalable and extensive networks that could be accessed on the demands of parties involved. The user benefits from these networks not only by interacting but also in transactions resulting from the creation of markets and community-based networks (Moazed, 2024). For instance, Etsy connects buyers and sellers of handmade goods, whereas Uber connects drivers and riders without driver ownership.

16.4.2 Circular Business Model

The rationale to formulate, deliver, and capture values to a wide number of audiences (aka stakeholders) in an attempt to reduce social and ecological costs is regarded as a circular business model. According to Atasu et al. (2021), there is increased attention among manufacturing organizations to use a circular business model so that they can develop a supply chain, which would help in recycling the incorporated resources previously used in the creation of the product. However, according to Atasu et al.'s argument, this could not be extended to the service industry. Nonetheless, it reflects that reducing the footprints formed on the environment, minimizing operational waste, and efficiently and effectively using expensive resources (Atasu et al., 2021). Hence, it is a more attractive option for entrepreneurs. It is important to note that the incorrect approach could prove highly costly if the circular model is not developed adequately, thus making a circular business model more challenging (Atasu et al., 2021). Moreover, the success of a circular business model heavily relies on the strategic management of top management (Atasu et al., 2021). This would enable the entrepreneurial venture to find the right balance between resources and capabilities while addressing operational constraints.

The circular business model helps the entrepreneurial venture attain long-term sustainability and ensures that practices remain ecological, thus improving the scope of business in the long term. One of the real-world examples is Patagonia. To reduce their environmental impact, companies such as Patagonia use circular models that prioritize product recycling, reuse, and refurbishment (Lacy and Rutqvist, 2016). Thus, the circular business model helped Patagonia attain long-term sustainability.

16.4.3 Peer-to-Peer (P2P) Model

Direct interactions between consumers are the primary focus of the P2P model. Individuals provide services such as furniture assembly via TaskRabbit, whereas accommodation rentals are managed through Airbnb, all within a peer-to-peer framework (Botsman and Rogers, 2010).

16.5 Customer Development Model vs. Product Development Model

The understanding of customer requirements and the validation of the business concept are emphasized by the importance of the Customer Development Model (CDM), proposed by Steve Blank before significant resources are invested in product development. In the startup ecosystem, its significance is deemed particularly crucial, as uncertainty regarding market fit can lead to the misallocation of time and resources.

16.5.1 Customer Development Model

Steve Blank developed the CDM containing four important phases (Ries, 2011). The core of this model is to reduce market risk (Blank, 2005). The Lean Startup model is an expansion of the CDM (Ries, 2011). Interestingly, the lean startups used by entrepreneurs call for the use of continuous cycles and minimum viable products (MVPs) – a testing ground to take into consideration feedback from the customer so that products and/or services can be refined and improved (Ries, 2011). The model consists of four key phases:

16.5.1.1 Customer Discovery

In this phase, customer concerns and requirements are identified and comprehended. Interviews and surveys are conducted by entrepreneurs to gather insights regarding prospective users. A startup that creates a new fitness app, for example, might interview fitness enthusiasts to learn about their preferences and pain points regarding current solutions (Blank, 2005).

16.5.1.2 Customer Validation

During this phase, hypotheses about the customer and their needs are tested by the entrepreneur through MVPs. Feedback on the product's value proposition is gathered through this approach. For example, a simple video demonstration of its service was initially offered by a company such as Dropbox to assess interest prior to the full product's development. Dropbox acquired early adopters and refined its offerings based on user feedback (Ries, 2011).

16.5.1.3 Customer Creation

After the product-market fit is validated by entrepreneurs, they then shift their attention to expanding their business. A variety of marketing strategies have been developed to generate demand for the product or service available. One prominent example is Airbnb, which initially utilized social media and word-of-mouth marketing to generate demand among travelers seeking unique lodgings (Zeng, 2016).

16.5.1.4 Company Building

In this concluding phase, the company evolves from a startup to a structured organization. The emphasis shifts to maximizing the efficiency of business processes and expanding the scope of operations. In the case of Warby Parker, for example, once the eyewear model was validated through customer feedback, retail locations were established, and an online presence was expanded. All of this was done while maintaining a commitment to social responsibility by donating glasses to those in need (Ries, 2011).

16.5.2 The Product Development Model

In contrast, the initial development of a product is centered on the Product Development Model (PDM), often based on the entrepreneur's vision or assumptions about market needs. According to Raeburn (2024), product development appears to be exciting; however, it is not free of challenges. It is evident that from the ideation stage to the launching stage, all products require different strategies to be successful (Raeburn, 2024). Thus, this makes the process more challenging for entrepreneurs. Nonetheless, the basics of the product development model could help entrepreneurs to some extent, such as knowing the breakdown structure and ensuring ways to develop cross-departmental collaboration (Raeburn, 2024). This approach is considered riskier since it may lead to products that fall short of the needs or expectations of the customer. The traditional stages of the PDM include:

16.5.2.1 Idea Generation

New product ideas are generated by entrepreneurs based on their vision, market trends, or competitive analysis (Raeburn, 2024).

16.5.2.2 Concept Development and Testing

The product idea is further developed, and prototypes are created for testing. Feedback is often gathered (Raeburn, 2024); however, it frequently occurs after substantial resources have been allocated to development.

16.5.2.3 Product Development

Following internal validation of the concept, full development is undertaken by the product, and resources are allocated for manufacturing and launch preparations (Raeburn, 2024).

Table 16.1 Difference between Customer Development Model and Product Development Model

Aspect	*Customer Development Model*	*Product Development Model*
Focus	Customer needs and validation	Product features and specifications
Approach	Iterative and feedback-driven	Linear and sequential
Risk Management	Reduces risk by validating before investing heavily	Higher risk due to assumptions about market needs
Example	Dropbox's MVP testing	Microsoft Windows development

Source: *Own illustration*

16.5.2.4 Market Launch

The product is introduced to the market, often with significant marketing efforts being made to draw in customers (Raeburn, 2024).

Microsoft's Windows operating system is a classic example of the PDM. The company developed the system according to its vision of an ideal operating system, frequently leading to the launch of versions that garnered mixed user reviews. The risks associated with assuming market fit without direct customer feedback are highlighted by this approach (Teece, 2010).

16.5.3 Comparison of Models

Table 16.1 outlined the key differences between the CDM and the PDM:

The comparison shown in Table 16.1 indicates that the CDM focuses primarily on the needs of customers and their validation, whereas the specifications of the product, along with features, remain the focus of the product development model. Additionally, the approach in the product development model is linear and sequential by nature, whereas a continuous (iterative) and feedback-driven approach is demonstrated in the CDM (Table 16.1). MVP testing of Dropbox is an example of the use of the CDM. On the other hand, Microsoft Windows development is based on the product development model framework, as the specification improves over time (Table 16.1).

16.6 Sustainable Entrepreneurship in the Modern Era

In addition to business objectives, environmental and social goals are integrated into sustainable entrepreneurship. For example, sustainability has been prioritized by companies such as Tesla and Beyond Meat, which emphasize clean energy and plant-based alternatives, respectively (Schaltegger and Wagner, 2011). Through this approach, consumer demands for environmentally friendly products are met, and these companies are positioned as leaders in innovation.

On the other hand, challenges such as higher initial costs and the difficulty of reconciling profitability with environmental objectives are encountered by sustainable entrepreneurship. For sustainable practices to continue to be profitable in the long run, entrepreneurs must ensure ongoing innovation.

16.7 Conclusion

The swift evolution of business models defines the contemporary entrepreneurial environment, encompassing traditional wholesale and retail models as well as digital platforms and circular economies. As external pressures from globalization, technological advancements, and changing consumer preferences are addressed, entrepreneurs must be flexible in their adoption of these models. Through the comprehension and implementation of frameworks such as the CDM, entrepreneurs can navigate challenges with greater efficiency, thereby ensuring that they achieve profitability and continue to align themselves with the requirements of current consumers.

The constantly changing environment will continue to pose challenges, and entrepreneurs will respond by reinventing their business models. To survive and thrive, entrepreneurship must embrace change.

Bibliography

Atasu, A., C. Dumas, and L. N. Van Wassenhove. "The Circular Business Model." *Harvard Business Review*, July 2021. Accessed November 2, 2024. https://hbr.org/2021/07/the-circular-business-model.

Blank, S. *The Four Steps to the Epiphany: Successful Strategies for Products That Win*. Wiley, 2005.

Botsman, R., and R. Rogers. *What's Mine is Yours: The Rise of Collaborative Consumption*. HarperCollins, 2010.

Cusumano, M. *Staying Power: Six Enduring Principles for Managing Strategy and Innovation in an Uncertain World*. Oxford University Press, 2010.

Evans, D. S. "The Antitrust Economics of Multi-Sided Platform Markets." *Yale Journal on Regulation* 20, no. 2 (2003): 325–381.

Faizan, R., and A. U. Haque. "The Relationship between Societal Attributes, Feminine Leadership & Management Style: Responses from Pakistan's Urban Region Female-Owned Businesses." *European Journal of Business and Management* 8, no. 23 (2016): 171–191.

Johnson, M. "Amazon's Smart Innovation Strategy." *BloombergBusinessweek*, April 2010. Accessed November 2, 2024. www.businessweek.com/innovate/content/apr2010/id20100412_520351.htm.

Lacy, P., and J. Rutqvist. *Waste to Wealth: The Circular Economy Advantage*. Palgrave Macmillan, 2016.

Laudon, K. C., and C. G. Traver. *E-commerce 2018: Business, Technology, Society*. Pearson, 2018.

Mintzberg, H. *Rebalancing Society: Radical Renewal Beyond Left, Right, and Center*. Berrett-Koehler Publishers, 2015.

Moazed, A. "Platform Business Model – Definition | What is it? | Explanation." APPLICO, 2024. Accessed November 2, 2024. www.applicoinc.com/blog/what-is-a-platform-business-model/#:~:text=PLATFORM%20BUSINESS%20MODEL%20DEFINITION%3A%20a,the%20way%20linear%20businesses%20do.

Osterwalder, A., and Y. Pigneur. *Business Model Generation: A Handbook for Visionaries, Game Changers, and Challengers*. Wiley, 2010.

Parker, G. G., M. W. Van Alstyne, and S. P. Choudary. *Platform Revolution: How Networked Markets Are Transforming the Economy and How to Make Them Work for You*. W. W. Norton & Company, 2016.

Raeburn, A. "Product Development Process: The 6 Stages (with Examples)." ASANA, 2024. Accessed November 2, 2024. https://asana.com/resources/product-development-process.

Rappa, M. "Business Models on the Web." North Carolina State University, 2004.

Ries, E. *The Lean Startup: How Today's Entrepreneurs Use Continuous Innovation to Create Radically Successful Businesses.* Crown Business, 2011.

Rubin, P. H. "The Theory of the Firm and the Structure of the Franchise Contract." *Journal of Law and Economics* 21, no. 1 (1978): 223–233.

Schaltegger, S., and M. Wagner. "Sustainable Entrepreneurship and Sustainability Innovation: Categories and Interactions." *Business Strategy and the Environment* 20, no. 4 (2011): 222–237.

Teece, D. J. "Business Models, Business Strategy and Innovation." *Long Range Planning* 43, no. 2-3 (2010): 172–194.

Zeng, M. "Airbnb: Business Model Overview and Key Financials." *Journal of Business Models* 4, no. 1 (2016): 51–59.

Case Study: Post-COVID Innovation – The Rise of EcoUnited and Its Circular Economy Venture

Diya Nitinbhai Patel, Harmandeep Kaur and Adnan ul Haque

Post COVID-19, worldwide environmental concerns increased significantly, and consumer preferences shifted, opening the door to opportunities for EcoUnited. As a small-scale, eco-friendly startup that primarily focused on grocery delivery, EcoUnited decided to move from a conventional online marketplace model to a dynamic circular business model. Although the company had always delivered organic produce to consumers, post COVID-19, it adopted a circular economy business model that emphasized subscription-based services, local sourcing, and zero-waste packaging.

Alternative Business Model

With an emphasis on sustainability and community integration, EcoUnited's new business model ensured that all products were locally sourced to achieve a substantial reduction in the carbon footprint. This aligned with the company's zero-waste policy, which encouraged customers to return used packaging for future use. This change strengthened EcoUnited's position as a leader in employing sustainable trends on a global platform while helping them in cost reduction by eliminating waste.

Critical Success Factors

Sustainable Sourcing

Through local sourcing, all produce was acquired from local farmers, which not only supported the domestic economy but also reduced transportation emissions.

Zero-Waste Operations

EcoUnited minimized plastic consumption, encouraged packaging return, and adopted sustainable strategies to inspire customers to adopt eco-friendly practices.

Digital Transformation

To anticipate customer needs and avoid food waste, EcoUnited used AI-driven predictive analytics on its digital platforms.

By serving the increasing number of environmentally conscious customers, this sustainable business model enabled EcoUnited to prosper in the post-pandemic era.

Reflection Questions

- Explain the impact of COVID-19 on the initial business model of EcoUnited.
- List the circular economy business model's key attributes as adopted by EcoUnited.

- Reflect on how increased customer loyalty and engagement resulted from the adoption of the new business model.
- Post COVID-19, what role did sustainability play?
- How did EcoUnited's operational efficiency increase due to adoption of digital transformation?

Index

Note: Tables are shown in **bold** type.

FSC
www.fsc.org
MIX
Papier | Fördert
gute Waldnutzung
FSC® C083411

Kolibri 360 GmbH
Ferdinand-Jühlke-Straße 7
99095 Erfurt, Deutschland
produktsicherheit@kolibri360.de